Praise for *Somewhere S*

"*Somewhere Sisters* is stirring and unforgettable—a breathtaking adoption saga like no other; a provocative exploration into the ideas of family and belonging; and a deeply meaningful meditation on what makes us who we are and what connects us to one another."

—Robert Kolker, *New York Times* bestselling author of *Hidden Valley Road* and *Lost Girls*

"Expertly reported, this tale of Vietnamese twins separated in infancy and raised in a world apart challenges perceptions of international adoption." —*People*

"Hayasaki reveals the racial and class prejudices at the root of such adoptions without losing sight of the complexities of human emotions and family ties. This is a clear-eyed and well-grounded take on a thorny social issue." —*Publishers Weekly*

"Well researched and compassionately written, *Somewhere Sisters* is a journey from separations to reunions, from individual lives to the history of adoption. Urgent and compelling, this book asks important questions about responsibility and ethics and will inspire all of us as we work toward a more responsible and inclusive society."

—Nguyễn Phan Quế Mai, author of *Dust Child* and *The Mountains Sing*

"Hayasaki contextualizes [the sisters'] stories in the larger history of transracial and transnational adoption, as well as nature-nurture science, making for a nuanced portrait." —NPR, "Best Books of 2022"

"Fascinating and moving on its own, the sisters' complex story of growing up, both together and apart, is complemented by Hayasaki's illumination of the personal, psychological, and sociocultural realities of adoption." —*Booklist*

"Deeply researched, artfully woven, and lyrically written, *Somewhere Sisters* explores the harsh reality behind international transracial adoption. Hayasaki is a master storyteller, and her compassion for her subjects is evident on every page. Her meticulous exploration into the dark legacy of nature-nurture studies, American saviorism, and the science of attachment is a powerful addition to our understanding of the lifelong impact of adoption."

—Gabrielle Glaser, author of
the *New York Times* Notable Book *American Baby*

"Hayasaki explores the many dimensions of transracial and transnational adoption in this moving account of families torn apart."
—*The Cut*

"Hayasaki, a journalist who spent five years tracing the girls' diverging paths, writes a sensitive, well-researched account of the years before and after their emotional reunion." —*The Washington Post*

"Hayasaki weaves their reflections about belonging, heritage, and identity—gleaned from hundreds of hours of interviews with the girls and their birth and adoptive families—with a broad consideration of adoption and twin studies that aim to shed light on the extent to which genes and environment shape human behavior, personality, and development. An engaging portrait of intersected lives."
—*Kirkus Reviews*

"Journalist Erika Hayasaki chronicles the unbelievable timeline of twin sisters Isabella and Hà ... A heart-wrenching tale told with compassion."

—*BuzzFeed*

"[Adoption] is often portrayed as a magical ending whereby a family is finally complete. But in *Somewhere Sisters*, Erika Hayasaki dispels this idea ... Unwinding the narratives of our culture isn't a fanciful pursuit: It makes space for new meanings and new ways to live."

—*The Atlantic*

"Erika Hayasaki has produced an elegant exploration of race and nationality. This intimate, meticulously reported portrait of an impoverished Vietnamese mother and her twin daughters, who were separated by adoption, is not only a compelling story, but one that touches on profound questions of human identity."

—Barbara Demick, author of
Eat the Buddha: Life and Death in a Tibetan Town
and *Nothing to Envy: Ordinary Lives in North Korea*

"A talented journalist, Hayasaki has meticulously reported this story, touching on complex topics such as the ethics of adoption, Asian American identity, how siblings reunite, and more."

—*Shondaland*

"*Somewhere Sisters* should be required reading for anyone considering intercountry and/or transracial adoption. Even-handed and balanced, Hayasaki's book is a vivid, searing portrait of the complex realities behind the simple saviorism that is so often the impetus for foreign adoptions."

—*Washington Independent Review of Books*,
"Our 51 Favorite Books of 2022"

"Erika Hayasaki lays out what happened to both twins, and what their story can teach us about family, nature and nurture, and adoption."

—*Bustle*

"*Somewhere Sisters* is a heartbreaking, many times maddening tale of three adoptees, two of whom are twins separated at birth, who find themselves at the intersection of nature and nurture, fighting against fate and circumstance to carve out their own destinies. Seamlessly weaving historical context with brilliant reportage, Hayasaki delivers an incisive and poignant exploration of the world of transracial adoption and twinship, bearing witness to the profound struggles of those caught between two worlds, trying to define themselves."

—Ly Tran, author of *House of Sticks*

"This incredible true story is as fascinating as any novel . . . Journalist Erika Hayasaki interviewed family members extensively in order to write this nuanced tale of transracial adoption, nurture versus nature, and sisterhood."

—*BookBub*

"[*Somewhere Sisters*] raises many critical questions about the responsibility of wealthier countries and their attitude toward adoption in countries that they often left after years of colonization and war. This book is ultimately a very emotional and human account of finding out what the meaning of family is."

—*The San Diego Union-Tribune*

⬡⬡⬡ SOMEWHERE SISTERS

ALSO BY ERIKA HAYASAKI

The Death Class: A True Story About Life

SOMEWHERE
SISTERS

ՀՐՀՐՀՐ A Story of Adoption,
Identity, and the
Meaning of Family

ERIKA HAYASAKI

ALGONQUIN BOOKS OF CHAPEL HILL 2023

Published by
ALGONQUIN BOOKS OF CHAPEL HILL
Post Office Box 2225
Chapel Hill, North Carolina 27515-2225

an imprint of WORKMAN PUBLISHING CO., INC.
a subsidiary of HACHETTE BOOK GROUP, INC.
1290 Avenue of the Americas
New York, New York 10104

Printed in the United States of America. Design by Steve Godwin.

The publisher is not responsible for websites (or their content) that are not owned by the publisher.

Library of Congress Cataloging-in-Publication Data
Names: Hayasaki, Erika, author.
Title: Somewhere sisters: a story of adoption, identity, and the meaning
  of family / Erika Hayasaki.
Description: First edition. | Chapel Hill, North Carolina : Algonquin Books of Chapel Hill,
  [2022] | Includes bibliographical references. | Summary: "Isabella and Ha, identical twin
  girls born in Vietnam, were raised on opposite sides of the world, each having no idea
  that the other existed. Erika Hayasaki's deeply reported, intimate story of their journey
  back to each other upends common conceptions of adoption, family, and identity"—
  Provided by publisher.
Identifiers: LCCN 2022018472 | ISBN 9781616209124 (hardcover) |
  ISBN 9781643753423 (ebook)
Subjects: LCSH: Vietnamese American girls—Illinois—Barrington—Biography. |
  Twin sisters—Illinois—Barrington—Biography. | Twin sisters—Vietnam—Biography. |
  Solimene, Isabella Louise, 1998—Childhood and youth. | Nguyễn, Thị Hồng Hà, 1998—
  Childhood and youth. | Solimene, Olivia Claire, 1999—Childhood and youth. | Adopted
  children—United States—Biography. | Adopted children—Vietnam—Biography. |
  Intercountry adoption—Vietnam. | Intercountry adoption—United States.
Classification: LCC F548.9.V53 H39 2022 | DDC 362.7/789592207731 [B]—dc23/eng/20220615
LC record available at https://lccn.loc.gov/2022018472

ISBN 978-1-64375-536-6 (PB)

10 9 8 7 6 5 4 3 2 1
First Paperback Edition

To my grandmothers who survive within me, to my mother and daughter who sustain me, and to understanding that we all try to do right with what we have and know

If you look deeply into the palm of your hand, you will see your parents and all generations of your ancestors. All of them are alive in this moment. Each is present in your body. You are the continuation of each of these people.

—THÍCH NHẤT HẠNH, *Present Moment, Wonderful Moment*

CHARACTER FAMILY TREE (VIỆT NAM)

Nguyễn Thị Thanh
(grandmother)

Nguyễn Thị Kim Liên
(daughter)

Nguyễn Thị Kim Rô
(daughter)

LIÊN'S FAMILY

*First daughters born to
Nguyễn Thị Kim Liên
(Thanh's granddaughters,
Liên's birth children)*

Nguyễn Khánh Kim Loan
(Isabella Solimene) &

Nguyễn Thị Hồng Hà
(identical twins)

RÔ'S FAMILY

Nguyễn Thị Kim Rô &
Trần Thị Tuyết
(same sex partners)

RAISE

Nguyễn Thị Hồng Hà
(adopted Liên's birth child)

Phan Văn Quý
(Liên's husband, Ha's stepfather)
& Liên

RAISE

Phan Hoàng Ngọc &
Phan Nữ Hồng Hà
(aka Baby Hà)
(Liên & Quý's daughters)

CHARACTER FAMILY TREE (UNITED STATES)

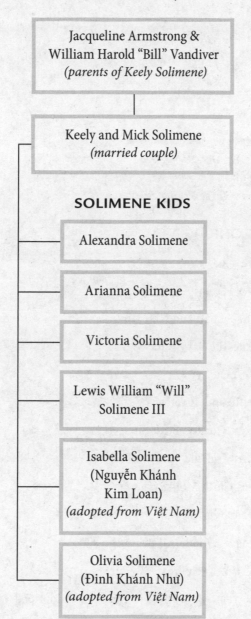

Jacqueline Armstrong &
William Harold "Bill" Vandiver
(parents of Keely Solimene)

Keely and Mick Solimene
(married couple)

SOLIMENE KIDS

Alexandra Solimene

Arianna Solimene

Victoria Solimene

Lewis William "Will"
Solimene III

Isabella Solimene
(Nguyễn Khánh
Kim Loan)
(adopted from Việt Nam)

Olivia Solimene
(Đinh Khánh Như)
(adopted from Việt Nam)

CONTENTS

Prologue: Three Triangles

PART ONE

ONE 1998 9

TWO Hà 14

THREE Loan and Như 21

FOUR The Baby Lifts 26

FIVE Liên 33

SIX Rô and Tuyết 39

SEVEN Cuckoo Birds 46

EIGHT Isabella 51

NINE Cloth Monkeys 59

TEN Olivia 64

ELEVEN Wonderful Beginnings 70

TWELVE Keely 79

THIRTEEN Baby Brokers and Viral Adoptions 88

FOURTEEN "Is the Baby Okay?" 91

PART TWO

FIFTEEN A Twin Who Walks Alone 102

SIXTEEN Blindly Searching 106

SEVENTEEN Fairy Tales 110

EIGHTEEN The Letters 115

NINETEEN Storms 122

TWENTY The Fog 129

TWENTY-ONE "I Got Her" 134

TWENTY-TWO Strangers in the Village 139

TWENTY-THREE "They Love Her" 144

TWENTY-FOUR They Are Coming 148

TWENTY-FIVE Motion Sickness 153

TWENTY-SIX The Cold 155

TWENTY-SEVEN The Night 163

TWENTY-EIGHT "Harder than This" 167

TWENTY-NINE Always Loan 174

THIRTY "Where I Am From" 179

THIRTY-ONE "Be with Us" 187

THIRTY-TWO Goodbye 191

THIRTY-THREE "I Will Come Back" 199

PART THREE

THIRTY-FOUR America 207

THIRTY-FIVE "We're Still Here" 214

THIRTY-SIX Switched 225

THIRTY-SEVEN Powerful Marks 232

THIRTY-EIGHT Similar Scars 237

THIRTY-NINE Unspoken 243

FORTY Grandma 249

FORTY-ONE Where It Feels Safe 254

FORTY-TWO Climb Out 258

Epilogue 263
Notes on Sources 269
Selected Bibliography & Suggested Resources 293
Acknowledgments 301

Three Triangles

THREE YOUNG WOMEN share a booth in a noodle restaurant on a frigid evening in 2018 in the Chicago suburb of Arlington Heights. Each wears a winter windbreaker over a sweatshirt, covering their identical tattoos. Inked below their rib cages, the girls bear the same image: a row of three simple and unadorned triangles, a design they came up with together. One triangle to represent each of them, overlapping like their lives, standing in symmetry, as if hooked arm in arm. They are sisters, each with her own original adoption story, connected to one another.

"The three of us have this huge bond," explains the youngest, "because we're different. And we get that." They went to the tattoo shop together in 2017, riding home with tender torsos.

The sisters recount this story inside of the franchise restaurant, Noodles and Company, where they eat dinner. The girls, all born in Việt Nam and now living in the United States, do not know it yet, but the next couple of years will involve periods of intense self-discovery for each of them, questions about individualism and what it means to be part of a diverse nation in which differences can be celebrated while also deemed inferior. Or blotted out.

On this night, they are not yet college students. But over the next few years, they will grapple with the elasticity of identity and family. They will embark on college adventures and personal awakenings. This will take place as a racial and social justice movements take hold across the United States and as the world reels from a devastating coronavirus pandemic and rising displays of anti-Asian hate.

In the middle of it all, the trio—Hà, Isabella, and Olivia—will live together and lean on one another. Few others could truly understand the dynamics of their interwoven lives or how they got to this place together that required such emotional sustenance from each other. Their family bond has never been a traditional one.

HÀ NGUYỄN AND Isabella Solimene are identical twins, but they did not grow up together. Separated shortly after birth, they barely knew of each other until they were preteens.

In Việt Nam, Hà was adopted as an infant by two women, one of whom is her biological aunt. The women built a life together as romantic and domestic partners, raising their cherished child. Hà's aunt worked as a village babysitter, while her other adoptive mother worked in the rice paddies. An only child in her household, Hà grew up in the coastal mountains with sparse electricity and seasonal monsoons.

A wealthy white family in Illinois adopted Isabella, along with another child from the same orphanage, whom they named Olivia. Isabella and Olivia are not biologically related. The family gave both girls their last name, replacing their Vietnamese names with Western ones.

Nguyễn Khánh Kim Loan became Isabella Louise Solimene.

Đinh Khánh Như became Olivia Claire Solimene.

Born in 1999, Olivia is ten months younger than Isabella and Hà. She was adopted on the same day in Việt Nam as Isabella.

Both Olivia and Isabella were raised by Keely Solimene, a homemaker and philanthropist, and her husband, Mick, an investment banker. They lived in a house in an affluent suburb lined with equestrian trails and enormous homes on vast acres of land. Out of six Solimene children raised together, Isabella and Olivia are the only two Asian Americans and adoptees. Hà would not meet the Solimenes until years later.

I FIRST LEARNED about the sisters in 2016, six months after giving birth to my own identical twin boys. As part of a science journalism fellowship, I was researching stories about environmental interactions with genes. The project led me to Professor Nancy Segal, the head of the Twin Studies Center at California State University, Fullerton, who connected me via email to various twin pairs around the country, including Hà and Isabella.

The history of twin research, I would learn, is a long, dark tale of nature-nurture science. Fueled by twin studies, as well as adoption research, the field of genetics has throughout history tilted toward a view of DNA as fate. Can any of us choose who we become? Or is our fortune, with every fathomable twist and turn, already chosen for us?

As monozygotic (or identical) twins, Hà and Isabella have the same genes, the same interior blueprint. Yet for most of their lives, they existed in entirely different environments. Isabella learned to ride a bike, play soccer, speak English, all alongside Olivia, with whom she shared no genes at all but instead shared experiences, circumstances, surroundings.

Within a few months, I was on a plane to Illinois, where I would meet the sisters. Like many of us, I was familiar with the popular narratives about twins, adoptions, and biological family reunions, which had seeped into my subconscious since childhood. Twins separated at birth only to find each other. Fairy-tale adoption journeys. Happy endings, after some turbulence. But I have also long known that a nonfiction story is fragile, sometimes seemingly more unbelievable than fiction. Like folds of origami, its face changing with each new angle. Their story, I would come to understand, involved an entire world of incongruity, unease, resilience, and sometimes aching love.

As I got to know more about the nonbiological sisters raised as a duo in Illinois, my own life experiences also pulled me toward wanting to know more about theirs. I was born in Illinois, raised for part of my life not too far from where Olivia and Isabella grew up. My father is

Japanese. My mother is white. As a child out in public with my mom, if my dad was not nearby, people often assumed I was adopted. We lived in a small town surrounded by cornfields. There were few Asian Americans in my school or in my neighborhood. I was teased about my eyes and called a chink, jap, and gook. I thought about growing up in the Midwest, looking and feeling different from everyone else, and wondered if Isabella and Olivia had experienced the same.

This is a work of nonfiction, a chronicle of identity, poverty, privilege, and the complex truths of adoption. The sisters' experiences push beyond the confines of the nature versus nurture debate. There is a difference between fate (a future that is fixed and unchangeable) and destiny (a future dependent on experiences and choices). Their story is about what happens when people believe too blindly, or too narrowly, in just one or the other.

The sisters found themselves drawn to triangles, minimalistic and meaningful, a fitting symbol to capture their merged lives. In math, the delta symbol represents change. Religions and mythologies have claimed triangles as representations of birth, life, and death. Among the Sepik people of Papua New Guinea, triangles are found throughout artifacts and within the underlying patterns of their homes, an expression intended to capture a reality made up of opposite forces that are not separate but instead exist within the same form.

Political scientist Claire Jean Kim, of the University of California, Irvine, created the theory of racial triangulation, which challenges Black-white conversations about race in America. Asian Americans, Kim explained, have been pulled outside of a historically binary race discussion, like a point on a triangle—used as pawns or "model minorities" in a system designed to uphold racial hierarchies of white dominance while oppressing Black people and silencing the struggles of Asian Americans. Adoption systems have also been subject to these racial dynamics, according to Liz Raleigh, a sociologist of race and family. Model minority stereotypes, she teaches, have influenced the high rates of adoption from Asia, a kind of ranking system of sought-after children according to countries, cultures, and race.

Within the adoption community, the term *adoption triad* refers to the intersections of adoptee, first family, and adoptive family. One adoption symbol, which also shows up in some tattoos, depicts a heart interwoven around a triangle. But today, some prefer the term *adoption constellation*, which pushes back against notions of equally balanced family arrangements and neat relationships and acknowledges the systems and societal forces involved in creating those notions.

In this book, three girls grow up and learn to love and rely on one another at different times, in different ways. Few others could truly understand the dynamics of their sisterhood.

They are interconnected angles, shared lives within the same story.

PART ONE

ONE

1998

THE BABIES ARE crying. Nguyễn Thị Kim Liên treks through the clogged city streets of Nha Trang. She is exhausted, carrying two newborns in her arms in a double clutch. It is 1998. A hip malformation that she's had since birth forces her weight to rest more heavily on her right side and her legs to curve outward like the body of a harp. It was hard to find a job before she gave birth. Now it is impossible. Even if someone offers work, there is no one else to care full-time for the children.

Liên has no permanent home and no money. She brings her babies to an open-air marketplace, where she searches for a high-traffic spot to plant herself and her daughters on the ground. They had been entangled inside of her belly, perceived to be a single soul for weeks, until a doctor's visit revealed it was a pregnancy of two.

Delivered prematurely and now five months old, the twins are still far too small for their age. Both are starving. One is so sick, she may die.

WHEN LIÊN RECALLS that period of her life two decades ago, she sees her twenty-six-year-old self, pushing each child out of her body inside of a clinic in the city. Like many mothers, she remembers the physical pain only vaguely, but she could see her girls clearly, each less than four pounds at birth. They emerged swiftly—probably, she said, because they were so small. Unable to pay for a prolonged hospital stay, she bundled them up and left after only two nights.

As she tells it, the twins' father, a man whom Liên dated briefly, had disappeared months earlier. Liên had since fallen in love with a new man, but he was not pleased to learn that she was pregnant by a former boyfriend. Now the babies were here. She temporarily took shelter with family members, but no one could keep her and the twins for long. Liên's mother could not afford to help; the aging woman had already reared twelve children.

That was how Liên found herself, just months after giving birth, sitting on the ground of the outdoor marketplace, hoping that passersby would stop for the woman with two hungry newborns and hand over money. Liên had tried many times before to get both babies to nurse simultaneously, but it required unbearable positions for everyone involved, so she rotated. One squirmed on her lap, while she pressed the other to her breast in a constant rotation. Even if they mustered the strength to suckle, they could not drink enough. Liên was hungry too. She could not afford to eat what was needed to nourish two more humans.

Liên tried boiling rice grains and giving the twins the leftover cloudy water. She returned to the doctor who had delivered them, who took pity on Liên and her daughters. The doctor gave her 300,000 đồng and told her to buy milk. He diagnosed both twins with rickets, a skeletal disorder caused by a lack of vitamin D and calcium that results in soft bones, stunted growth, and deformities.

On the street, a stranger approached. "There is an orphanage nearby," the woman told Liên, explaining that one of her family members had been unable to care for a child and had gone to that same facility. "You can take your babies there too."

Liên scooped up her daughters and carried them to the entrance a few miles away. A big brown sign in front read CENTER FOR KHÁNH HOÀ SOCIAL PROTECTION in English, and TRUNG TÂM BẢO TRỢ XÃ HỘI TỈNH KHÁNH HÒA in Vietnamese (Social Sponsoring Center

Khánh Hòa), but Liên could not make out the words. She never had the opportunity to learn to read or write.

Once inside, staff greeted Liên and examined her daughters. One was too sick, she told her. The facility could not accept such an ill child, but the other appeared healthier. The orphanage would admit her.

THAT DAY AT the Center for Khánh Hoà Social Protection, Liên dictated a letter in Vietnamese (later translated by the government agencies into English). It read:

I have twin born daughters, born July 24, 1998 my children born out of wedlock, due to the condition, the situation being very difficult I couldn't guarantee to bring up my two daughters so that their health is often weakness, illness, malnutrition, I haven't the family, the house, the stable employment for having the income in order to bring up my daughters. Currently my health condition is still weak, I have to rear my little daughters, every day I must carry my daughter in my arms for to be as a beggar. . . . Please, the various competent authorities consider, settle and create the condition for my daughter to have a good future.

She signed the letter with the ink prints of her left and right forefingers. With that document, her daughter, Nguyễn Khánh Kim Loan, became a resident of the orphanage. They would call her Loan. With one less baby in tow, Liên would soon set off to see her sister, who lived in a mountain village.

Liên would eventually turn over child-rearing for her other twin daughter to her sister, whose partner named the child Nguyễn Thị Hồng Hà.

Versions of this story were passed down over the years, as told from various family members' memories. But memories are fickle, subject to shifts in environment, time, and point of view.

As at least one version goes, the villagers prepared for the baby Hà's funeral. They planned to build a box from wood, small enough to hold a tiny body. They waited. But to everyone's astonishment, the child did not die.

Hà

Right before I came to the US, I went to my temple. The monks told me that in my past life I was a monk. They said something bad happened to me in my past life, so I got so sick, and then I passed away at a young age.

They said, "You were reborn into a human, and you had to clean and clear that bad karma from your past life before you could be reborn."

When they told me this, I was sitting there shaking. They told me, "You will become great but only if you put the work into it."

If I don't work for it, nothing is going to come to me. And they emphasized this. They said that I'm going to hit a lot of roadblocks. But eventually, if I do the work, I will become a very successful person.

I remember I asked my monks, "Where do all the blessings come from?"

And they told me they come from my past life. "You created good karma for yourself when you were a monk, but you did not get to use it because you passed away so young. So, in this life, you will be able to use those blessings."

TWO

Hà

NGUYỄN THỊ HỒNG Hà grew up knowing an incomplete story of her birth. She believed she was born on July 2, 1998, according to the calendar that follows the cycles of the moon. Hà was told that she had been a sickly infant with a distended belly and swollen, runny eyes when the two women of the mountain village of Khánh Đông, on the southern central coast of Việt Nam, took her in.

Hà's aunt, Rô, is a short and shapely ever-smiling woman who wears pink lipstick and bangs; her hair is partly swept up in a half ponytail. Rô's partner, Tuyết, smokes cigarettes while squatting, wears her hair cropped short, and prefers trousers and short-sleeve button-downs from the men's sections of stores.

When Hà was an infant, they fed her formula and a powdery wheat cereal that tasted like vanilla, purchased from local merchants with money Tuyết earned from working in the rice paddies. As Hà grew stronger, they fed her spinach or pumpkin soup, noodles, mangos plucked from trees in their yard, and milk straight from their cow's udder. Hà learned to crawl on the dirt. She learned to waddle chasing the chickens. To stave off sickness, Rô and Tuyết made hot rice soup with pepper and onions.

Their home stood high on a hill, at the top of a dirt path shrouded by bamboo and banana tree leaves. It was a four-hundred-square-foot one-room dwelling constructed of planks of wood, corrugated tin, leaves, clay, and an earthen floor. Small animals slipped between the gaps and crevices, and heavy rains soaked everything inside. They washed their clothes in the river behind their home and cooked over a firepit, their outdoor kitchen a smattering of buckets on a patio where Hà loved to scoop up dust and rocks, creating her own play cafe.

The government turned on electricity in the village sporadically, but not always in the fierce heat of day. If switched on at all, it was often unexpectedly. There were only so many lightbulbs, electric fans, rice cookers, televisions, or refrigerators around the village. With power so unreliable, such items frequently went unused. Hà's family did not need them.

The stars and moon were their lights at night, and on summer days, when the sun was high and bright, Hà stayed in the shade, waiting for the sky's breath. She bit her nails. She drifted off to sleep in the afternoon, near her big, smelly, devoted dog, May Mắn, which translates to "Lucky" in English. He was black with two white spots on his temple, which made him look like he had four eyes.

Though Hà did not have siblings in the village, there were plenty of other kids around to play with. Sometimes the local children made fun of Hà, told her she was the girl whose father did not want her, the girl whose own mother gave her away.

"Why do you live with two women?" kids asked. "Why does one of them look like a man?" Some asked if Tuyết was a lesbian. Hà did not even know what that meant.

"You must have been born from a rock," other kids told her.

For years Hà wondered if this were true, until she was old enough to learn about biology, but she learned to ignore the questions and comments, especially if she wanted to play with the village kids. They were the only children around, so like them or not, she saw them every day. She acted like she didn't care or couldn't hear them. The more she ignored, the less they taunted.

Despite these moments, Hà lived happily in Khánh Đông, shielded from the complications of outsiders. She harbored no desire to leave.

In Khánh Đông, she was never lost. The main road that cut through the village was visible from the top of the dirt path where Hà's house stood. Every so often on an otherwise quiet afternoon, police would wait at the point where the dirt path intersected with the road to catch motorists breaking the speed limit. When this happened, the residents made a spectacle out of it. They shouted to each other to join in the audience—"Come right away!"—and settled in the shade near the base of Hà's house.

Soon there were uncles and aunts, brothers and sisters, and babies. The onlookers would pick papayas from trees planted by Hà's aunt, rip open their skin and bite into the sweet, buttery flesh. They cheered and made bets every time an unsuspecting driver came close to getting snarled in the officer's trap.

But the real playtime in Hà's neighborhood began at nighttime. After dinner, as darkness cloaked the countryside and the moon began to brighten, Hà slipped outside onto the patio of gravel and dust that surrounded her home. The neighborhood children trickled over to join her. They concocted games with chopsticks, spoons, and pots. They filled cups with river water. Hà pretended to be a saleswoman peddling bottles of wine and bánh mì. They picked leaves from the jackfruit trees and made believe they were đồng, exchanging the make-believe dollars for play goods.

As the night stretched on and the moon grew radiant, Hà would venture deeper into the brush. Twigs snapping beneath her feet, she trekked farther from home, but never too far. She'd often climb onto a slab of wood that a neighbor had hung from two ropes knotted around a thick tree branch. She gripped the twine with both hands, kicking her legs into a steady swing.

Hà delighted in the thrill of telling scary stories with other children, then racing through the brush squealing as if being chased by ghosts. The night sky held her happiest childhood memories.

The moon was more to Hà than a source of light. It was her friend, her confidant. She believed that the moon had a soul, a dark side and a bright side, much like people. It listened to the ghost stories she shared with other kids. It knew of mysteries she never spoke of, too, like the one about her long-lost sister.

WHEN HÀ WAS four, Tuyết and Rô told her some startling news.

"You have a sister."

They explained that her first mother, Liên, had given birth to another child on the same day that she had had her.

Hà tried to grasp this new information. A sister? From the same parents? The same age as her? It was so hard to picture someone she had never met.

At the time, barely preschool age, Hà knew a pair of sisters in her village who looked almost exactly like each other. Rô explained they looked alike because they were twins. Rô told Hà that her sister was also her twin. "If you meet your sister in the future," Rô said, "she's going to look like you too."

How do you know she looks exactly like me? Hà thought. *How is that possible?*

Days after receiving this news, Hà found herself wedged between Rô and Tuyết, riding on a borrowed motorbike heading somewhere. As Tuyết drove for what felt like a long time, Hà looked out at the open highway. They passed rice paddies; green hills; shrines; cemeteries; rose, turquoise, and orange buildings with lavender roofs; airy cafes with red plastic chairs; and grazing cows, muscular with russet-colored hides.

They arrived in Nha Trang, the city where Liên lived, but they were not there to visit her. Liên had reestablished herself in Nha Trang, where she had married a new man and given birth to two more kids. It was also the city, Rô told her, where Hà's sister had been taken in by an orphanage. For four years, Hà's twin sister had lived there, Rô said, for as long as Hà had lived in the village. And now they wanted Hà to meet her. The girls had not seen each other since they were babies.

Arriving in Nha Trang, everything felt electric. In the alleyways, hundreds of residents lived tucked away from the busy main streets, their homes hidden down zigzagging paths, like veins running beneath the city's skin. Follow one, and it led down a soapy thoroughfare, wet from dumped laundry water running toward the street drains. Rows of dwellings sat behind steel doors that were propped open, moving pictures of the lives of strangers. From the alley, passersby could catch a glimpse of families eating dinner, drinking beer, or sleeping shirtless in a hammock. Clotheslines stitched buildings together. It was a city on a beach, far different from Hà's village.

Tuyết parked her bike near the orphanage. Rô held Hà as they entered the sliding gates.

"We are looking for a child," Rô told the director at the front office. "Her name is Nguyễn Khánh Kim Loan."

She explained that she was the aunt who had been raising Loan's twin.

The director informed her that yes, Loan had lived in this orphanage, but she had recently been adopted. They could offer no more information, except this: "She was adopted by Americans." Rules forbade the orphanage from providing contact information for Loan's new caregivers. They had come too late; Loan was gone.

Tuyết and Rô boarded the motorbike again, disheartened but also reassured. If the child had made it to America, they reasoned, she would grow up living a prosperous life. Hà journeyed back to Khánh Đông nestled between Rô and Tuyết, slipping into the routine of her life almost as if the misadventure had never happened.

Yet as the years passed, she found herself wondering more and more about the sister she did not know. She did not want to go to America. It triggered no tangible image for her mind to hold onto. She couldn't yearn for a place she didn't know.

The villagers told her it was a rich country, but Hà didn't know what it meant to be rich or poor. Hà knew only that she was a child who never went without shelter or love, and on most days, she was well fed. Even during the slowest, stormiest, toughest months, when Tuyết could not find work in the fields and didn't have enough money to buy rice or noodles, they could visit a neighbor's house in the village to borrow some. Everyone knew one another, and besides, there were often pineapples from the trees, okra and spinach growing in their garden, white fish in the river, and endless eggs from their two dozen chickens.

As a child, Hà had never ridden in a car, or a bus, boat, or plane, and she did not feel the need to. America could have been as far away as Hồ Chí Minh City, another place she had heard of but had never seen. Sometimes, though, her wonder about her twin turned into something stronger.

During the day, Hà heard purring above and peered through the fingers of the trees to spot an airplane slicing through the clouds. It looked so small from far away, she thought, how did those metal machines carry people?

Hà screamed into the sky: "Bring me my sister!"

Isabella

I think about this all the time. How I would have turned out? Growing up, I had such extreme questions and ideas. I was so curious about everything. If I stayed in Việt Nam, would I have wondered the same way?

I believe in science. I think our genes play a role in who we become. They do determine who we are from birth. But I also feel like you can have all these predetermined factors, but there are no specific rules in how you will get to be who you are.

We're born with certain predetermined parts of us, but how those parts play out in our own lives is unclear. I believe part of life is about figuring out how you are going to reach your own destiny.

THREE

Loan and Như

NEARLY EVERYTHING THAT Isabella Solimene remembers of her early childhood in Việt Nam is shaped by photos and videos taken by the Solimene family. She does not have many felt life experiences of being Nguyễn Khánh Kim Loan. Instead, she recalls scenes on tape, watching herself as Loan years later. She holds images in her mind of the orphanage, the gates, the dirt courtyard, the babies doing tummy time on patterned linoleum floors. She recognizes scenes from when the Solimene family came to adopt her. They gave her lollipops and a black-haired doll. It was all recorded.

Isabella also has visions of encountering a man at the orphanage. Toothless and one legged, he terrified her. Was he real? Or part of her imagination? If the man did exist, she realized years later, he must have lived in the state-run center that held the elderly and disabled. Perhaps, when she was a resident of the orphanage, she saw him occasionally hobbling through the shared courtyard. Perhaps he was harmless, yet she had still felt afraid. What does a child with no mother around do when she is afraid?

Long after leaving Việt Nam, during her childhood in Illinois, the one-legged man appeared in Isabella's nightmares, the ones in which she was sent back to her birth country and forbidden from returning to the only home she could fathom, in America. She would wake up with her heart racing and find her mom, Keely, at her side, cradling her, trying to soothe her back to sleep. Somewhere in her subconscious this man, real or not, represented her idea of the place where Loan's life was overturned and Isabella's began.

Even though Isabella had watched the adoption home videos often over the years, new details emerged with each viewing. "You start watching them over and over again, and start to create a memory," Isabella told me. "It was really hard to watch because I get motion sickness, and the videotaping made me nauseous. It was very jiggly and wobbly. My mom thought it was making me upset, making me have anxiety, but it was not that."

The videos revealed part of the story of that life-altering day in July 2002 when orphanage caregivers prepped four-year-old Loan for the moment she would leave the Nha Trang orphanage for good. As Isabella viewed this tape, she tried to put herself back into that moment. She tried to imagine what Loan thought and felt knowing her new mother was coming.

First, the American family would visit, and Loan would spend a few days with them outside of the orphanage, returning to the facilities in the evenings to sleep, until the paperwork and formalities had been completed. It was a process that could take days or weeks. Then Loan would go home with her new family on an airplane.

Loan had met the Solimenes before, three months earlier, when the family had traveled to Việt Nam. She cooperated with the orphanage employee, who squatted on the floor dressing her for the visit with her adoptive mom, an American woman named Keely Solimene.

The orphanage caregiver pulled a white lace dress over the top of Loan's head. She spun Loan around and tied a ribbon into a bow at her back. Then she smoothed down the dress around Loan's waist and fluffed it at the edges.

Keely lifted Loan up and rested her on her right hip, flipping through a photo album and began showing pictures and speaking words in English.

"House," Keely said, pointing to a photo of their home in Illinois.

"Ma," she said, pointing to herself.

"We're going to take care of you," said one of Loan's soon-to-be new sisters.

Loan sucked in her cheeks and rolled her tongue. The entire Solimene family would convene in Việt Nam for the adoption: Keely, with her American daughters, Arianna, Alexandra, and Victoria, and son, Will. Mick, whose sister also made the trip to Việt Nam, would soon arrive, too.

The Solimenes gave Loan a blinking, beeping plastic toy, and she clutched it, jabbing at the buttons. Everything about this foreign world where Loan was headed was unfamiliar. With one exception: Loan would not be inaugurated into the Solimene family alone. The Solimenes were not adopting just one child from the orphanage in Nha Trang.

They were adopting two.

LOAN HAD ALWAYS watched out for and played with a girl ten months younger than her, not biologically related. The child's name was Như.

Như had arrived at the orphanage at two months old, on Loan's first birthday, July 24, and the two girls took to one another, even though they were opposites. Loan was fun loving, adventurous, and protective. Như was timid and unsure.

The orphanage had tried to prepare Như for her soon-to-be new family's arrival as well. Như had also met the Solimenes before, on their visit three months earlier. But this time when they arrived with lollipops, toys, and clothes, Như took one look at the Americans, turned around, and ran back to her dorm. She hid behind a staff caregiver until the Solimenes came for her again, this time with Loan by their side.

When Loan entered Như's wing of the orphanage, the children flocked to her, poking at her blinking toy. Off in the corner, a caregiver grabbed the other ribbon-trimmed dress, pulling this one over Như's head. Như wriggled in the ruffles and frowned. She reached for the hand of her caregiver, who was trying to pull a pink sun hat over her head. Then the orphanage employee ushered Nhu along to join Loan and the Americans.

Nhu looked nervous, but Loan, wearing a baby-blue sun hat, extended her left hand to Nhu's right one. Loan and Nhu held each other all the way down the steps, across the courtyard, making their way out of the orphanage in their matching outfits.

They were sisters now. Not twins—but from that day forward, "I mean, they were my twins," Keely said years later. "For all intents and purposes, Isabella and Olivia were twins."

LOAN AND NHU spent the next week at the Evason Ana Mandara hotel in Nha Trang with the Solimenes. Adorned with swimming pools and a koi pond, the beach resort was frequented by Westerners as well as Russian and Chinese tourists. Multilingual Vietnamese residents staffed the front desk, bar, and restaurant, cleaned the rooms, and tended to the gardens. But locals did not stay at the Ana Mandara, nor did they dine in the restaurant or swim in the pools. Staff watched curiously as Loan and Nhu, in their matching green and blue swimsuits, clung to inner-tube floaties and ate sliced watermelon and egg rolls. The girls spoke only Vietnamese, while the American family sang "Row, Row, Row Your Boat" to them in English.

Inside the suite, the girls lounged on the two double beds. Now they wore matching purple sundresses and white bloomers that Keely had brought for them. The older Solimene kids watched as Loan and Nhu rolled around on the beds, grabbing their feet as if in a happy baby yoga pose, bopping on and off the mattresses. Loan and Nhu chitchatted and snickered with each other, gesturing toward Victoria, Keely's third daughter, who was sprawled on her belly atop the other bed, grinning at their cuteness.

None of the Solimenes could understand what the girls were saying or what exactly they found so hilarious as they pointed to Victoria and babbled in her face.

Years later, the footage would be translated: "You're fat! You're smelly! You're fat! You're smelly!"

The older sister Arianna turned to the camera and said, "This is how nap time is going."

By night, Nhử would burst into tears, begging to return to the orphanage. The Solimenes had hired a driver for the trip, and they loaded the girls back into his vehicle and dropped them off at the orphanage to sleep, returning the next day to do it all again. Their wait for the paperwork approval stretched on for days upon days until finally it cleared: Loan and Nhử would leave the orphanage for good.

On that official day, July 15, 2002, Keely beamed as she carried a straight-faced Nhử out of the government building on her right hip. Keely held one of the black-haired dolls in her other arm, her purse dangling from her wrist. Mick emerged smiling, holding Loan on his right hip.

Keely and Mick lowered the girls onto a stone patio to take photos in front of the building, which was lined with motorbikes. Both Loan and Nhử stood there looking bewildered, in matching white dresses now, holding matching dolls. Keely snapped photos and Loan smiled for the camera, as if she had become practiced at it.

"Nhử, smile!" Keely called out. "Big smile."

Loan grinned wider, but Nhử looked around sullenly.

Nhử wrapped her left arm around Loan's shoulders and neck in a tight embrace, pulling her sister's head closer to hers until there was nothing between them but skin and air.

"Isabella-Loan. Isabella-Loan," Keely said. "Olivia-Nhử. Olivia-Nhử. You girls are little Solimenes now."

FOUR

The Baby Lifts

ON APRIL 4, 1975, a windowless, hot flight took off from Sài Gòn's Tân Sơn Nhất International Airport. The US Air Force's C-5 Galaxy cargo plane was packed with around 120 infants strapped two to a seat on the upper level and more than a hundred children on the bottom level. Another four dozen adults on board stood and braced themselves as the plane took off at 4:15 p.m. They began handing out bottles of sugar water and cartons of milk to the toddlers.

President Gerald Ford had recently allocated $2 million in humanitarian aid to support the evacuation of Vietnamese children, who were said to be orphans, as part of the US-backed mission Operation Babylift. The kids were on their way to the United States, where American families were preparing to adopt them into their homes. The American war in Việt Nam was coming to an end. In three weeks, Sài Gòn would fall.

Just fifteen minutes into the air, the rear of the plane blew up. The force sent ceiling insulation, glassware, paper, and debris shooting through the cabin.

Someone screamed, "Oh my God! My Jesus, God, no!"

The air pressure began to plummet, and everyone struggled to breathe. Some of the babies began to turn blue. The pilots fought to keep the plane steady, but just after 5:00 p.m. it careened into a rice field, breaking apart, parts of the plane bursting into flames. Of the 313 people on board, 138 perished, including 78 children.

The lead of a story in the *New York Times* quoted a South Vietnamese lieutenant: "It is nice to see you Americans taking home souvenirs of our country as you leave—china, elephants, and orphans. Too bad some of them broke today, but we have plenty more."

Investigations would later find that the military plane had a history of problems. Yet in the hours after the crash, the United States continued to shuttle Vietnamese children to America. "Our mission of mercy will continue," Ford said in the aftermath. "The survivors will be flown here when they are physically able. Other waiting orphans will make the journey."

The day after the Galaxy exploded, another 324 children—including survivors from the previous doomed flight—were loaded onto a Pan Am flight headed for the United States. The infants were put into cardboard boxes lined with airline blankets, then wedged between seats.

When the first flight of children arrived in San Francisco, Vietnamese interpreters began interviewing them, explaining they were going to live with their new families. But some children looked confused and tried to explain that they were not orphans. They had family in Việt Nam and did not want to be adopted. A few asked: "When can I go home?"

A public statement issued immediately after the crash, signed by ethics and religion professors across America, denounced the airlifts, noting that many kids had relatives who might still be alive. The statement also noted: "The children would be happier growing up in Vietnam with Vietnamese, rather than in America with Caucasians," adding, "The only reason for bringing the children here is to salve our conscience, and children should not be used that way."

The criticism did not deter the operation. An ad that ran in the *New York Times* days later read: "Last Friday morning an air force transport crashed, stranding hundreds of orphans fleeing Vietnam. By Friday afternoon we'd chartered a Pan Am 747. . . . Your dollars can literally buy these kids their ticket to a new life."

Many Americans, including protesters who had decried US involvement in the war in Việt Nam, had turned to adoption to cope with their country's culpability and failures. For them, choosing to adopt was not just an act of religious faith or generosity. It was a direct reaction against US negligence in Việt Nam. After the Galaxy crash, and the media coverage that ensued, calls to "rescue" Vietnamese children grew even louder.

The children from Operation Babylift would be part of the first wave from Việt Nam adopted into families in Western homes, in countries such as America. The fall of South Việt Nam, and the danger and chaos that ensued, drove their evacuations. But in the decades after the war, there would be many other Vietnamese children raised in American families. Their adoptions would not be spurred by war but instead by chronic issues like poverty.

These children would be raised under the legacy of Operation Babylift, which continues to shape modern transnational adoption systems and is often driven by the same kind of assumptions about what constitutes and creates a better life.

"WE HAVE A saying in Vietnam," Nhu Miller, a Vietnamese researcher, told Marjorie Margolies, an American journalist who documented their conversation in her 1976 memoir. "If your father is dead, you still have an uncle. If your mother is dead, you have an aunt."

Margolies had decided to adopt from Việt Nam. Miller explained to her: "We never had orphanages until the French came, and then the Americans. We always had the extended family, and if there was no living relative, there was always a friend of a neighbor who took you in. . . . I still think that's the best solution for most of our children. I am not really enthusiastic about having our children adopted and taken out of the country."

Historically in Việt Nam, many families sent their children to orphanages during times of turmoil, to protect them from war, starvation, and peril. They thought of the facilities as boarding and feeding centers or as temporary foster homes. Though some children did not have surviving family members, others did have relatives who planned to return for the children when they could earn enough money or when it was safe to bring them home.

By 1972, the Nixon administration had dropped more than 155,000 tons of bombs on North Việt Nam, demolishing villages, schools, and medical facilities and sending waves of displaced residents fleeing to other regions in search of safety and shelter. In the final months of war, the North Vietnamese military began seizing South Vietnamese provinces, sending refugees fleeing in search of getaway boats. Some desperately waded into the sea, including mothers holding their babies, only to drown or be trampled trying to reach barges and fishing boats.

The US military's deadly policies and practices in South Việt Nam gave rise to more refugees and vulnerable children, including "Amerasian" children with Vietnamese mothers and American fathers who were US soldiers, who filled the orphanages, which by early 1975 held approximately twenty thousand kids. As Americans tuned into the news about Việt Nam, many began to worry about the youngest survivors, left to fend for themselves, as they saw it, under brutal communists.

After the crash of the Galaxy cargo plane in April 1975, two dozen more planes full of Vietnamese children took off over the following weeks, evacuating twenty-seven hundred children from South Việt Nam. Operation Babylift became a media spectacle, drawing in famous supporters like *Playboy* founder Hugh Hefner, who provided his own plane, the *Big Bunny*, to transport the children to the States and deployed *Playboy* models to stay with the babies en route.

While some in the media at the time hailed Operation Babylift as a massive rescue and relief effort, others assailed the operation as child exploitation, reflecting the same "kind of wrongheaded thinking that led to our involvement in Vietnam in the first place," as Judith Coburn of the *Village Voice* put it. Another journalist, Gloria Emerson, took aim at white parents, particularly "middle-class women," who she said welcomed their new "dark-eyed children" while giving them new names like "Phyllis and Wendy and David." The ACLU issued a statement saying Americans mistakenly assumed that "growing up in a good American home is the best of all possible solutions for the children." As one scholar, Jonathan Patrick Thompson, who studied white saviorism's role in the evacuation of Vietnamese children, wrote: "This Western sense of knowing what is best for non-white cultures was at the core of America's involvement in Vietnam and Operation Babylift."

In the years leading up to the end of the war in Việt Nam, Black leaders in the United States linked the struggles of Vietnamese citizens to their own, in seeking economic, cultural, and political freedom. They saw the Vietnamese as victims of Western imperialism. Around this time period—the peak of antiwar protests—the formation of the term *Asian American* as an identity and political ideology began to emerge on campuses like the University of California, Berkeley and San Francisco State College. Inspired by the Black Panthers and other contemporary political activist groups, the Third World Liberation Front and the Asian American Political Alliance came into being as social movements, encompassing a broad range of pan-ethnic groups under the designation of Asian American.

Meanwhile, Martin Luther King Jr. joined a chorus of other Black activists, scholars, and writers, including Malcolm X and James Baldwin, who understood the conflict as seeking to expand US economic power and political control over parts of Asia. "We are a racist society, racist to the very marrow, and we are fighting a racist war," wrote Baldwin in 1967. Baldwin believed that his own condition as a Black man in America told him enough about what white Americans really wanted, for him and for Asian people. "Therefore, every bombed village is my hometown."

Just as Langston Hughes and W. E. B. Du Bois had viewed the decision to drop atomic bombs on Japan as racially motivated, connecting Japan's nonwhite victims to the freedom struggle, King and Baldwin understood that the extraordinary military spending on the war in Việt Nam meant fewer resources for poverty, housing, and educational initiatives at home. In his 1967 "Beyond Vietnam" speech King declared:

"The Western arrogance of feeling that it has everything to teach others and nothing to learn from them is not just."

In the brutality and aftermath of the war, adoption advocates claimed the "babies were unwanted," as Dana Sachs documented in *The Life We Were Given: Operation Babylift, International Adoption, and the Children of the War in Vietnam*. But in sifting through archives of notes posted by families looking for their lost kids, Sachs wrote: "Clearly, some of the children were wanted. Deeply wanted, even after 30 years had passed." Of the two thousand to three thousand orphans evacuated and sent to Western families, as many as fifteen hundred of them were estimated to never have been abandoned.

"But what about the mixed-race children—abandoned by GIs in South Vietnam?" Margolies asked Miller. "If they're going to be rejected, aren't they better off coming to America? Coming to a home where they'll find love, not rejection?"

Miller replied, "Black children are discriminated against in America, too."

"But Nhu, this is a war-torn country. It's very important to get children out of an orphanage into a family, especially in these crucial years."

Miller told Margolies that America had spent hundreds of billions of dollars in Việt Nam. Yet only a sliver of that money went toward the country's kids. "Why don't they take some of the money and use it to help families stay together in Vietnam," she said, "so we can take care of our children?"

Some family members in Việt Nam had enlisted their children to be a part of Operation Babylift, with hopes of reclaiming them as soon as they could make their own way to the United States. It was a desperate but temporary attempt to save them from suffering in the aftermath of war. Some Vietnamese parents did come to America, immediately setting forth to find their children upon arrival. Some even filed lawsuits to get their children back.

Amid the war and tumult of 1975 in Sài Gòn, Vietnamese mother Lê Thi Sang arranged for an American helicopter pilot to transport her son, Tuân, to America. The pilot's family, the Knights, ended up adopting the child and renaming him Dean.

Lê Thi Sang eventually migrated to the United States, as historian Allison Varzally documented in *Children of Reunion: Vietnamese Adoptions and the Politics of Family Migrations*. Lê Thi Sang got a job as a hotel maid and wasted no time trying to recover her son, but the American family caring for him said he no longer wanted to speak Vietnamese. He had become a proud "American boy," who enjoyed sports and family pets.

The custody battle went to court. A judge ordered that Tuân live with his biological mother for three months. After that trial period, he would be free to choose which parents he wanted to live with. Tuân left the American family's home reluctantly.

At first, Lê Thi Sang worried she could not compete with the Knights, who had provided clothes, toys, and other comforts to the boy. Instead, as Varzally reported, Lê Thi Sang decided to feed her son Vietnamese food in hopes that he would remember his roots. She took him fishing. She told him that she loved him. After three months, to the Knights' dismay, Tuân made up his mind: he would live with his mother.

"Foreigners, who see only orphanages and assume the Vietnamese don't care for their children, do not hear about mothers struggling alone to care for ten children," Nhu Miller said in 1975. She added that they also don't consider women caring for others' children, who would never think of putting them in an orphanage.

As Varzally pointed out, "Miller's portrait of maternal struggle and adaptation disrupted prevailing images of Vietnamese women that had shaped US assertions in South Vietnam"—images of Asian women as "victims or vixens." These caricatures ignored the real Vietnamese women, "individuals making tough but deliberate choices amid arduous circumstances."

FIVE

Liên

LONG BEFORE SHE gave birth to twin girls, Nguyễn Thị Kim Liên grew up in Nha Trang with three brothers and eight sisters (another sister passed away young). They all lived in a single-room home with walls made of soil and reeds, and a roof thatched with rice straw. They slept on four beds made of bambusa balcooa. Liên slept with her sisters in one bed, the brothers in the other.

Liên was born in Đất Sét, Diên Khánh, in the Khánh Hoà Province. Liên's father gambled, buying rice and fish with his winnings. He often brought Liên along, and she remembers those trips fondly, because these were rare moments when she received so much of his attention. Liên's mother, Nguyễn Thị Thanh, worked constantly to provide for her kids, making bánh and selling it at local market. Later, Thanh worked as a caregiver for affluent mothers who had just given birth, helping them bathe their babies and cooking and cleaning for them.

When Thanh was a baby, her own mother died. Thanh never knew her real parents. Like her granddaughter, Hà, Thanh was adopted and raised by two women. When she grew up, she married Liên's father, who was supposed to fight in the war alongside the Việt Cộng, against the government of South Việt Nam, Thanh explained, "but he was always hiding because he did not want to fight."

Thanh fended for herself and her kids at a time when Việt Nam's landscape had been ravaged by land mines and bombs. The napalm dropped by the United States set jungles ablaze and destroyed villages, causing mass death and devastating hunger. Food staples like rice, meat, and milk were in short supply, and families relied on ration coupons. Starvation led to vitamin A deficiencies, blinding children. Malnourished populations ended up with stunted growth.

Liên was three when Sài Gòn fell. After its troops withdrew from the country, the United States imposed a trade embargo on Việt Nam, cutting off exports and imports from America. Other nations also denied assistance to Việt Nam, under US pressure. Hundreds of thousands of Vietnamese refugees fled the country over the next decade, thousands dying at sea as they embarked on a mass exodus by boat.

Thanh stayed in Việt Nam, devoting every day to finding or buying food for her family. She fed Liên and her siblings rice grains that fell from trucks onto the cement, mixing the grains with cassava. She sold noodles to make a living. She did not have official government identification documents, which would have afforded her more opportunities like an education.

There were days when the family didn't have any food, and despite her mom's efforts Liên ate anything she could find. She remembers having worms in her stomach. Even during the holiday Tết, there was no special meal. The family was hungry like any other day. When they did manage to salvage some rice, the family members would divvy it up after cooking it with cassava. Wood burning beneath the brick stove heated the pot. The bitter taste made Liên cry.

When their mother was not home, most of her siblings forgot to feed Liên and gobbled up the little food they had themselves. When Thanh was home, she gave the children rice before eating any of it herself. Liên's hunger was prioritized.

Like her mother, Liên did not have the government identification documents needed to enroll in school. Due to her hip injury from birth, Liên was never able to walk or move around like her siblings, but when she was nine, she tried to work to help her family. She got a job tending to other people's cows. Once, while she was driving the cows, they began to run. Liên was so unsteady on her faulty leg, they swiftly knocked her down and a cow stepped on her neck. She ended up in the hospital and would bear the scar from that day forever.

Liên was twenty-five when she met the man who would become the birth father to the twins. He was visiting his brother in the house next door to where Liên was living with another sister in her family. As Liên recalled, she learned he was divorced and had a teenage son. He courted her, but Liên's sisters did not care for him and discouraged the relationship. Liên fell for his charm anyway; just weeks into dating, she believed she was in love.

Her boyfriend came and went, stopping by to see her when he visited his brother, then disappearing for stretches of time. When he was away, Liên relied on his brother to give her rides to the store or work. She could not walk far or ride a bike by herself. When Liên's boyfriend learned that his brother had been giving her bike rides, he grew jealous and enraged.

Three months into the relationship, Liên began to feel tired and ill, and the discomfort did not dissipate for days. Her sister advised her to go to the hospital, where the doctor told her she was pregnant. At a follow-up months later, she learned she was carrying twins. She and her boyfriend had been dating for only a few months, and when Liên told him the news, he disappeared.

Liên's family blamed her for being careless enough to carry on with a man who was not her husband. One sister insisted that Liên terminate the pregnancy—she dragged her out of the house, telling her to go to the clinic and get an abortion, but another sister stopped them. She told Liên it was morally wrong to abort, and she must keep the children and raise them. Liên knew what hunger felt like. She didn't want her children to grow up knowing that ache.

To Liên, in the earliest days of the twins' lives, they were two creatures crying, peeing, and breathing in tandem who depended on her to stay alive. She never named the twins herself. It was hard to tell them apart, except one was sicker.

When she went to the orphanage with her twin girls that day in 1998, she did not want to give away either child. If she'd had money, Liên said years later, she would have kept both, raised them herself. "I had to work and buy milk from outside to feed them. But it wasn't enough, so I had to give one up for adoption," Liên said in Vietnamese. "The adoption agency gave me some money, so I could buy milk for the other one." She explained that someone from the orphanage ended up naming her daughter Kim Loan. Liên knew that Loan was the healthier daughter and that her child might be adopted by another family. She accepted that reality and vowed to visit the orphanage when she could until that day came.

In those initial weeks after signing over the care of Loan to the adoption agency, Liên realized that having one child was still impossible for her to manage. It was then, as she grew more committed to her new romantic relationship, that Liên made her decision. She was aware that her sister Rô, and Rô's partner, Tuyết, wished to raise a child together.

Liên had always been closest to Rô, who was four years older and a natural nurturer, sometimes salvaging food for Liên or giving her attention in a household where it was easy to get overlooked. She knew she could trust Rô with her child.

WITH HÀ SAFELY in the care of Rô and Tuyết, Liên got to witness them caring for her. She also visited her other twin daughter in the orphanage at various times during the first three years of her life. She gave Loan earrings on one of the earliest visits, a gift she hoped her daughter would keep to remember her by.

Then came the day when Liên arrived at the orphanage and was told that Loan had been adopted. "When I came again to see Loan," Liên said, "she was already gone." According to Liên's memory, the orphanage never warned her that the proceedings were under way, much less with an American family. All Liên can remember is crying for a long time. She always knew it was a possibility, but her daughter's sudden disappearance crushed her. "I was happy for Loan," she recalled, "but I also asked myself if and when I could meet Loan again." She hoped Loan was allowed to bring the earrings to her new home. She hoped Loan knew she had a mother who loved her. As the years passed, Liên said she thought about her lost daughter every day. "I missed Loan a lot. I wondered, 'Where is Loan? How is her life? Does she still remember me?'"

The twins, Liên explained, received opportunities she never had. "If they still had lived with me, they would end up like me. They would have no chance to study," Liên said. "They would not have a bright future and sometimes even nothing to eat."

When Hà and Isabella were around seven, Liên tracked down the Solimene family's information through someone locally connected to the adoption agency. She asked an acquaintance in Việt Nam to write a letter to the family, translating her Vietnamese words into English. The Solimene family received the letter, which was postmarked February 19, 2006.

It read:

I am very sad. I miss my child very much. But I don't know what to do. Our lives here are very unstable, we are here one day and there the next because I don't have a house. . . .

I sincerely don't know what to say except for thanking you from the bottom of my heart. . . . No parents can leave their child but because of our situation we had no choice. I know you both are good people; Loan is very lucky to be able to be raised by you. Do you know that not all Vietnamese are rich? Many are forced to live in poverty, living day by day. I am hoping you can help us out so we can start a small business. I will be grateful for your help.

The reasons I am writing this letter is first to ask how you are doing and Loan, second I want to let you know how grateful I am, third I am hoping for your help so my kid here can have a better life. . . . I wish and dream that one day Loan will return to Việt Nam, but I don't know if this dream will come true. . . .

My children here don't have a chance to go to school. My husband drives a cyclo, he makes just enough to buy rice for day-by-day meal. As for me, I am handicapped so I can't do much. This forces us to share the living space with other family. I don't know why I am in such poverty, this is my destiny which I have to accept.

It was a good thing you came along for Loan, she will have a better future not like her younger sibling. . . . I am hoping my child will have a bright future, that is the most important any parent can wish for.

SIX

Rô and Tuyết

LIÊN'S SISTER NGUYỄN Thị Kim Rô was pregnant once. She mostly remembers the blood. Rô was twenty-one at the time, and she knew it could not have been her period, though she never went to a hospital to find out for sure. Many years later, Rô did go to a Buddhist temple, where she asked one of the spiritual guides about the day of the blood. She believed they could see into the past, and she'd never let go of that day, how scary it was. The guide told her she had peed out her baby boy.

Rô's worries were confirmed. It had been a miscarriage.

Three months earlier, Rô had been in an arranged marriage, but it was not real love. She didn't get along with the man or her mother-in-law. It took only a couple of weeks of being his wife for Rô to know she didn't want any part of it. She fled.

Rô remembers crossing a river at midnight, hiding in the forest. She snuck into her family's house when daylight came, asking if her husband had come to find her. They told her to keep running—he was looking for her. She begged for money and collected enough to buy a bus ticket to the city, but her husband eventually tracked her down and carted her back to the countryside. She stayed for a few days, then ran away again, for the last time.

Rô knew the pregnancy that resulted in a miscarriage had been her one chance at growing a child in her own body. She knew nothing of IVF or any fertility medical procedures. Rô knew only that she had never been with a man before her husband. And she never would again.

Born in 1968, Rô grew up in the same single-room hut as her younger sister Liên, sleeping on the same bambusa balcooa beds, eating the rice-and-cassava mixtures, often starving too. But she worked for others for as long as she could remember, mostly as a babysitter and housecleaner. Rô was among the most sensitive and nurturing of the siblings, a contrast to Liên, who was reticent and reserved. Rô cried at goodbyes and cuddled. She tried to protect Liên. This is why their mother assumed Rô would make the ideal wife for a man.

Two years before her arranged marriage, when Rô was nineteen, she met a friend's sister, Tuyết, then eighteen. Rô and Tuyết did not take to each other immediately. The two women were so different—Rô was doting and girlish; Tuyết, steely and serious. Tuyết would pick at Rô's daintiness, even throwing pebbles at her to try to get a rise out of her. Meanwhile, Rô looked at Tuyết with disdain. *Why*, she would think, *does this girl look like a boy?*

Rô, who had moved to the countryside with her parents and four sisters (two of the twelve siblings had passed away), left for Nha Trang for a few months to earn money working at a restaurant and cleaning homes. When she returned, flush with groceries purchased from her earnings, she invited Tuyết to her family's home for dinner as an act of good faith. Tuyết agreed, and the two began to grow closer.

Tuyết played the guitar, and Rô would follow her around listening to her music. They spent many evenings this way, until Rô was suddenly married off, forced to be with a husband.

When Rô fled her husband the final time, she did not return. She went straight to Tuyết.

"Run away with me," she told her. Rô knew that her husband, who lived in the next village, could still find her if she stayed.

Tuyết did not hesitate.

The two of them ended up in Long Khánh, in the southeast region of Việt Nam. They spent two years on the road together, working in coffee fields and harvesting dragon fruit and rambutan on farms.

When they returned, Rô's husband had found another woman, and Rô and Tuyết had made up their minds: neither of them would ever need another partner. They were in love and would build a home and a life together. They even talked of one day adopting a child.

TRẦN THỊ TUYẾT was six when the American War ended. She remembers waking up to the sound of an explosion. A bomb had fallen nearby, and more continued to drop. Her mom whisked her to an underground hideaway, where they stayed overnight. Tuyết cried as her mother tried to reassure her. She told Tuyết the sky was pooping.

Tuyết is the youngest of twenty siblings (her father had two wives). Of the eleven siblings her mother gave birth to, only four survived. Tuyết explained that some of them died in a bombing during the war, while others died from malnutrition.

Her father worked for the North Vietnamese Army. After the North conquered the South, he returned to Nha Trang, but since so many of Tuyết's siblings had passed away, her father believed her mother had bad spirits inside of her. He married another woman to reset this fortune and build a new family. Both wives lived in the same three-room house together with all the kids, and Tuyết does not recall the women ever quarreling, though the children argued all the time. Tuyết's father had his own room. He would spend one night with one wife, then spend the next with the other.

Tuyết was never close to her father, but it was his government position that enabled her to attend school. She also had official government identification, those coveted legal documents that Rô and Liên's family lacked. Everyone in Tuyết's family was listed in the sổ hộ khẩu, a government-issued household registration book, along with each person's age and address.

Due to her father's status, Tuyết's siblings also each had giấy chứng minh nhân dân, citizen identification cards. This legal system allowed the government to keep track of its citizens' whereabouts, but it was also crucial for accessing subsidized medical care and public welfare and being allowed to attend a public school. A resident could apply for the documents, but it was a notoriously complicated and potentially pricey system to navigate, with each missing document depending on another. Being born into a family with all this already in place was a privilege. For most, the system seemed impossible to wade through. Liên and her family members never did.

Tuyết's family was never poor in any way comparable to Rô and Liên's family. The government also gave Tuyết's father, along with his kids, various plots of land on which they could build homes. When Tuyết was ten, her mother moved with her four surviving kids away from Nha Trang to the village of Khánh Đông, where they lived on one of those government-provided pieces of land. Tuyết's father remained in the city with his second wife and her children.

Tuyết's mother sold sticky rice to support her family. Her brother went to work on the sea catching fish, returning once a week to visit. Tuyết's only sister stayed behind to do the housekeeping and cooking, and Tuyết, along with another brother, went to work in the sugarcane, cornfields, and rice fields. She would begin at 7:00 a.m. and get off at 5:00 p.m. It was hard work in hot, humid weather, the kind that built muscles and hardened hands. Tuyết did not have enough education to work in an office, and she never saw herself as a housekeeper, so she took whatever physical jobs came to her.

When Tuyết fell in love with Rô, she was first attracted to her beauty and sweetness. She loved how Rô appreciated her guitar playing, how she looked beyond Tuyết's hard exterior and saw the fellow nurturer inside. Rô had also always held jobs, including one at a brickmaking company, where she hurt her back. She couldn't work in the rice fields as easily as her partner. Tuyết added Rô's name, birthday, and shared address into her số hộ khẩu. With their partnership, Rô was able to break free of life without identification cards.

ONE DAY, RÔ and Tuyết's neighbor returned to the village from a hospital in Nha Trang, where she had given birth. The neighbor told them that she had seen Rô's sister, Liên, at the same hospital and that Liên had given birth to twins. Rô had not talked to Liên for months, and though she had heard her sister was pregnant, she had no idea it was with two babies.

A few weeks later, Rô and Tuyết traveled to the city to pay Liên a visit. They brought twenty kilograms of rice as a gift. When they found Liên, she was temporarily staying with both babies in home of another sister, the same one who had stopped Liên from getting an abortion.

Tuyết examined the infants. They were naked and hungry. Rô kissed and cuddled the twins through the night. Tuyết and Rô could not forget how malnourished they looked. One was particularly weak.

Not long after that visit, Tuyết returned to Nha Trang to run errands and stopped by again to see Liên and her twins. Rô stayed back in the village. This time, Tuyết saw only one baby. Liên told her she had given the other to the orphanage. Tuyết picked up the remaining child and cradled her. She seemed sicker than before. Liên had no money for diapers, and the infant pooped on Tuyết's shirt.

A few weeks later, Liên appeared in Khánh Đông on a rainy winter day. She had traveled with the baby to ask Tuyết and Rô for help. Their sister could not care for them. The grandmother could not either. Liên had brought along someone else too: her new boyfriend, Quý. He loved Liên and wanted to provide for her—he even wanted to support the twins eventually—but Quý had no job at the time.

Tuyết and Rô fed their visitors. Then Tuyết made Liên an offer: If caring for this baby was too difficult, why not let Rô and her look after the child for one month? They had plenty of food, and enough money to pay for milk. They could nurture her back to stronger health. If, after that time period, Liên wanted to take the child back, she could. Or, if after one month, Liên decided she wanted to give the baby to Tuyết and Rô forever, she could do that too. The choice was up to her.

Liên and Quý stayed at Tuyết and Rô's house with the baby for three days. On the third day, Liên told Tuyết and Rô she had already made up her mind. She would give the child to them. But she did not want to lose contact with her daughter forever. Tuyết understood. She offered to let Liên and Quý stay for a while in a house nearby, on land owned by her brother.

Tuyết named the baby Hồng Hà. It means "Red River," after a famous waterway flowing from Southwest China through northern Việt Nam.

Liên got pregnant again shortly after relinquishing parental rights to the twins, this time with Quý's child. In the first years of Hà's life, Liên got to see Rô and Tuyết parenting her in the village, how good they were at it. Liên always considered herself to be Hà's mother, regardless of who raised her, but she never doubted how much they loved Hà.

In Rô and Tuyết's village, Liên gave birth to Quý's daughter, whom she named Phan Hoàng Ngọc; she was a year younger than the twins. Again, Liên wondered, what would this child's future bring if she had been unable to care for her previous two? But this time, Liên had Quý, a committed father, and he pledged to find work.

RÔ HELPED LIÊN take care of her newborn for twenty days. Meanwhile, Quý went to work to earn money in the sugarcane fields with Tuyết. After a period of living on loaned land, and seeing how devotedly her sister and Tuyết raised Hà, Liên decided to move back to the city with Quý. There, Liên and Quý had another daughter, Liên's fourth.

Tuyết added Hà into her family registration book. From then on, Hà would have all the benefits bestowed upon a legal, documented resident. Most important to Tuyết, Hà would get to enroll in school.

Hà

If I had grown up with Liên, my life would be very different. Tuyết and Rô made sure I got an education. When I was young, I did not care about school. But my moms who raised me made sure I worked hard in my studies.

I don't know how much genes play a role in how we think. But I know my environment growing up shaped me into a person who cared about getting a good education.

I don't think you can measure intelligence without thinking about the environment someone grows up with too.

SEVEN

Cuckoo Birds

IN THE NINETEENTH century, Francis Galton, the younger cousin of Charles Darwin, grew fascinated by the cuckoo bird, those long-tailed animals for which the clocks are named. He thought there were lessons for humans in the cuckoo's refusal to adapt to the environment of another species.

Adult cuckoo birds are known to sneak their eggs into the nests of other birds—of a different breed of bird entirely—tricking strangers into raising their young. The foster cuckoos are reared exclusively by adoptive mothers. As soon as the bird is old enough, Galton noted, it cries its distinct two-syllable "coo-cooo," despite a lifetime of being nurtured by birds who made other sounds. "It is probable that nearly every young cuckoo, during a series of many hundred generations, has been brought up in a family whose language is a chirp and a twitter," Galton wrote in 1875. "But the cuckoo cannot or will not adopt that language, or any other of the habits of its foster-parents."

To him, this indicated that "much more is inherited than educability, namely the propensity to act in the same way under similar circumstances which characterizes all animals of the same race, whether they have been reared from eggs and had no maternal teaching; or otherwise." The cuckoo bird, Galton noted, "leaves its birthplace as soon as it is able, and finds out its own kith and kin, and identifies itself henceforth with them."

To Galton, this peculiar animal behavior (while not universal to all birds) mimicked what he believed to be a biological inability in humans to shed the genetic predispositions they are born with, or to fully embody different learned traits or behaviors from another gene pool, simply because they were exposed to alternate environments.

In 1875, Galton announced that he had discovered a "new method" by which to weigh the effects of nature and nurture. Galton published "The History of Twins," the first detailed attempt to tease apart the influences of nature and nurture by focusing on twins. Galton sent questionnaires to twins, examining traits like height, weight, strength, voice intonation, and handwriting, and received back replies for eighty cases. Nine twins in the paper (which was not peer reviewed) described "seeing his or her reflection in a looking-glass and addressing it in the belief it was the other twin in person"; one set of twins reported: "We were extremely alike, and are so at this moment, so much so that our children up to five and six years old did not know us apart."

Transfixed by possibilities of intellectual talent and mental ability being passed down through bloodlines, Galton took note of cases of twins experiencing identical toothaches and extractions, hair loss, death of the same disease, simultaneous contraction of the same contagious illness, such as whooping cough, chicken pox, and measles. Others reported making the same comments at the same time, singing in the same moment, finishing each other's sentences. "It would be an interesting experiment," Galton wrote, "for twins who were closely alike to try how far dogs could distinguish them by scent."

His theories expanded from birds and gene lines into grandiose templates for designing a superior human race. Eight years after his paper was published, he proposed the selective breeding of people in order to create stronger, smarter, more desirable individuals, and he called this *eugenics*.

If genes proved predetermination, as many accepted in the early part of the twentieth century, it made sense to US social workers to screen orphans with IQ tests or to probe the biological family's medical, psychological, socioeconomic, and academic histories, so children could end up with parents who came from similar intellectual, behavioral, and physical stock. At a time when adopting across racial lines rarely occurred in the United States, adoption was administered through a eugenics-shaped "matching" system.

Social workers hardly had to ask if prospective parents wanted a child as close as possible to their own hair or eye color. Some parents even appealed for a child that might have similar musical talents or college potential. For such requests, social workers made predictions based on intelligence tests and psychological screenings of children and their relatives. "For social workers, infants were not blank slates upon which adopters would write their own scripts," Barbara Melosh wrote in *Strangers and Kin: The American Way of Adoption*, "but rather were disturbing ciphers to be painstakingly decoded."

THE FIRST PAIR of identical twins separated at birth to be "studied" were known as "Jessie and Bess." In a 1922 paper in the *Journal of Heredity*, Paul Popenoe wrote of the case of a mother in Arizona who gave birth to identical twin girls. The mother died eight months later, and the girls ended up living with two different families. The twins did not see each other again until they were eighteen. The case would be cited as science in literature for years to come despite (or perhaps because of) the insidious views of its author.

Popenoe was also a white supremacist and a supporter of eugenics. He led calls in California for forced sterilization of people living in psychiatric hospitals. As many as seventy thousand Americans—minorities, poor, women, people who were deaf, blind, or mentally or physically ill—were forcibly sterilized during the twentieth century under eugenics-fueled policies. In 1927, the US Supreme Court ruled that the forced sterilization of the handicapped did not violate the US Constitution. In the words of Supreme Court Justice Oliver Wendall Holmes, "Three generations of imbeciles are enough." In 1942, the ruling was overturned but not before thousands of people underwent the procedure.

Eugenics would eventually fuel Adolf Hitler's mass killings of Jewish and other groups in Nazi Germany. Under Hitler's regime, three thousand identical and fraternal twins were held captive at Auschwitz, where they were tortured, starved, injected, drained for blood, mutilated, and killed as part of Nazi experiments conducted by Josef Mengele, who seemed to be trying to find evidence of biological superiority or inferiority within different groups of people.

Popenoe wrote that Bess lived with her adoptive parents on a ranch until she turned five. The family then moved to Helena, Montana, where she attended public school. She ended up in a business career, working as a secretary and clerk. Her sister, Jessie, attended rural schools and trained as a nurse, before having a "physical breakdown," as Popenoe wrote. She taught school, then married and had a son.

After they reunited, the sisters appeared to resemble each other. Same height, voices, hair. Both had weak lungs. "We are both high strung and do not seem to conserve our energy as we should," one sister noted. "We both favor history, social study . . . and politics. Neither of us cares for mathematics, and I would not call either of us a good student. We are too 'smattery,' although we learn rapidly and with very little effort."

Popenoe determined from this single case study: "Such mental similarity in two individuals brought up together is striking enough. But when two individuals are separated in infancy, brought up as differently as are the twin sisters described above, and still manifest such mental similarities, it is impossible to resist the conclusion that the psychical make-up of the individual is very largely settled by the time he is born."

IN THE 1930S, adoption agencies across the United States began implementing closed adoptions, cutting off all contact between birth and adoptive families. For generations, families with adoptees lived in the dark, without access to birth records or genetic profiles. The complete severing of child from birth parent turned out to be a boon for scientists seeking to isolate biological influences from environmental.

Like twin studies, adoption studies became a cornerstone of the field of behavioral genetics. In the early part of the twentieth century, adoption research was also used to try to measure intelligence, with findings again co-opted by white supremacists (some of whom happened to be scientists) to advance theories that racial differences in behavior have a genetic basis.

Science is a reflection of a particular social and political moment. It has never been immune to bias, bigotry, xenophobia, and racism of its times or its practitioners. Even today, some researchers cling to the science of inheritance and continue to push specific hypotheses and assumptions. "The concept of genetic determinism has made some succumb to the illusion that every one of us has a racial destiny," wrote Angela Saini in *Superior: The Return of Race Science.* "In reality, as science has advanced, it has only become clearer that things are more complicated."

By the 1950s, eugenics continued to charge adoption debates, yet beliefs in genetic determinism were on the precipice of falling out of fashion. Social scientists and anthropologists pushed new research supporting ideas that culture and nurture shaped human character and individuality, not a person's particular bloodline. Another extreme theory was taking hold—behaviorism—sharply tilting public support away from the power of nature and toward the belief that environment dominates the narrative in shaping who a person becomes.

EIGHT

Isabella

GROWING UP IN Illinois, Isabella used to sit in the bedroom that she shared with Olivia and play with her favorite toy, an interactive globe that came with a touch pen. She tapped the pen on a different part of the world, and the globe spoke to her, offering facts about the place's history or engaging her with games about cultures.

Her mom decorated their bedroom. Isabella had a purple blankie; Oliva had a pink one. They slept in a trundle bed and, later, in twin beds draped with canopy veils. They watched cartoons on a purple and pink Disney princess television. As little girls, Isabella and Olivia spent hours using their imagination while tinkering with their giant toy castle and its majestic kings, queens, and knights, all the stuff that fairy tales are made of.

The girls also had a Barbie house with a pretend hot tub and an automated toddler-size Barbie jeep, which they would climb inside and steer around the block. It would take an entire afternoon, the toy vehicle moved so slowly. And the Barbie dolls? Olivia and Isabella gleefully ripped the heads off and flushed them down the toilet.

"Been murdering dolls since '98," Isabella wrote years later under an Instagram photo of her and Olivia taken during their adoption, when both girls were dressed matching white sundresses and given identical black-haired baby dolls. Olivia held hers in a football clutch. Isabella held hers by the neck.

The Solimenes lived in Barrington, Illinois, one of the wealthiest communities of its size in America, home to investment bankers and lawyers who commuted forty miles southeast to Chicago. The family's Cape Cod–style house on West Sunset Road had gray and white trim, five bedrooms, and a plush, manicured lawn—more than four thousand square feet of house on a half-acre corner lot. The 2000 US Census counted 10,047 residents. Ninety-six percent of them were white. Asian Americans made up 2 percent.

Their mother, Keely Solimene, had never wanted to move to Barrington. She grew up with parents who struggled financially. Still, the family ended up there at Mick's suggestion, staying for nearly a decade after Isabella and Olivia were adopted.

The Solimene family adored Isabella and Olivia, providing all the elements of an upper-class American life. Birthday parties, private-school educations, toys, books, bikes, and puppies. Keely shuttled kids from school to appointments. She took care of homemaking duties, with Mick often away. Her four biological kids were spread among elementary, middle, and high schools when Isabella and Olivia were preschoolers. Keely was the nurturing force in the family, tending to homework and extracurricular schedules, illnesses, injuries, cooking, cleaning.

They were a close and supportive family. Growing up, Isabella's parents and siblings cheered her on at soccer matches as she played with red and white bows in her hair. For Halloween, Olivia and Isabella dressed up like mosquitoes with wings. The family went on trips to Holden Beach, North Carolina, where they all raced go-karts and devoured ice cream. Isabella and her siblings rode horses at Broken Bow Ranch in Texas, and went on ski trips in Maine and Colorado. Sometimes, their older brother, Will, would pick up Isabella and Olivia, carrying them over his shoulders through the snow as they squealed with laughter.

Looking back on her childhood, Isabella cherished these moments of joy. Family dinners, celebrations, holidays. Whatever the world outside of their household thought about them, Isabella remembers feeling like she was an integral part of their tight-knit family circle, starting with her very first days as a Solimene.

WHEN ISABELLA ARRIVED in the United States, the Solimene siblings would chase her around the house trying to get her attention. "Loan! Kim Loan!" Soon she learned to answer to Isabella, but she never felt like the name fit her.

She and Olivia also did not appreciate their mom's tendency to dress them alike. The sisters abandoned this practice as soon as they had any say in the matter. Years later, a college-age Isabella would post a photo of herself and Olivia when they were preschoolers on Instagram. Both girls had matching retro-style lime-green polka-dot dresses with high, round collars, white bobby socks with black Mary Jane–style shoes, and star-shaped purple sunglasses.

"Killer outfit, mom," Isabella captioned the photo.

Keely enrolled the girls in a preschool in Barrington, where they were immersed in English. Isabella and Olivia still played with each other speaking Vietnamese until one day Isabella woke up refusing to speak at all. Instead, she pantomimed. She pointed to food, to her stomach, to the sun, hugging herself to express that she was warm. This enraged Olivia. Isabella had abandoned their private language. Yet eventually, Olivia did too. Within a year of living in America, Isabella and Olivia communicated with each other, and everyone else, in English. They even dreamed in English.

Growing up, Isabella had a favorite book, which she learned to read on her own: *The Story of Ferdinand*. In the book, a Spanish bull named Ferdinand lives peacefully in a pasture with his mother. While the other young bulls around him like to run and buck, Ferdinand prefers lounging under a tree and smelling the flowers. One day, Ferdinand is stung by a bee and begins jumping around wildly. A group of men spot the bucking bull, mistaking him to be tough and mean. They capture him and cart him off to a bullring. But sitting in the middle of the ring, Ferdinand won't fight. The picadors, the banderilleros, and the matador do their best to convince Ferdinand to fight, but he will not become what others expect him to be.

The children's classic was written by Munro Leaf in 1937 and published in the lead-up to the Spanish Civil War, when Fascist military forces began rebelling against the leftist republic. Ferdinand the gender-nonconforming bull became a political character, criticized by all sides. He was called "subversive," "Red propaganda," "Fascist propaganda." The book was banned in Spain, and Hitler demanded it be burned in Nazi Germany.

But *The Story of Ferdinand* survived and endured for generations across the world, making its way into the small hands of Isabella, inside of her fairy-tale princess bedroom, where she absorbed the tale of the animal plucked from one existence and dropped into another, refusing to go against his true nature.

BY SECOND GRADE, Isabella began getting bullied by a peer. "She had siblings that were friends with my siblings. So of course, my mom was like, 'They're good people, she's just a kid.' My mom had a relationship with her parents. So did my dad."

Isabella got into fights with the girl. "She would bite me in my own house," Isabella said. "Then at a certain time in my life, I'd be like, 'Wait, no, that's actually not okay.' Because now I have bruises. Now my skin is broken from her."

Isabella remembered how her mom gave her "a little slap on the butt," and said, "Go play with her." To Isabella, it was like telling her, "Get over yourself."

Her mom didn't understand why Isabella didn't care to play with the other kids at school or in the community. Many years later, Keely would speak to Isabella about her regrets over not sticking up for her, about punishing her daughter for not wanting to be friends with a bully. "I feel so bad, because I remember yelling at you," Keely told her. She apologized for spanking her.

Still, it bothered Isabella for years. "I felt really forced to create these relationships," Isabella said, "because I went to school with these girls, and I've never truly wanted to be friends with them. They were extremely mean to me." Looking back on it, Isabella was happier alone. She would rather play by herself at recess. Eat her goldfish crackers alone.

There were days when kids at school would pull back their eyes in that clichéd mocking that has persisted and plagued Asian Americans across generations. Isabella didn't fight back; she endured the insults. She acted like she couldn't hear them, but over and over kids would ask questions: Where are you from? Are you Chinese? Where is Việt Nam? Can you speak the language? Why are your eyes different?

Once, in a typing class, the computer offered an option to write in Chinese characters. Two boys sitting near her began banging a string of random characters onto the screen, then turned to Isabella and asked, "Can you read this?"

Isabella found herself at a loss for answers. Back then, she did not call herself Asian American. To her, that implied being from a family of immigrants from Asia and that wasn't her story. Keely had Dutch roots; Mick, Italian. She felt no tangible connection to Asia. When people asked, "What *are* you?" Isabella began to say she was Asian and Italian. That felt a little more accurate. But not totally right either.

Sometimes Isabella joined in with the same kids poking fun at her. She would pull back her own eyes in response and make the same ching-chong sounds as them. This caused the kids to crack up. They were laughing with her now, weren't they?

Once, Isabella ran home crying to her older brother, Will, explaining she had been playing outside when the neighbor boy started making fun of her for being Asian. Will was an athletic kid, four years older than Isabella, a protector of his family. He always told his sisters, "If anyone ever makes fun of you, come tell me right away."

"Where is this kid?" Will demanded.

Will marched outside to track down the neighbor. He confronted the boy and knocked over his french fries. "If you make fun of any of my sisters again, you're going to have an issue with me."

The boy left them alone, but Will could not shield the girls from every comment.

WHEN ISABELLA WAS in second grade, she watched a clip from a documentary at school about the September 11, 2001, terrorist attacks against the United States, which had occurred a year before she and Olivia were adopted. Isabella could not shake the images of the planes hitting the twin towers in New York, how those buildings buckled into billowing clouds of dust and smoke. Years later, she watched more scenes from the attacks and felt haunted by the images of blood- and debris-covered survivors.

The Solimenes raised her as Catholic, but she found herself wanting to learn more about the Muslim faith and Middle Eastern culture. It didn't seem fair, she thought, to categorize a huge segment of the world population as "terrorists." Yet she knew that all around her many people did. She wanted to understand why people in America seemed so afraid of those they saw as brown or assumed to be Middle Eastern.

Since Isabella was ten months older than Olivia, she began school a year ahead of her, which meant she had to make friends in her own grade. Isabella was no longer the outgoing toddler she had been in Việt Nam. She kept only a couple of close friends at a time. One was a girl named Mirelle, whose family was from India. Keely was friends with Mirelle's mom, and they invited the Solimenes over for dinner.

Isabella loved everything about Mirelle's family—the way her house smelled like curry, the saris her mother wore, the tunics her father wore. The family seemed deeply connected to a culture that Isabella wanted to immerse herself in. Perhaps, she would later realize, Mirelle's family made her somehow feel closer to a culture she had lost herself. While other kids thought of Mirelle's family as odd and even frightening, assuming ridiculously that they were somehow connected to extremists, Isabella found herself instinctively drawn to them.

"I had a playdate with Mirelle," Isabella would tell other kids at school, and her classmates asked questions like "Aren't you scared of her family?" and "What does her dad wear?"

Isabella and Mirelle sat together during lunch, while other kids stayed away.

Mirelle gave Isabella some of her food: basmati rice, roti bread, and potatoes cooked with turmeric, garam masala, and coriander. Isabella liked the food so much more than her own peanut butter and jelly sandwiches that Mirelle's mother began packing a second lunch, just for her.

Isabella's world revolved around Mirelle until third grade, when Mirelle and her family moved. Outside of school, Isabella played with her cousins and the children of another family who had adopted kids from China and Việt Nam. But that family, close friends of the Solimenes, soon moved also, to California, partly to live somewhere more diverse.

"I think about that a lot," Isabella would say years later. "I definitely think it would have been easier had I grown up where everyone was like me, or where I wasn't the minority."

AT SOME POINT in elementary school, Isabella learned that she had a biological twin. Her mother explained to her that she did not know where this twin might be. It should have been a huge moment, but Isabella, looking back on it years later, could remember nothing significant about the day she found out, or even how Keely revealed it; the magnitude of having a long-lost sister wouldn't sink in for a long time.

As a child, Isabella found the thought of having a twin as unfathomable as the idea of having a biological mom or dad in another part of the world. In the initial years after her adoption, Isabella tried to fantasize about Việt Nam, and about her birth mom, closing her eyes to picture the scene. She could pull details only from home videos the Solimenes took, but the images never seemed to fit together in any logical way. Faces had no definition. Voices had no sound. Places did not sparkle with familiarity. It was exhausting to live in an imagination so void of texture and light.

Isabella would daydream aloud with Olivia too. The girls wondered if they resembled their birth mothers or shared the same habits of some unknown biological relative. They mused over what their lives would be like if they were still in Việt Nam. Or if they had not been adopted by the Solimenes.

"Would we still be kicking a ball around together like this?"

"Would we be in the orphanage, or somewhere else?"

"What do you think happened to those other kids in the orphanage?"

"Would we still be together?"

NINE

Cloth Monkeys

BY 1939, THE British psychologist John Bowlby argued that environment mattered in early maternal separation, and so did a caregiver's cold attitude toward an infant. He believed lack of nurturing could lead a child to become emotionally detached or develop irreversible behavioral disorders. Even though early researchers in the field of behaviorism were ridiculed or mostly ignored, he theorized that a newborn's need for nurturing was biologically instinctual, like hunger, a human trait that increased its evolutionary chances for survival.

Bowlby observed how babies would protest out of anxiety and anger, sometimes for hours, if they felt abandoned, clinging, weeping, and searching for their mother. Once the babies found their caregiver again, the desperate behavior would cease. If separation went on for longer periods of time, once again despair would set in. Bowlby believed such children had difficulty loving and trusting and would be at risk for future juvenile delinquency and criminal behavior. His theories took more than a decade to emerge into the public eye when they were included in the World Health Organization's report on the mental health and needs of homeless children in postwar Europe.

Despite such arguments that nurturing mattered to the healthy development of a child, by the mid-twentieth century many psychologists and doctors still rejected the notion that children needed affection or love to thrive, and parents were told to refrain from cuddling in order to promote independence.

In 1958, a professor of psychology at the University of Wisconsin–Madison, Harry Harlow, began breeding rhesus monkeys, which are about 94 percent genetically identical to humans, for research. In an experiment so cruel it would not be repeated today, he separated sixty infant monkeys from their mothers at birth, raising them in isolation from one another. Graduate students rotated in and out, giving the infants bottles and blankets and changing their diapers. Harlow noticed the baby monkeys that clung to their gauze diapers, as well as to the padding that covered the floor, grew up physically normal and without diseases. Yet they acted like they were mentally ill, pacing, swaying, or staring nowhere.

Harlow began to wonder if the baby monkeys were experiencing depression or mental illness because they had no primary caregiver to show them attention. Harlow then separated eight more rhesus macaques from their mothers at birth, this time raising them in cages with two "surrogate mothers," the first, a block of wood covered in sponge rubber and terry cotton and fitted with a feeding nipple, and the second made of wire mesh and a bulb, also fitted with a nipple. He placed warming devices inside of the contraptions.

The behavioral patterns of the baby monkeys proved eye opening. Regardless of which fake mother was associated with the feeding, the babies spent nearly their entire day hugging, stroking, kissing, sleeping, and nestling with their cloth mothers. The monkeys mostly ignored the fake-eyed wire mothers, besides occasionally feeding from them when the cloth mother ran out of milk.

The baby monkeys would fill their bellies with food from a nipple attached to steel, then scurry back to nuzzle the soft towel and suck their thumbs. Even after being separated from their cloth mothers for a long period of time, the baby monkeys returned to them without hesitation. Harlow's findings motivated researchers like Bowlby. It was not just a matter of who or what gives a baby food, researchers argued. And it did not matter if the caregiver was a biological relative, a nurse, or an orphanage employee. If children received consistent affection and nurturing, he believed they could flourish.

Harlow's research opened the floodgates for future behavioral research, furthering Bowlby's theories. A colleague of Harlow's, Stephen J. Suomi, discovered through medical exams and spinal taps of monkeys that aggression was linked to low levels of serotonin; calmer monkeys had high levels of the hormone. Monkeys born with low levels yet also raised by nurturing mothers turned out normal. Meanwhile, monkeys with similar low serotonin levels but raised by fake mothers, like Harlow's cloth versions, turned out to be more violent. "Nurture," as one reporter wrote, "had overcome nature."

These findings invigorated behaviorism, reinforcing scientific beliefs that a person's development was influenced most by the environment and the caregivers within it. This shift helped overturn adoption practices from the 1920s, which had prohibited infants from being adopted by strangers until they were at least six months old (the allotted time needed to conduct all the testing and assessments required for matching). The earlier the attachment to a nurturer, the new conventions suggested, the better.

"Give me a dozen healthy infants, well-formed, and my own specified world to bring them up in and I'll guarantee to take any one at random and train him to become any type of specialist I might select," wrote John B. Watson in 1958, "doctor, lawyer, artist, merchant-chief and, yes, even beggar-man and thief, regardless of his talents, penchants, tendencies, abilities, vocations, and race of his ancestors."

Today, across the internet a version of that quote has been shared, retweeted, copied onto coffee mugs and tote bags, and quoted in journalism pieces and some research. When I looked into it, I found the repurposed quote—originally built off a Jesuit saying, "Give me a child until he is seven, and I will give you the man"—is not attributed to Watson but instead to his famous behaviorism couterpart, B. F. Skinner.

When I searched academic archives, I could find no credible books or academic papers, nor any of Skinner's own writings, confirming that he ever directly uttered the words now attached to memes with his face on them: "Give me a child," as the viral adage goes, "and I will shape him into anything."

This Instagram-ready phrase embodies the fatal flaws and assumptions of early views of behaviorism. You cannot so easily take children and shape them purely as a reflection of their environment. You cannot ignore where they come from and expect them to so easily adapt.

Olivia

I was in the closet for so long. Years. And it was hard, you know, growing up in a conservative yet also accepting family. But we were surrounded by, you know, white supremacist–type people.

I went to a Catholic school, learning about God, reading the Bible, being taught that homosexuality is just not right. Especially in the Bible, however you interpret it. So of course I'm like struggling with myself, and I just became someone that was not happy.

In our private school, my sister and I were among the only Asians. And so there was this whole thing where I grow up and feel different already. I'm already different because of my ethnicity. And then there's another part of me that's different. My sexuality.

Basketball was my escape route, you know, burning off some steam from fighting internally with myself about how I'm different. You know how in March Madness every team has the same goal? To "survive and advance."

That is what I told myself. Survive and advance.

TEN

Olivia

WHEN THE GIRLS were little, Isabella and Olivia often wondered how many biological siblings they had, what their relatives looked like, and if they resembled them at all. Sometimes Olivia asked aloud if she had a sister in Việt Nam. She would make a noise that sounded like "naa-auu!"

Olivia had always been the goofy one, the class clown able to make everyone laugh. Isabella giggled, thinking it was another Olivia joke.

She said it again. "Naa-auu!"

But why, Olivia once asked Isabella, did she associate that sound with the thought of having a sister in Việt Nam?

Isabella didn't have an answer. It would not be until years later that they learned Olivia did indeed have a sister in Việt Nam, two years older than her. Her name was Ngà—pronounced "Nau."

At a certain point in elementary school, Olivia stopped talking about their past, just as Isabella had decided as a toddler to stop speaking Vietnamese. Olivia told herself that this life in Barrington was her life now. The Solimene family was her family. Her only parents and her only siblings. This was her America. Calling herself Asian American did not seem to fit Olivia's version of herself either. She was American. She loved the name her parents had given her.

Olivia hated when anyone asked, "Where are you from?" She was from Illinois. She didn't want to go through the explanation again.

"What if we go back to Việt Nam one day?" Isabella asked.

Olivia shrugged. She was not waiting for that day. As far as Olivia was concerned, her biological family gave her away. She didn't need to know any more about them, not in the way that Isabella seemed to.

Olivia settled into being the youngest of the Solimene family. She got joy out of making the rest of them laugh. Once, at a restaurant in North Carolina, she hopped on stage alongside a guitarist, grabbed the microphone, and started singing: "The Wheels on the Bus" her voice echoing through the speakers. It became a cherished family memory.

When they were old enough, Olivia and Isabella would ride their bikes twenty minutes to the convenience store and spend $20 on Warheads, Now and Laters, lollipops, cans of Peace Tea, and Pop-its firecrackers that explode when thrown on the sidewalk. Back at home in their big backyard, they played soccer, baseball, and football. Olivia liked playing with boys. She could compete with them in sports as an equal. She could also fight them if she had to.

When provoked, Olivia defended herself. One icy winter day on the playground, a kid tormented Olivia with racial slurs. He called her "yellow" and asked, "Why are you such a different color than all of us?"

She punched him in the face and tackled him. She ended up getting scolded in the principal's office along with him.

The day that Isabella ran home to tell their older brother that a neighbor was making fun of her for being Asian, Olivia teamed up with her brother to put a smoke bomb made of sparklers inside his family's mailbox. It exploded, and the entire mailbox turned green.

In elementary school, Olivia had crushes on girls. She remembers in fourth grade another schoolmate seemed to be exploring her sexuality in the same way. Olivia found out this girl liked another girl.

Huh, Olivia thought. *That's interesting. If this person feels it, then I feel it, too, and I guess it's somewhat normal?*

Then the girl transferred to another school. "So there I was," Olivia recalled years later, "just me by myself again."

She already felt different because of her ethnicity. "So I struggled a lot. Like, yeah, I'm Asian. I'm yellow, however they wanted to perceive me."

Olivia felt like her parents wanted her and Isabella to assimilate into white neighborhoods and Catholic schools, to fit in like their white children before them had done. "They didn't want to treat us differently," Olivia said. "But I feel like they needed to realize that we are different."

One girl in school picked on her "nonstop," Olivia said. "She bullied me about hanging out with the boys, about not being white and being gay." Years later, Olivia would look up the girl on social media and realize that she, too, is queer. She must have been battling her own self-hatred and identity crises in elementary school, Olivia realized, but that was no excuse. "She didn't have to take it out on me."

It was in sixth grade that Olivia told her mother about a girl she had a crush on. They were in the car when Olivia said to Keely: "I want to date this girl."

At this point in her life, Olivia had not revealed herself in this way to anyone else in the family, not even Isabella. "I was just offering so much honesty about my sexuality."

"You want to date her?" Keely asked. "You like girls? What does that mean?"

"She was defensive about it," Olivia told me, reflecting on that moment. "I'm sure she was very confused, as much as I was. I think she was trying to protect me. She was being a mom, and I was in such a bad place, getting bullied."

As the same time, Olivia was learning about the Bible in her Catholic church and school, "being taught that homosexuality is just not right," she said. "So of course I'm like struggling with myself, and I just became someone that was not happy."

After that day in the car with her mom, Olivia said: "We absolutely stopped talking about it." That same year, Olivia told a girl at school that she liked her and thought she was pretty. "Please don't tell anyone," she said to the schoolmate. But the girl told her mom. And that mom called Keely. "My mom had to deal with her mother calling and say-ing 'Your daughter is a disgrace' or whatever. 'Keep her away from my daughter,'" Olivia said. "I felt awful."

Not long after, Olivia went onto a group Skype chat. A kid said there was going to be a party at the house of the girl that Olivia liked. "Okay, I'll be there," Olivia said. "I show up at a party. It was all a joke." Nobody else showed up. "I was really hurt. I was so embarrassed. I just felt so ashamed." Rumors spread that Olivia had showed up to the girl's house. The mom of the girl got upset again. "She was like, 'Stop stalking us.'"

That was when Olivia withdrew from sixth grade in-person classes. She homeschooled for the rest of the year. "People thought I was sick, but I wasn't. I just hated everyone."

Olivia returned for seventh grade. That was when "Olivia started having boyfriends," Keely told me. "It wasn't like we were saying, 'Go have a boyfriend.' I mean we were not encouraging it at all." Yet, to Keely, it seemed like the relationships were genuine.

From Olivia's point of view, she cycled through relationships with boys, and when there were no boys of interest left in school to try out, she started seeing one who lived out of state, in Georgia. "Still nothing," Olivia said. "I wanted to be normal, or at least the way society sees nor-mal." But she couldn't find a spark—there was no attraction.

"I wanted a wedding, and to be married, to be like my sisters who have boyfriends, without being judged," Olivia said. "There were moments where I was trying to convince myself, 'Oh, I love this guy. Oh, he's the one.' But it was all a lie."

By high school, Olivia doubled down on school, her social life, and sports. Olivia became a local basketball star. She excelled in academics. Olivia took after their dad, whom she looked up to. She knew Mick had been a star soccer player and top student. "I always had this goal to be like him, to be successful, to play a sport in college like him," Olivia said. "I never wanted to let him down. He's very hard when it comes to grades. He'd be in the car, and say, 'Good grades, good college, good grades, graduate, good job.' He would always say that to us."

Olivia wanted to live up to his example. Mick almost never missed her basketball games, and Olivia could tell how proud he was when she scored and when she got good grades. This motivated Olivia to keep working harder. But inside, she was in pain.

"I would get in a lot of fights with people just because I was just so angry with myself for being different," Olivia recalled. "There were moments when I was just completely unhappy. Like, 'Why am I still here? When I don't know my own way. Why bother to continue on?'"

Olivia became the girl in school who said hi to everybody, giving high fives, even if she knew they did not particularly like her. "When you're nice to people," she learned, "they'll be nice back to you." By high school, Olivia was not just figuring out how to fit in anymore; she was becoming popular. She could be friends with everyone. To the outside world, it looked as if Olivia was thriving in her high-school environment.

Sometimes today Olivia looks in the mirror and thinks to herself: "I can't believe I'm still here because, to be completely transparent, I didn't want to be here. I didn't want to be alive anymore."

Olivia tried desperately to go against her own nature, contorting and denying herself until she barely recognized herself at all. She didn't open up to her siblings, but says that family dinners with them, movies, and trips "are the reasons I'm still here."

"I don't want to say that I'm mad," Olivia said, looking back on her childhood. "But there were moments where I could feel the tension, definitely with my dad and mom. I could sense they thought this wasn't going to last. Like being gay was a phase, something I was trying on."

When Olivia finally told Isabella that she was gay, she received an unsurprised response: "Oh yeah," Isabella said. "I already knew that."

Their other siblings reacted similarly, all love, no judgment. But that initial experience of "coming out" to her mom weighed on Olivia for years.

For so long, Olivia realized that other people had made her reality more complicated than it really was. "I am a lesbian. I'm Asian. I'm an adoptee. Nothing about that is going to change. That's who I am." And even when she finally accepted herself, some people chose not to acknowledge her truth at all.

"I'm in front of you. See me. *See* who I am. It's really not that complicated," Olivia said. "Come on, dude, *you* are making it complicated by refusing to see me."

ELEVEN

Wonderful Beginnings

FIFTY-THREE YEARS BEFORE the Solimene family adopted two girls from Việt Nam, a white mother in Washington, DC, gave birth to a son. She raised him on her own for the next three years, as the boy's white biological father never came around; she didn't know where he was. The mother eventually fell in love with a Black man who worked as a taxi driver and was in law school. The couple married and raised the boy together. Her new husband provided for the family financially, while she stayed home as a homemaker. He soon decided to file a court petition to legally adopt the child whom he and his wife supported.

The judge denied the petition in the district court. "Ordinarily such an adoption should be not only approved but encouraged," he wrote, referring to a child born out of wedlock and raised by a stepparent. But in this case, he continued, "a problem arises out of the fact that the stepfather is a colored man, while the mother and boy are white people. This situation gives rise to a difficult social problem. The boy when he grows up might lose the social status of a white man by reason of the fact that by record his father will be a negro."

Throughout the nineteenth and into the early twentieth century in the United States, adopting across racial lines was illegal in many states, though African American families during those periods were among the first to do so, caring for mixed-race children (usually Black and white), often informally—community members taking in children in need, for example. But when it came to Black families raising white children, this was deemed impermissible.

In 1851, the Adoption of Children Act had become the first law requiring that child placement promote the welfare and needs of the child instead of the wants of adults. By the 1920s and 1930s, as middle-class white families in the United States turned to adoption as a way to build a family, it was not generally hard to find homes for white children, but Black children were frequently labeled "hard to place."

Eventually, in the 1940s, white parents who could not have their own biological children and struggled to adopt in-demand white children began crossing racial lines and adopting Black children—almost exclusively children of mixed Black and white descent. Only then did the practice take on the term *transracial adoption* within the public and adoption circles.

Still, "although some adoption agencies assisted in these adoptions," wrote Valerie Phillips Hermann in the *National Black Law Journal*, despite legal efforts to promote child welfare first, "they were not deliberately advocating the development of transracial adoption. They were merely serving those who were in need of a child."

In a post–World War II society, some Americans reacted to this national climate by trying to build their families around more inclusive values, intentionally seeking out children whom they believed had been cast aside, impoverished, or born to families fragmented by war and upheaval. As the pattern goes, adoption was increasingly embraced as a political act and a humanitarian one. For some Americans, it was a step toward creating a unified country, made stronger by its diversity. But it also rooted itself in an overly rosy narrative about race in America, one that erased or overlooked the realities of oppression. Multicultural societies, mixed-race children, and color blindness would never be the antidotes to structural racism or global imperialism.

"It is evidently common for white adoptive parents to minimize racial traits and to accept the 'biracial' adoptees into their families as just children needing love and care," wrote F. James Davis in *Who Is Black? One Nation's Definition*, assessing the early years of transracial adoptions. "Apparently the majority of these white parents prefer to describe their adopted children by some term other than black—and often as 'racially mixed'—a rejection of the one-drop rule. Many seem to assume that their child will not be subject to the rule, especially if the child looks almost white, and that people will simply accept the child as another human being. However, neither the white community nor the black will allow the 'mixed' child to be an exception to the one-drop rule."

While some white families adopted Black and Native American children, others began looking overseas instead, adopting European orphans from Germany, Italy, and Greece after World War II. They eventually turned to orphanages that housed mixed-race children born to Japanese or Korean mothers and US servicemen during World War II and the Korean War. Hundreds of mixed-race children were abandoned by their American fathers, many of whom returned to their wives or girlfriends in the States after the wars.

In Japan and Korea, mixed-race children were often rejected by the local communities because they were not birthed within the confines of marriage, and their features did not fit into racially homogenous societies. Their Asian mothers were frequently written off in history as prostitutes, even though some of these sexual relationships were acts of love and romance. Some Japanese and Koreans tried to advocate for tolerance and acceptance of their mixed-race orphans, while others supported adoption from overseas as a solution.

In 1952, there were around five thousand mixed-race children reported in US-occupied Japan. The US government did not openly acknowledge its role in creating these orphans, nor deem it necessary to go out of its way to help the birth mothers. Yet the country's leaders understood that stories and images of abandoned sons and daughters of US servicemen in Japan could stir anti-American sentiments, reinforcing negative views of US imperialism, at home and abroad. Some

Americans felt guilty for their country's decision to drop the atomic bombs on Hiroshima and Nagasaki, believing the United States had a responsibility to help the kids abandoned by wars. Others saw America as a savior and champion of world progress that had the humanity to take in outsiders, particularly deprived and forgotten children.

In 1949, the white American writer and Nobel Prize–winner Pearl S. Buck founded the international adoption agency Welcome House, which placed mixed-race children from Asia with American families. Raised by Presbyterian missionaries in China, Buck's secular adoption efforts were guided by anti-imperialist views, her politics inextricable from her humanitarian work. Buck transracially adopted seven children herself.

In a shift that would penetrate American society, Buck opposed intellectual, racial, or religious matching in adoption procedures and instead helped popularize the notion that a family was not built or bound by ethnicity, ancestry, or nationality but rather that a family could be a patchwork of people, as well as a nucleus for political and social change. Buck's agency was successful in placing thousands of mixed-race children. "Amerasian" children, as Buck wrote, were "a new breed, without family, without country. Yet it is we who have cre-ated them. We have a responsibility, however much we may deny or neglect it."

In the United States, her ideas were met with both admiration and alarm. Some xenophobes worried that an influx of children from other countries and interracial families might encourage more race mixing in the United States. Meanwhile, another American, Harry Holt, a Korean War veteran and evangelical Christian, adopted eight mixed-race Korean orphans, raising them in the 1950s with his wife. The Oregon farmer was driven by religious ideals. He soon devoted himself to finding homes in America and elsewhere for other Korean adoptees, organizing mass adoptions of several hundred children from Korea, which were publicized enthusiastically and hailed as patriotic and pious acts. The Holt Adoption Program appealed particularly to born-again Christians, who were encouraged by religious leaders to adopt from overseas. In her book *To Save the Children of Korea*, Arissa Oh called this "Christian Americanism," a religious and patriotic ideology that turned the adoption of Korean GI babies into missionary work.

This movement would end up propelling changes to US immigration laws in 1961, which made transnational adoptions possible and allowed the global industry to flourish. Around thirty-five thousand children were adopted from outside of the United States by American families from the mid-1940s to the 1970s, including many from South Korea. Bringing orphans to the States became a highly publicized undertaking, a sentimental, religious, and political plotline of relief and rescue, benevolence and altruism. But the adoptive families and agencies did not always fully consider how these children could face psychological detriment and discrimination in the United States.

Meanwhile, for decades Asian immigrants remained ineligible for US citizenship under racist, exclusionary laws. It was not until 1965 that Congress ended historical exclusions based on race and nationality, approving the Hart-Celler Act. But even then, when Asian immigrants began to increasingly obtain US citizenship, LGBTQ immigrants were often deemed "sexual deviants" under Hart-Celler and were intensely scrutinized by immigration authorities or flat-out denied entry to the country. And until 1967, Asians—like other groups of color in America—were also prohibited by law from having sex with or marrying whites under antimiscegenation laws in fourteen states. The Supreme Court decision in the case of *Loving v. Virginia*, centering on a Black and Native American woman who married a white man, finally lifted prohibitions on interracial marriage, which were ruled unconstitutional across the nation.

Throughout this period, American media continued to hold up the creation of blended families as stories with "wonderful beginnings and happy endings," wrote University of California, Berkeley ethnic studies professor Catherine Ceniza Choy in *Global Families: A History of International Adoptions in America*. The denouement arrived when the child was adopted. Few stories detailed how adoptees themselves adapted to the trauma of assimilation as the country itself struggled, often violently, with its own identity. Some voiced concern over the wisdom of uprooting a child, questioning whether it would be better to find ways for them to be cared for in their birth country. But Choy, also a historian who studied records of the International Social Service, USA from 1929 to 1995, wrote that they later dismissed those worries, believing that if they were not adopted internationally, the kids would "not live or [would] have nothing to live for."

Some transracial adoption debates in the United States from the 1950s to 1970s centered on whether it was appropriate for white parents to raise minority children at all. Critics of transracial adoption argued that white parents were not prepared to raise Black children, citing cases in which minority adoptees were not taught about their racial history or ancestry, or others that were passed off as white. In the 1950s, the National Urban League and other organizations began recruiting more Black adoptive parents to adopt Black children.

Between 1958 and 1967, under the Child Welfare League of America's Indian Adoption Project, nearly four hundred Native American children were separated from their families and reservations—without home studies or investigations—and placed with white adopters. Reasons for removal often included "neglect," which throughout adoption history has been an extremely broad and problematic category, encompassing everything from children living in shoddy homes or vehicles to homelessness, poor hygiene, lack of food, absent parents, or drug abuse. Neglect is not the same as abuse. But it has long been used as legal justification for separating children from poor families.

The Indian Adoption Project lasted nine years, but white families' interests in raising Indigenous children continued to snowball in its wake, as churches and religious organizations—from Catholics to Mormons to Pentecostals—flocked to the adoption industry. Once adopted, Native children were conditioned to blend into white society. They lost connections to their families, origins, and traditions. By 1972, an estimated 25 to 35 percent of Native children had been removed from their families and communities and placed with predominantly white families. For Native communities in the United States, adoption systems have long been viewed through a clear-cut lens: as a form of forced subjugation and cultural erasure.

The Indian Adoption Project echoed assimilationist practices of the nineteenth and twentieth centuries, when government institutions forcibly removed thousands of Native children in the United States and Canada from their families, enrolling them in boarding schools with harsh labor and discipline policies, stripping them of their culture, language, and heritage. The schools aimed to remove them from tribal influences, in some cases cutting off their braids and replacing their family names with Western ones. Many children in these boarding schools died from tuberculosis, pneumonia, starvation, physical abuse, or under mysterious circumstances, like drownings or shootings. Their bodies were buried in unmarked graves.

By the 1960s and 1970s, the adoption landscape was again moving with the political and social pulse of the country. The number of white babies up for adoption dwindled with the US Federal Drug Administration's approval of birth control and legalization of abortion, and the National Children's Bureau estimated that about fifteen thousand American families had adopted transracially by 1972. "The supply of white children for adoption has all but vanished and adoption agencies, having always catered to middle class whites[,] developed an answer to their desire for parenthood by motivating them to consider Black children," the National Association of Black Social Workers wrote in a position statement on transracial adoption in 1972. Amid growing opposition to adoptions of Black and Native American children by white families, the National Association of Black Social Workers denounced the practice, adding: "Only a Black family can transmit the emotional and sensitive subtleties of perception and reaction essential for a Black child's survival in a racist society."

Sociologists Rita Simon and Howard Altstein studied 206 middle-class families who had adopted transracially before 1972. Most were Christian, living in predominantly white neighborhoods. They praised transracial adoption, finding it to be an enriching experience for children and their families. These early studies and others in the same vein implied that most transracially adopted children adjusted to their environments without any major problems. Such findings would become a bedrock of early transracial adoption research.

But the researchers overwhelmingly focused on interviewing the white parents of the children of color—not the children themselves, as Kim Park Nelson wrote in *Invisible Asians: Korean American Adoptees, Asian American Experiences and Racial Exceptionalism*. Many adoptive parents "wanted their children to racially identify as raceless or as white. This being the case, it is hardly surprising that many parents and children then reported either having no racial identity or having a white identity." This de-emphasis on race likely was an attempt to "protect their families from the difficulties of difference." Nelson added: "But in creating an imagined racelessness, they were unwittingly whitewashing their children." Such parent-focused studies throughout the 1970s, Nelson wrote, failed to capture the adoptees' feelings of loneliness and alienation from both adoptive and birth cultures.

In 1978, the Indian Child Welfare Act passed by Congress sought to keep Indigenous children with their families. Against the backdrop of this dialogue, three decades after World War II, foster care system reforms made it tougher to adopt children in the United States. And while fewer babies were being adopted from Japan, more Korean kids continued to arrive.

In the wake of the civil rights movement, enthusiasm for an integrated society, as well as the emerging academic studies that seemed to tout the benefits of adopting across racial lines, spurred more transracial adoptions. Patterns also adjusted depending on foreign conflicts and natural disasters, as transracial overseas adoptions rose. In the years leading up to 1975, Americans could not ignore what was taking place in Việt Nam.

By the 1990s and into the 2000s, newborns from Asia were again in high demand in the West—especially in France, Ireland, Denmark, Italy, Spain, the United Kingdom, and the United States. Many parents signed up to adopt overseas without realizing how vulnerable the process was to corruption or how little effective regulation or oversight there was.

TWELVE

Keely

KEELY SOLIMENE ALWAYS knew she wanted a life filled with kids. Born in Indiana, she had been raised in a family of four children. Keely was the second oldest, with two brothers and one sister. Her father was a pharmaceutical salesman, while her mother was responsible for raising and caring for the children. They moved to a housing complex in Justice, Illinois, over an hour southwest of Chicago. Then the family later settled another twenty miles west, moving into a house in Bolingbrook, Illinois.

Her father, Bill, was outgoing, a real charmer. The first to arrive to a party, last to leave. He drank scotch. Keely's mother, Jacqueline, did not party or drink alcohol, and thought her husband drank too much. They were, as Jacqueline put it, a mismatched couple.

Bill moved from job to job. "He had a strong personality," Jacqueline told me. "He tended to get bored." The financial insecurity weighed on Jacqueline. "I learned to make the food dollar really stretch." They lived off Hamburger Helper, tuna casseroles, and powdered milk.

Keely's defining childhood memory is her first day of first grade at the neighborhood elementary school in Justice. The children on her bus arrived late and the school was already full. Staff told Keely and the kids from her bus to sit on a heat register near a window. They would be going to a different school. Keely felt like even though she was not wealthy, she should not have to settle for less than what she believed she deserved. She thought the other school was for students with less privilege. "We had all came from the apartment complex. And they didn't want us there. They chose the other kids to stay in that school instead of us."

Keely was adamant. She was not going to get on the bus or attend a different school. She told the adults she had to speak to someone about this situation. "I marched into the principal's office and told her that the randomness of how I wound up on that register should not dictate the quality of my life. I remember just feeling like this is not right. This is not fair." The principal granted her permission to stay. She was five.

Keely's mother described her daughter as "one of those people who just doesn't give up. That's her. It can be one of her best qualities. And it can be not so good at times." And Keely agreed with this assessment. It was a kind of tunnel vision that led her life. "To my mom's point, when I do something, I do get pretty intent on doing it."

To earn money, Keely started babysitting when she was not yet in middle school, taking multiple jobs in a single day. She would work a few hours before school taking care of the kids in one family and a few more hours after school with another family in the neighborhood, ending the night caregiving for a third family. Keely was happy around children. She sensed that they just wanted to be loved and paid attention to. Kids saw goodness all around them, even though that innocence would not last forever. Keely called herself a "Pollyanna" and wanted to hold on to that faith in human goodness for as long as she could.

She believed her father embodied this goodness. Keely would never forget how he taught her to dance in their basement. She was planning to attend her school's first big social event and had no idea how to respond if a boy asked her to dance.

He taught her how to two-step to Neil Diamond's "Song Sung Blue": ". . . When you take the blues and make a song / You sing them out again."

It was a song about sadness, but it didn't dwell; it focused on harnessing the gloom to feel better. Throughout her life, Keely's father told her: "Hold life's possessions with a loose grip." His own parents had divorced and struggled financially. As a child, he changed residences thirty-three times. As a result, he never valued big homes or fancy cars. He wanted his daughter to know that human connections mattered more than money and things.

Once, her father knocked on doors in the neighborhood holding a Polaroid camera. When each neighbor answered, he snapped a photo without warning them beforehand. He handed them the photo as an invitation to his "come as you are" party. Whatever they wore in that photo, whatever they looked like in that moment, he told them, that is how he expected them to show up to his party. No pretense, no judgment.

"I don't want people getting all dressed up," he said.

Keely remembers it was a great party.

When she was twelve, her father called her into the sitting room upstairs, along with her siblings. He sat in chair holding a glass of scotch.

"Your mother and I are getting a divorce," he said. "I'm moving out." It had been her mother's decision.

Jacqueline had long suffered from depression and overall unhappiness in the marriage. Her kids were in elementary and middle school. "These were terrible ages for a family to explode," she said. "It is one of my deepest regrets. I wasn't able to take better care of them at their most vulnerable ages."

Keely's dad seemed crushed, not wanting his family to break up. She cried and begged him not to leave.

"It's going to be okay," he said. He would move into his office in the village, where he held a local government position. It had a couch.

"I want to go with you," Keely told him.

He explained that the office was no place for a kid to live.

"In those moments," Keely recalled, "when time stopped, I knew it was the beginning of something that was going to change my life, a fork in the road." Her entire life, just like that, she thought, could swerve left or right in an instant. This divorce was going to happen, she told herself. Her family would end up in the right place. She would end up in the right place. Fate would decide. "I am going to let go, and however this goes, it goes."

Her mom was Lutheran, her dad Presbyterian, though church was not at the center of their lives. But Keely paid attention to signs or messages; she believed people crossed her path for a reason, and there was a purpose to this life, even if she had not yet figured it out.

Jacqueline took temporary jobs to make ends meet, so Keely took on the role of caregiver to her younger siblings, taking care of them when they were sick, waking up to feed them Cheerios in the morning before school. She left her own school early to pick them up and walk them home from theirs. She made Tuna Helper dinners on an electric skillet.

Growing up, Keely and her siblings wore thrift store outfits long before thrifting became cool. One year, she really wanted to buy herself a purple velvet skirt that had built-in pants beneath it from Zayre, a discount retail chain store. Her mother had agreed to take her in the family's brown Ford Pinto that Saturday, but when Keely woke up, she looked outside and saw someone hooking the Pinto up to a tow truck to haul it away. They had fallen behind on payments, and the car was repossessed. Still determined to buy her skirt, Keely walked about three miles to Zayre, and purchased it for a dollar earned from babysitting.

Keely knew college was on the horizon for her, even though her parents could not afford it. She did not know what she would study or where she would go, but she was determined that she would get there. She had always been curious about the world, even though she had seen very little of it. College was her chance to explore. She ended up at Western Illinois University in Macomb, about four hours away, because it was one of the only schools where she could get financial aid and housing. To make ends meet, she also took out student loans and juggled classes while working at McDonald's and washing dishes in the dorm cafeteria.

One day, she noticed a young man in the cafeteria who had a head of thick, brown, wavy hair. He was carrying so much food on his tray she thought it might topple over. He reminded her of the teenage son from the television version of *Little House on the Prairie*. Not long after, Keely was at a campus bar, the Moon, having a conversation with a goalie from the university's soccer team. The same cute guy with the thick hair approached. The goalie introduced them. The young man's name was Mick, and he also played on the team.

Mick's father was a vice president of marketing and sales for Technical Tape, Inc. and ACCO International, Inc., responsible for the sale of a office products to hardware and office supply chains. His mother cared for Mick and his two sisters when they lived in a suburb of Texas and then a suburb of Chicago.

In high school, Mick was an avid soccer player but he not particularly popular. He was on the shorter side, reserved and shy. As he explained it, "I never went to prom or dances. I was in the wallpaper category. It was hard to differentiate me from your average geeky kid."

But he had a strong work ethic. Though his family was middle class, Mick understood that if he wanted anything extra, he had to work for it. In the summers, he worked as a golf caddy, as a busboy at Beef'N'Barrel, as a shoe salesman, and on the overnight shift in a factory assembling car parts. "I'm a big believer that you can sleep when you die," Mick said. "I've always believed success often involves luck, but the only way to achieve luck is to put yourself in the position to encounter luck."

As a sophomore majoring in finance at Western, Mick was a year older than Keely. He had an athlete's intensity about him but also a sharp sense of humor. He told her she had a "beautiful smile." They got to know each other over the dorm-room phones each night and eventually began dating.

Keely eventually transferred to the University of Illinois at Urbana-Champaign, a college town amid cornfields, two hours south of Chicago. It was not until she arrived at the University of Illinois that Keely's lot in life, as a lower-income student, clicked into place for her. She remembered many of her classmates came from much more affluent backgrounds compared to the students at her previous campus. Their families sent care packages stuffed with goodies, and students had extra spending money to eat out, buy drinks at bars, or purchase clothes without the stress of balancing weekend work shifts and classes.

Mick graduated from Western as the valedictorian of his class and landed a job in a training program at Continental Bank (which later became Bank of America). He was also going to school at night to earn his MBA at the University of Chicago. Keely graduated in May 1983 from DePaul University in Chicago (a car accident had forced her to transfer schools). She got a job a few months later at the Midwest Stock Exchange in a bank building in downtown Chicago. Three years into her career, Mick proposed. They married in May 1986, and she was pregnant by summer. They were excited to learn they were having a girl.

By September, Keely was nauseous, cramping every day. She started spotting. The spotting turned into bleeding. She went to the doctor and the nurse drew her blood, which revealed that her hormone levels had dropped. She was having a miscarriage.

The whole experience was crushing—to want a baby so badly and then to lose it so abruptly. Keely dreamed that her unborn daughter's name was Stephanie. She cried for days but decided she wanted to get pregnant again right away.

Five months later, she was. Alexandra was born in November 1987. Keely decided to leave her job and become a full-time stay-at-home mother. By now, they had moved into a condo in Chicago overlooking Lake Michigan. Keely gave birth to her second daughter, Arianna, in 1989. Mick had been raised Catholic, and though he didn't attend church regularly, Keely wanted to embrace the religion and decided to convert and baptize their children.

With a growing family, they wanted to buy in the suburbs and settled on Barrington, an hour's drive northwest of Chicago. In 1993, they moved to a home with dated wood-paneled and wallpapered walls and blue and goldish shag carpet throughout. The family would not remodel right away. While other Barrington residents lived in million-dollar homes, "the land of McMansions, owned by titans and CEOs," as Mick put it, the Solimenes tried to live unpretentiously. Keely gave birth to two more children, Victoria, and a son, Lewis William III (whom they would call Will).

Keely shouldered many of the child-rearing and home responsibilities. There were days when the house was a mess, days when she and the kids didn't leave home or even change out of their pajamas. Keely watched a lot of kids' movies. Plenty of days, everyone's hair went uncombed. She remembers lining the girls up and going down the row to french-braid their hair. Each night, she would dump all four kids in the bathtub, wrestle each one out and into their pajamas, and put them to bed. She conked out next to them while reading bedtime stories. "It was all exhausting," she said, "physically exhausting."

Mick coached the kids' soccer teams and imparted lessons about focus and commitment. He planted in them a drive to achieve. But he also knew he was away far too much. He listed that under his own "bad characteristics column." Keely would look back years later, when her kids were grown, and wonder why she didn't question the fairness of the division of household labor in her marriage. She felt she did what was necessary at the time and didn't challenge the roles.

"He was not home anymore," Keely said. "He was working all the time. He was traveling on 9/11. I didn't even know where he was. This was our life. I mean it was like that for decades, and I didn't like it. I begged him to quit his job. I knew that he was making a choice, career versus family."

KEELY REMEMBERED HOW Barrington reeled from the September 11 attacks, along with the rest of the nation. Businesses closed. Sports games were canceled. Will was now in first grade, Victoria in fourth, Arianna in seventh, Alexandra in eighth. Keely wrote daily affirmations in her journal:

Oct. 23, 2001:

—Thank you for Arianna's ability to express her feelings about the September 11, 2001, tragedies after a month of saying nothing, several nightmares and her not wanting to be in public without me. Arianna finally said, "Isn't it so sad that so many people are still so sad. . . ."

—Thank you for my ability to comfort Victoria who has been so afraid. . . . She told me recently that "it is so nice that the television isn't showing the pictures anymore of the World Trade Center on fire," but she continues to be afraid every time a train passes or a plane flies low. When I hug her, she trembles with fear until it passes.

As the weeks passed, slowly, conversations among Keely's neighbors began to revert to their kids' extracurricular activities, birthday parties, and caretaking duties. Keely knew people would soon start planning their holiday cards where families stage smiling festive photos to send to relatives and friends. Keely did not send a traditional family photo card in 2001, instead making a card with her kids' backs facing the camera as they stared at the White House. Under an image of a red bow, she printed the caption "May the spirit of our nation bring peace and compassion throughout the world."

While waiting in the parking lot one October morning in 2001, Keely spotted her neighbor, Sue Fallon, marching toward her. Sue was humble and unflashy, one of the few moms in the community with whom Keely felt like she could connect. Four years earlier, Sue had brought home her first adopted child from Việt Nam.

Today, Sue had a proposition for Keely. She knew of a girl who lived in an orphanage in Việt Nam. Her name was Loan. "This little girl should be a Solimene," Sue said to Keely. "She is an amazing soccer player." Sue gave Keely a printed-out email with a photo of the child staring toward the camera. The paper photo was wrinkled, the quality of the image dull. Keely took in Loan's bowl cut, her bright yellow pants and white shirt with a yellow collar and a pink and blue flower pattern.

Keely was now forty-one. Before September 11, the thought of adopting never went beyond a glimmer of possibility, but now she wanted to do something good and meaningful. If the child needed a home, Keely thought, she and Mick had a big home to offer. If the child needed love, she had plenty of that too. She looked at that photo of Loan, who sat on a laminate floor, holding her right foot with her hand. This, Keely thought, could be her next child.

THIRTEEN

Baby Brokers and Viral Adoptions

IN THE UNITED States, a "viral" Christian adoption movement took off through the early decades of the twenty-first century.
Evangelists began mobilizing churches and online communities and
holding conferences, which drew thousands, promoting a message and
a mission: "save" the world's orphans. Adopting a child from overseas cost a family on average between $30,000 and $50,000, and some
Christian leaders helped secure loans or grants for evangelicals to adopt,
according to investigative journalist Kathryn Joyce, author of *The Child
Catchers: Rescue, Trafficking, and the New Gospel of Adoption*. Pushed
by this mass adoption movement, American money began flowing into
poor and developing countries, including Việt Nam.

An illicit international adoption underworld emerged, with stories
of child "brokers" trawling villages looking for families who might send
their children overseas for adoption. From Việt Nam to Cambodia,
South Korea, Russia, Guatemala, and beyond, reports surfaced of adoption facilitators paying off mothers and pressuring or bribing pregnant
women to give up their newborns.

In 1999, nine people from Việt Nam's southern province of An
Giang were found guilty for their roles in smuggling 199 babies abroad
for adoption, from mostly poor families who lived in rural farming
communities. The defendants, who received sentences ranging from a
year to two decades, included a hospital doctor who helped identify

potentially vulnerable babies, an orphanage director, a ringleader who brokered the adoptions, and a government official. The children, all under a year old, were sold for a total of $112,000. The trial raised alarm bells abroad, and France, which had been averaging about twelve hundred Vietnamese children adopted into its country annually, suspended all new applications from prospective parents. In Việt Nam, more arrests followed.

"By heading to a poor, underdeveloped, or war-torn country to adopt a baby, Westerners can inadvertently achieve the opposite of what they intend," investigative reporter E. J. Graff warned in 2008. "Instead of saving a child, they may create an orphan." Children had become precious resources caught up in a profit-making industry, which often exploited birth parents. "The large sums of money that adoption agencies offer for poor countries' babies," Graff reported, "too often induce unscrupulous operators to buy, coerce, defraud, or kidnap children from families that would have loved, cared for, and raised those children to adulthood."

In 1999, the *Wall Street Journal* published an on-the-ground look at the baby trade industry in Việt Nam. Journalist Sam Marshall mapped out the various middlemen and fixers in the adoption web, explaining how adoption racketeers persuaded mothers who lacked the funds to pay their hospital bills, or who could not read or write, to sign over their babies. Some of them did not realize they would never see their child again.

After adoption fixers passed along word to their network of affiliates "that a baby boy was on the market for an unspecified fee," they worked as a team to hook a prospective foreign parent. Everyone in the chain would get a cut of the fee an American parent was expected to pay for a Vietnamese child, including a man named "Mr. Adoption," who bragged that he could push the process through in a fraction of the time of "by-the-book adoptions." The birth mother would also get a payout, though hers was often less than the lead broker's.

By this point, an estimated ten thousand Vietnamese children had been adopted by foreigners since the 1970s. These scandals and others forced the Vietnamese government to work to tighten rules and implement a supervisory unit to oversee the process. By 2003, Việt Nam's adoption program would be halted by the United States, citing concerns over adoption fraud. Adoptions resumed three years later after the two countries reached an agreement to try to do more to protect children and families. But by 2008, those agreements had dissolved, and following a US State Department investigation, adoptions were suspended again.

But Việt Nam was not the only country facing scrutiny and pressure to curtail unsanctioned adoptions and crack down on baby stealing. Moratoriums on intercountry adoptions would come and go around the world over the next decade, but instead of curtailing baby trafficking globally, they often sent the problem rippling into other countries.

FOURTEEN

"Is the Baby Okay?"

KEELY'S NEIGHBOR, SUE Fallon, had adopted her first son as a toddler from Việt Nam, and in 1999 she and her husband decided they wanted to adopt again. Sue grew up in Michigan in the 1960s and remembered waiting for the local Sunday newspaper, which featured photos with blurbs about orphaned children. Sue would clip the photos and hand them to her parents. There was an orphanage near Sue's home, and she found out that a boy who attended her elementary school lived there. Sue saved her Twinkies and Ding Dongs and gave them to him.

By 1997, Sue had already given birth to two girls, so her growing desire to go through with the adoption process was not driven by an inability to conceive or a longing to experience motherhood. It was driven by the same empathy that she had as a child for those without parents or families.

Sue returned to browsing through worldwide adoption websites and photos of kids. The number of agencies offering intercountry adoption services had grown, even in the last ten years. There were organizations with names like Rainbow Kids or Precious in His Sight. Sue came across a baby from Việt Nam dressed in a white romper, her head resting on a striped blanket folded up like a pillow. The listing said the child was born in May 1999 and had been put up for adoption by September: "She was abandoned by her birth mother. A local village woman brought her to our orphanage. She has had her medical exam completed and is in great health. . . . Please help her find a loving home."

The bio listed the baby's name as Ly. The Fallons decided they would try to adopt Ly, and Sue began communicating with a facilitator who arranged intercountry adoptions for various agencies and often emailed Sue from Việt Nam.

A Santa Barbara, California, attorney's phone number was also listed on the adoption posting. She was working on international adoption proceedings and planned to travel to Việt Nam in October to meet Ly and help finalize the Fallon's adoption. But on October 10, Sue woke up to a cryptic email from the attorney: "I don't know what to say but things are wrong here and I am leaving as soon as possible."

Shaking, Sue wondered: *Did something happen to Ly? Is the baby okay?*

Two days later, the attorney sent another email, explaining that she did not feel safe. The attorney was told she could not see the child until the Fallons agreed to a payment. "They are only interested in money. I am not sure that Ly even exists at this point or if she could even be adopted."

Looking back, Sue believes she got caught up in a black-market baby operation. She later learned that the adoption facilitator, Mai-Ly LaTrace, they had been working with in Việt Nam was deported by the Vietnamese government under accusations that she was a child trafficker. Adoptive parents in the United States and in other parts of the world who had worked with the same facilitator had been posting their own suspicious experiences with her on the internet for several years.

The Vietnamese Embassy issued a statement about LaTrace, claiming she "illegally paid Vietnamese parents or other people to give up children for adoption." Sue later managed to adopt through a different agency that she trusted instead.

Though not every adoption case was corrupt, for those parents who managed to avoid the scandals, the headlines still stung. Being a part of a transracial and transnational adoption already raised questions from strangers: Which country is she from? Can she speak English? But now when people looked at a family, they might wonder if their adopted children were stolen, and some parents looked at their kids and worried the same thing, questioning the agencies and facilitators they used.

Thousands of overseas adoptions were still being conducted legitimately. But it was getting harder for governments to weed out nefarious adoptions from legitimate ones. In some cases, it made more sense to officials to shut all of them down. It was against this backdrop of transnational adoption uncertainty and scandals in 2001 that Sue first showed Keely the photograph of Loan. Sue had come across Loan through other parents within the adoption community. As Sue understood it, another American family had been planning to adopt Loan but changed their minds at the last minute.

Keely, a kindred spirit, felt connected to this child through a photo and worried that her chance to adopt from Việt Nam could end any day; it seemed like the window of time was closing. She had to act swiftly if she was going to adopt this little girl.

With the United States cracking down on adoption procedures, she was told nothing would be approved until a government representative verified that the child was indeed an orphan and that no one had been coerced into giving up their child.

Keely was in charge of gathering paperwork: home studies, agency contracts, fingerprints, bank statements, marriage license, birth certificates. In the middle of this prep work, the agency called Keely with another proposition.

There was the other child, Như, who had arrived at the orphanage on Loan's documented first birthday. The agent explained that Loan had become protective of Như and that the orphanage didn't want to separate the two girls—even though they were not biologically related.

The agency sent Keely a photo of Như. She had short-cropped hair and was barefoot, holding a yellow ball.

"Would you be willing to take the other child too?"

"Yes," Keely replied without hesitation. "Yes, of course we will."

DESPITE ALL HER preparations and enthusiasm, doubts about the adoptions still snuck in. Keely drove through Barrington one morning after dropping her kids off at school. She contemplated whether she could really mother a child whom she did not give birth to herself.

"I was still in a very selfish spot," she told me, explaining that she was focused intently on herself, her family, and how the children she would adopt would fit in with all of them. When it came to people outside of her family, or political issues beyond those immediate concerns, she did not allow herself to think too deeply.

Keely said she was "probably on the way to Starbucks or Target," when she caught herself thinking: *Can I love another woman's child? Can I do this?* She told herself in the moment that she could.

But any curiosity she may have had about birth families or mothers—about how or why they had given away their kids, who they were, where they had come from, what they looked like, or how they felt—she had to stifle and block out. She chose to rely, once again, on her enduring, blind faith in fate, her belief that everything happens for a reason.

"I had to go to this safe place in my mind," as Keely described it, "where the birth mother, the birth father, any birth siblings were not going to get my focus or attention." Without asking too many questions, she asked what she should sign and where she should go.

IN APRIL 2002, Keely boarded a cab in Hồ Chí Minh City, with three of her children by her side. Her oldest, Alexandra, did not come due to school commitments, and Mick could not get away from work. They arrived at the orphanage after a twelve-hour drive. The Solimenes removed their shoes. There were a few bare rooms with cribs. Each of the three buildings housed around fifteen kids, ranging from infants to teens.

Keely spotted a little girl playing in a group and recognized Loan. Keely and her kids walked over to her, offering Loan the treats from the Vietnamese shop, as well as a lollipop from America. They also gave her a toddler bike. Loan was timid around the Solimenes at first, but she immediately began scooting around the room happily with her bike and sweets.

Như was asleep in a crib in another room. She woke up as the Solimenes came in. She was sweaty and cranky, uninterested in the strangers smiling and staring at her. An orphanage caregiver swept the child up to give her a bath. Keely felt the water and was shocked—it was ice cold. After a caregiver toweled Như off, Keely gave her a baby buggy and a lollipop. Như didn't seem to care. But when they gave her crayons, Như began to color on a piece of paper. Keely noticed she was left handed.

The Solimenes spent a week in Nha Trang, getting to know both children. They took them on day trips and brought them to visit the posh resort. Loan seemed excited about the new adventures. She took to the Solimenes. But Như was always scared.

Then the Solimenes returned to Barrington to wait.

In July, they got a call from the adoption agency asking: "Can you return to Việt Nam as soon as possible?" Keely booked their flights immediately.

This time she brought all four of the Solimene children, along with Mick's sister, who left before the adoption was finalized. Mick showed up for couple of days.

On adoption day in 2002, when the process was finally complete, the Solimenes exited those towering gates of the orphanage one final time. Keely and Mick had Loan and Như, soon to be renamed Isabella and Olivia, at their sides—their children now.

Keely looked at her two new daughters in their matching dresses and sandals. She had planned to give them everything equally, the same advantages and assets she and Mick had given their own four biological children, down to the matching Corolle dolls they each held. The dolls smelled like vanilla. She had given one to each of her three biological daughters when they were little, except theirs resembled white babies. For Isabella and Olivia, Keely found Corolle dolls that looked Asian.

Keely looked around at the streets of Nha Trang. In that moment, for the first time in the adoption process, she began to panic. *What do I think I am doing? Taking these children from their country? Giving them new names?* She began to agonize and wonder if she had made a terrible mistake. Who was she to dictate anyone's destiny like this?

When they arrived back at the Ana Mandara hotel, she called the director of the adoption agency: "I just made the decision that will change their future. If I had not come here, they were going to grow up wearing the áo dài, and the gloves, and riding bicycles in the conical hats," she said. "I just took these two girls out of this culture."

"Keely, are you kidding me? What are you talking about? No."

The director, a white American woman who had adopted nine children from within and outside the United States, reassured her she was doing the right thing. These girls might never get adopted if Keely didn't go through with it, she reminded her.

And that, Keely said, was last she would worry about it. Keely would not look back on that day or those doubts. She did not plan to return to Việt Nam with them or on her own. "This is it. These are my kids. I'm going to raise them. They're Americans."

At first, Keely actually considered not telling them they were Vietnamese. "They looked to me as different as my biological kids looked from each other," Keely told me. "It's weird to say, but I don't see certain differences. I see more into their soul." She told me she tries to be guided by what she believes to be color-blindness. "It's not the color of our skin," Keely said. "It's the color of our thoughts."

Yet just days after stepping off the airplane from Việt Nam with both girls, as Mick sat with four-year-old Isabella in a Burger King in North Carolina, where they had gone for a family vacation, a white woman stared at them, turned to Mick, and said, "You don't look Oriental."

Two decades after adopting Isabella and Olivia, Keely would stand by her beliefs: "What if we could just all be okay with who we are and okay with who everybody else is?" she said. "Wouldn't it be such a healthy world if people could just see beyond the visible differences? I guess I came into the world sort of feeling this way, and I'll probably leave feeling this way."

A FEW MONTHS after settling back in Barrington, Keely began sorting through the girls' adoption papers. The stack of papers reached six inches high. Pages and pages stamped and sealed, some translated into English, some in Vietnamese. She had skimmed before, but most of the pages had gone unread in the pile.

This time, as she sifted through, she came across a letter written by Isabella's birth mother, Nguyễn Thị Kim Liên: "I have twin born daughters, born July 24, 1998 my children born out of wedlock . . ."

Twin daughters. Keely read it again.

Keely picked up another document. It was three pages long, listing Loan's milestones, like when she learned to walk.

She noticed two words: *twin birth.*

Keely would search her memories. Had she missed this in the confusion and thrill of navigating the girls' adoptions in Việt Nam?

Yet Keely felt certain that Isabella did not have any biological siblings living with her at the Center for Khánh Hoà Social Protection. Surely the agency would have made the Solimenes aware if she did. It would have been too glaring a detail to leave out. Olivia was always described as the closest child to Isabella.

Keely sorted through the paperwork, looking for documents from both birth mothers. She read over everything. Isabella and Olivia, according to the paperwork, definitely had two different biological mothers.

With that fine point tucked into the piles of pages, the significance hit her. If Isabella had a biological twin, as the documents suggested,

Keely thought she should ask where the child ended up. She called the adoption agency.

"We don't know anything about a twin," staff told her. No one could even say if the supposed twin was alive.

The thought of Isabella having a biological twin forced Keely to stop thinking of Việt Nam as a place she would never visit again. Instead, she began making plans to return. Keely believed what people said about twins having a "special bond," closer sometimes than with other siblings or their parents.

She asked Mick: "What are we going to do if we find her?"

PART TWO

Isabella

Even when I knew that I had a twin, it just never really hit me that something was missing.

I mean, I grew up being curious about it. There was another person out there just like me, but I didn't feel like I needed to know who it is.

It also scared me too. I just realized that this world is huge, and somewhere out there, there is another piece to me. Another piece, outside of my family here. It was this idea that my life didn't start here. It started somewhere else.

It just felt really, really scary. To think that my life could be disrupted by another person who thought like me. Looked like me. Did the same things as me.

To think there's another person out there that might have the same exact genes as I do.

FIFTEEN

A Twin Who Walks Alone

SCIENTISTS SAY THE biological bond between twins begins before birth. At fourteen weeks of gestation, when each fetus is the size of a lime, translucent and veiled in fuzz, they will begin grasping for each other.

By eighteen weeks in utero, they will stroke each other's heads, touch each other's backs in a kind of embrace, nuzzling together, entwining their arms, caressing their womb mate's tender eye area. They spend more time lingering in shared touch with each other than they will touching their own faces, heads, and bodies, or parts of the uterus. Some identical twins may share the same amniotic sac, depending on how early the fertilized egg divides. Twins who share one sac and placenta have even been shown to suck each other's thumbs.

Twins in utero will spend up to 30 percent of their time reaching out for the other sibling, before ever emerging into the glare of the outside world, according to researchers from the University of Padova in Italy, who launched a study of twin pregnancies using video technology. The scientists wanted to find out if pairs of fetuses intentionally directed their movements toward each other—rather than just accidentally poking and nudging in their inevitable knot of proximity.

Researchers speculated, based on these findings, that the twin relationship involves developing awareness of the self and the other. For twins, this perceptiveness begins long before birth, evidence of an innate desire for human contact that all of us share.

WHEN I FIRST visited psychologist and professor Nancy Segal, the head of the Twin Studies Center at California State University, Fullerton, we sat in her office, which was stacked to the ceiling with file folders and papers, its walls lined with copies of *Psychology Today* and the *New York Times Magazine* and dozens of other publications and books featuring her twin research. Photos of twin pairs hung on the wall alongside running bibs from her many marathons.

My newborn twins are identical, I told her, adding, "But I can already tell they're pretty different in their personalities."

"Well, moms are very sensitive to the differences," Segal said. "And you have to be, because you have to distinguish between them."

She explained how studies have shown that identical twins are more alike than all other pairs, and this is proof that genes are powerful. Segal herself has a fraternal twin sister. "Fraternal twins," she told me, "can be very different from each other."

Segal founded the Twin Studies Center over three decades ago. She often tells the story about one of the earliest pairs she studied. In 1979, Jim Springer and Jim Lewis, "the Jim Twins," were reunited at age thirty-nine after having no idea the other existed. Both had been adopted and raised by different families in Ohio, just forty miles apart from each other. Despite their separate upbringings, it turned out that both twins bit their nails, got terrible migraines, smoked Salem cigarettes, drove light blue Chevrolets, did poorly in spelling and math, and had worked at McDonald's and as part-time deputy sheriffs. One of the Jim Twins had named his first son James Alan. The other had named his first son James Allan. Both had named their pet dogs "Toy." Both had also married women named Linda—then they got divorced, and both remarried women named Betty. Since a shared environment growing up did not play a role in their behaviors, Segal and other scientists believe genetic disposition to certain behaviors did.

Another pair, nicknamed the "Giggle Twins," were raised in separate homes, both with rather serious adoptive parents. Until reuniting with each other, each twin believed she laughed more than anyone she had ever met before. They discovered they laughed alike (with arms folded), according to Segal's research. Both also realized they each had miscarriages, followed by the birth of two boys and a girl.

The Jim Twins and the Giggle Twins were all participants in the Minnesota Twin Study, conducted from the late 1979 to the early 2000s under the psychology professor Thomas Bouchard, whom Segal first worked with as a postdoctoral student. Researchers enlisted 137 pairs of twins, including 81 identical twins reared apart, putting them through a litany of tests and over fifteen thousand questions about their personalities, lifestyles, and tendencies.

Both adoptees and twins have long been the subject of fascination by scientists and treated as media spectacles and tropes. The less remarkable twin pairs, the ones who do not reveal shocking similarities, rarely make it into popular media accounts. People seem far more intrigued by uncanny connections.

I have a cell phone video of my sons playing at age three. In the footage, they are separated by a wall-like banister, unable to see each other. One bumps his head, immediately grabbing it in pain. In that same moment, his brother also reaches for the same side of his own head and says, "Owie." Yet the video does not show him bumping his head.

Friends and family became fascinated, watching the video over and over, assuming one brother felt the other's pain. Such rare, seemingly mystical, and probably purely coincidental stories are passed through different cultures and countries. They spur beliefs about the bond between twins and the power such pairs possess.

In Western cultures, some adults whose twin died in the womb or at birth speak of a life of loneliness or guilt, a perpetual void. My uncle, whose twin died at birth, felt his dead brother's absence his entire life. After my uncle suffered a massive heart attack, he told me believed he felt his twin's presence alongside of him while in that liminal space between life and death.

For twins who do grow up together, the death of one can be crippling for the survivor, Segal said. Identical and fraternal twins can feel the loss of their sibling more excruciatingly than any other loss, Segal teaches in her college lessons on twin grief. In 2007, identical twin Christa Parravani told the *New York Times* that her sister's death from a drug overdose caused her to stop eating. Cara tried to describe the loss: "It seems unusual to breathe now."

The Jicarilla Apache tribe in New Mexico sees twins as two people living out one life. In Mali, the Bamana and Malinke believe twins are powerful beings sharing a single spirit. The Nahani tribe in British Columbia believes twins are two halves of a whole, sharing the same breath. And on the Fijian island of Galoa, if one twin dies, the surviving sibling is believed to be dead, too, and must undergo a series of sacred ceremonies to return to life.

In the Karanga clan of southeast Africa, it is believed that a bereaved twin is destined to die of loneliness. Xhosa people, the Bantu ethnic group from southern Africa, will tell a surviving twin to lie facedown on their dead sibling's coffin or faceup in the freshly dug grave before the burial, or else they will die of mourning.

The Yoruba tribe in western Nigeria has one of the highest twinning rates in the world. One in eleven Yoruba people are born as twins, mostly fraternal. The tribe developed a system of rituals for when one twin loses another, involving the special carving of a small wooden figure that represents being born of two. It is believed to house the soul of the dead twin. The figure is worshipped, cleaned, and cared for like the living twin. This process allows the shared spirit of the separated siblings to endure. The twin connection among the Yoruba is captured in an oríkì praise poem: "Twin who cannot walk alone, who needs another with whom to walk."

SIXTEEN

Blindly Searching

KEELY'S TRIPS OVERSEAS began around the time Isabella was in preschool, in 2003, a year after she and Olivia were adopted. Keely was gone for weeks at a time, traveling for humanitarian missions, sometimes in India; but mostly she was in Việt Nam, searching for Isabella's twin.

Keely and Sue had decided over a coffee conversation in Barrington to venture back to Việt Nam together in the summer of 2003. First, they would stop off for two days in India to visit the sister of a Catholic priest from their town, and then they would fly to the Tân Sơn Nhất International Airport in Hồ Chí Minh City. It would be partly a charity mission, donating clothes and other items that the orphanage needed. But for Keely, it was also a twin-sister fact-finding mission.

From Hồ Chí Minh City they flew to Nha Trang, where they met up with Tuyết Hồ, a dress-shop owner whom Keely knew from her adoption of Isabella and Olivia. Tuyết Hồ had come to know many tourists through her shop and her work as a guide and translator. The day before Isabella and Hà were adopted in 2002, Keely had gone to the shop, where Tuyết Hồ sewed her a skirt and mock-neck blouse from white-gold silk.

In all, as Tuyết Hồ told me, she had worked with almost a dozen foreign families who came to Việt Nam to adopt over the years, interpreting, sewing, giving tours. She lost touch with most of them after the process was over, but a year after the Solimenes brought the girls from the orphanage to America, Tuyết Hồ learned that Keely would be visiting again.

During that 2003 trip, Tuyết Hồ accompanied Keely and Sue to the Center for Khánh Hoà Social Protection, where Keely had adopted Isabella and Olivia. At the orphanage, Keely met with the director, a woman named Hoa, though she felt nervous in her presence, particularly when it came to asking for any information about Isabella's twin.

"You were not supposed to go back and look for birth families," Keely said. Throughout her adoption process with the agency, she added, "it was very much ingrained: don't go search."

The visit with Hoa revealed no new information. Isabella's twin had never been enrolled in the center, so they would not have any records or official information on her whereabouts.

Keely's mind was already at work. Even without knowing anything about the child's life or who was raising her, she began to tell herself that perhaps she could find a way to adopt Isabella's twin, to bring her to the United States too. *I'm going to just find this little orphan girl, bring her here*, Keely thought. *And she's going to be child number seven in our family.*

KEELY RETURNED TO Barrington and sent emails to the director of the US adoption agency that she had worked with, inquiring about possible charity events, particularly for the kids who came from the same orphanage as Isabella and Olivia. She had also been in touch before with the director's daughter, Joy Degenhardt, who lived in Việt Nam, about finding Isabella's twin. In April 2004, Keely sent another email to Joy, with the subject line "Kim Loan's twin sister":

I have always felt that it would be important to know where her sister is, as they have a very special bond and they may want to see each other again. . . . I have exhausted my efforts and need your help. If she is with her mother, we may be able to establish a family to family arrangement to make sure they have what they need, or if she is available for adoption we would pursue adopting her. If she was adopted, we could have this information available for the girls at a later date. In any case, I would really appreciate any help you could offer. I left Kim Loan's birth records with Tuyết [Hồ] last summer, but she has not had much luck.

Joy wrote back, asking Keely to work with her instead:

Tuyết is a friend and many families want to have tailored clothing, so I introduced them to her. Sometimes she helps out in shopping, but that's about it. As for being involved with any of the adoptions, Tuyết is not familiar with this. As for Kim Loan's twin, I do remember the director saying that the 2nd twin was adopted at a later time to a French family doing a direct adoption. She did not give me any details.

Joy added that she would try to find out more.

Meanwhile, Joy's mother had suggested the children in the orphanage might enjoy a road trip. Keely got to work planning, enlisting Tuyết Hồ's help. The trip would involve sixty children and six caregivers, including the orphanage director, over three days in the hill town of Đà Lat. Keely and Mick would pay for all of it. It would also be a way to get closer to the director, in hopes that she might reveal something more about Isabella's twin.

In the summer of 2004, Keely returned to Nha Trang with her four older children and her niece. Isabella, now six, and Olivia, five, stayed behind with their aunt in North Carolina. Keely said they were too young to come along. Tuyết Hồ arranged van rentals for the orphans and staff to get to Đà Lat, a four-hour ride.

On that trip, Keely again asked Tuyết Hồ if she would again inquire about Isabella's twin. Tuyết Hồ spoke to the director in Vietnamese. Soon after, Tuyết Hồ told Keely there was a village in the countryside. Keely understood that they might find Isabella's twin there. Tuyết Hồ drove them to a village, but the search did not pan out.

SEVENTEEN

Fairy Tales

ONCE UPON A time in ancient Việt Nam, a dragon king from the water, Lạc Long Quân, had a love affair with a fairy princess from the land, Âu Cơ. "It is said that their brief union produced one hundred eggs—which hatched into the first Vietnamese children," wrote Indigo Willing, who studied the mythological story while earning her PhD in sociology at the University of Queensland.

One day, Lạc Long Quân told Âu Cơ: "I am descended from dragons, you from fairies. We are as incompatible as water is with fire. So we cannot continue in harmony."

The lovers parted, and each took half of their one hundred children with them. Despite their yearning to be together, it was their fate.

"It's such a beautiful story, how they fell in love in the heavens," Willing told me in a Zoom interview during the first year of the COVID-19 pandemic. "But they had to separate. So the king went down to the ocean and the fairy went up to the mountains, and that's the story of why the North and South and the Vietnamese people are continually apart."

This story represents a kind of collective longing for unity among Vietnamese people and an acceptance of what is meant to be. But in her research, Willing grew particularly interested in another strand of this legend not often recounted: In some versions, as she learned, it turned out a few of the fairy princess's eggs had accidentally been left behind.

As the tale goes, a European king and queen discovered the babies after the eggs hatched. "Thinking they were abandoned, the royal couple decided to take the infants back to their own soil and raise them," Willing wrote in a 2004 article in the *Michigan Quarterly Review*, "even though they looked different from the people in their land." The children, though loved, felt rejected by society because of their foreign status and wondered where they came from.

As a baby, Willing was classified as an orphan, adopted from Việt Nam in 1972, and raised by a white family in an Australian suburb. To her, these fictional children of Lạc Long Quân and Âu Cơ "represented the experiences of thousands of Vietnamese children who were adopted overseas, including many during the era of the war."

"As the adopted Vietnamese began to mature," she wrote, "they would come to feel curious about their birth country and the people they left behind." But in real life, the process of searching rarely leads to biological families, she explained. And when reunions do happen, they are often fraught with pain and confusion.

In her younger years, Willing did not feel so disconnected from her adoptive parents or their two biological sons. They loved her and always considered her part of their family. But when Willing started school, she began to question if she belonged.

"Why are you a different color from your family?" the kids would ask. "I just had no idea," she said, "because nobody said anything until then." Her parents told her about the war in Việt Nam, and from then on, "every time anything about the Vietnam War was on TV, [I] just watched it with horror." She remembers images with Vietnamese villains and women who were sexualized or portrayed as prostitutes. "The only thing I knew about Vietnam was that it was a land of poverty and orphanages," Willing wrote. "I was afraid to be associated with it."

For her master's thesis in sociology, Willing interviewed thirteen adults who had been adopted from Việt Nam as children between 1969 and 1975, all raised by white parents in Western countries. In her interviews with orphans, Willing noticed that when holes in their stories about why they were orphaned could not be supplemented with facts, the adoptees turned to fantasy-like tales and speculation passed on from parents, who often told them stories about the "Red Thread." Usually, these stories followed a variation of this quote: "The thread may stretch or tangle, but it will never break."

In Red Thread narratives originating in the East, a matchmaker arranged marriages by tying red strings between people who were deemed fated from birth to marry each other. In the West, adoptive parents reinterpreted the plot, which was repeated in internet forums and children's books targeting adopted children, elevating fate as its central theme, the idea that orphans were predestined to end up with their adoptive parents. It left birth parents out of the story completely, brushing aside social inequities that pushed parents to relinquish their children. "Fairy tales transform contingency into destiny," wrote one pair of researchers on childhood stories and adoption. "Their inexorable ending drives the message home that once things are what they were meant to be, they will stay that way forever."

Color-blindness fueled the fairy-tale narrative. For decades, psychologists and sociologists have argued that color-blindness denies and overlooks the painful, burdensome racial experiences of minorities, systematically and individually, ignoring clear racial disparities in education, health, income, poverty, and criminal justice.

Willing completed her PhD thesis in sociology at the University of Queensland, focusing on the experiences of Australian parents who have adopted children from Asia and Africa. She now runs the Adopted Vietnamese International community network dedicated to Vietnamese adoptees. Willing has also been active in film, literary, academic, and community projects that focus on cultural and transnational adoption communities.

Willing has yet to find her own biological relatives, as hard as she has tried over the years. Many adoptees who are now sharing their stories in podcasts, social media groups, books, and personal essays speak of a pervasive feeling of loss or loneliness. "Grief, you might feel very strongly one day, and then be fine for years. And then just one little thing will tip back into a fresh feeling of loss," she said. "It's lifelong for many of us. Sometimes I'm fine. And sometimes I'm disturbed, and unsettled, and sad."

Adoption stories, Willing points out, are often myths, crafted to fit a "rags to riches" narrative. Outcasts turned to royalty. Unwanted children turned into chosen ones. Babies born to nameless, poor mothers who are predestined to give their children to others with "better" living conditions. At the same time, adoption myths can also swing too sharply to the opposite extreme, steeped in the belief a child can fully assimilate and become the person their parents and environment shape them to be.

But as Willing and other transracial and transnational adoptee experts told me, when the painful layers get peeled back, the truth revealed is much more complicated. There are no neat and simple fairytale endings.

Isabella

My mom traveled a lot when I was growing up. I remember hating it when she left.

I remember being six years old and staying up late at night and doing laundry for soccer practice or a soccer game, or doing Olivia's laundry, or bathing Olivia because my siblings weren't always around, and neither was my dad.

I also remember staying up doing the dishes, because no one had done them for three days. I was really short in the kitchen, and I remember having to grab the stool so I could stand on it comfortably to lean over the sink.

Once, Olivia and I were home alone for the first time ever. I think my dad was golfing. The golf course was five minutes away. And I remember we were hungry for lunch. We had ramen, but I didn't know how to make ramen. We made it, and it was terrible. Like the ratio from water to like the seasoning packet was so off. I think we like went and sat and watched TV, like Sponge Bob, for the rest of the day.

It's like, "Mom does the laundry all the time. She does the dishes. She makes me lunch. She does this for me." I just had this greater feeling of appreciation for her. And I remember hating the feeling of missing her and having her gone for so long.

EIGHTEEN

The Letters

WHEN ISABELLA WAS in kindergarten and elementary school, during those stretches when Keely was away, she counted the days until her mom returned. She made "welcome home" cards and hung them around the house. Sometimes the kids were left under the charge of a nanny or their dad, other times with their aunt.

Keely gave Isabella and Olivia pebbles before leaving on one of her trips.

"When you miss me, hold this rock," Keely told Isabella. "You can scream at the top of your lungs holding this, and I'll be able to hear you from across the world."

There's no way she'll feel this, Isabella thought.

Still, the girls stood on the balcony of their aunt's apartment and yelled out into the universe, holding the rocks.

The next day, Keely called.

"Mom, did you hear me?"

She replied, "I heard you. I felt you guys hugging me."

Oh my gosh, she felt us for real.

From then on, Olivia and Isabella held their rocks and screamed every day that she was gone.

IN 2005, KEELY began planning another trip to Việt Nam, but she had to cancel at the last minute. Her sister had fallen ill. Keely asked Joy, the daughter of the adoption agency's director who still lived in Hồ Chí

Minh City, if she could instead travel to the orphanage in Nha Trang to find out more information about Isabella's twin. Keely would cover the expenses, and Joy could use the hotel reservations she had made.

A few weeks later, in June 2005, Keely emailed Joy to ask how the trip went. She learned that Joy had talked to the director about the twins' first mother.

Keely received this reply:

I went to the orphanage waiting for the birthmother to come to the center and she ended up not showing up. I talked to Hoa to see what the situation was with the family and as of now, the birthmother has gotten married to a cyclo driver. She has two children now with her husband. . . . They live in a shack and rome [sic] around trying to earn bits of money. Hoa has a hard time to find the birthmother. . . . Only the birthmother knows where the sibling is. Hoa says that some Vietnamese single lady is bringing her up. I hear she is also very poor but loves her. I saw a photo of the twin and thought I was looking at Loan. . . . It was the twin and they are identical!

SIX MONTHS LATER, in December 2005, Keely received a letter from Việt Nam written in English. It was dated two days after Christmas, from Isabella's birth mother.

Hi, this is Nguyễn Thị Kim Liên, Nguyễn Khánh Kim Loan's mother. I live in 15 Hoa, Van Thanh ward, Nha Trang city, Khánh Hòa province. I write this letter is to wish you best wishes. My family lives in poverty, we have no home, we can't bring our children up. Luckily, you adopted my daughter, Nguyễn Khánh Kim Loan. Thank you very much. We will never forget your charity. One more time we wish you good health and a Happy New Year. Sincerely yours, Nguyễn Thị Kim Liên

Another letter arrived around the same time, handwritten in English and signed with the same name: "If you return Việt Nam again, please notice before I can come."

Keely did not reply to any of Liên's letters. She denied that they were from Isabella's birth mother. "I was giving them very little weight," she said years later. "There was a tremendous amount of confusion." Sometimes she received letters written in Vietnamese. She asked a nail salon technician who spoke the language to translate for her.

If she *had* allowed herself to accept that these letters were from the twins' birth mother, the trail could have provided an immediate clue to finding Isabella's twin. "It totally would have," Keely admitted years later. "If I believed it. If it all seemed legitimate."

Keely had not even conceptualized the idea of the twins' mother. "I don't even think she was on the radar," she said. "I was so focused on just finding Isabella's sister."

IN 2006, ANOTHER letter arrived, addressed to the Solimene family. This one was signed by the grandmother of seven-year-old Olivia.

Dear the Godparents SOLIMENES . . .

I am Nguyễn Thị Mùa—the maternal grandmother of Khánh Như—the parents of Khánh Như they are deaf and dumb. Khan Như has 2 elder sisters and 2 younger brothers—all these children are childhood and schooling, therefore the family is always faced up with a lot of difficulties.

It is over three years, I have a chance returned the orphanage to visit Khánh Như and knew that you have adopted my granddaughter. Ms. Hoa said that you are the good-hearted persons. I am very glad and moved to tears. . . .

My family has an aspiration: Can we keep a correspondence together? How can we know about the Khánh Nu (health, education . . .)?

Because, this is the first time Khánh Như traveling to a remote place. Can you send us some photos about your family and Khánh Như? Or in some days in the future, can all your family come back Việt Nam to visit the old place? And we meet together?

We wish that all your family members are always happy and healthy. We also pray that God may grant all of you a long life with constant health. . . . Every night we always pray God blessing all of you. We are looking forward to hearing your reply.

Sincerely yours,

Nguyễn Thị Mùa

This letter from Olivia's grandmother affected Keely more than the others. "I was having a hard time," she told me. "When I finally realized these were birth mothers. Grandmothers. Birth families. When I finally realized that there were very, very painful feelings. It was terrifying."

Picturing this woman who so clearly loved her granddaughter visiting the child in the orphanage and then one day realizing she was gone, Keely said, "I was just feeling like, because I have money, I have this woman's grandchild."

Keely did not want to face the reality of other women. It would take her three years to write back to Olivia's grandmother.

These, Keely told herself, *are my girls.*

Nearly a decade later, when Olivia was nearing college age, Keely showed her the letter from Nguyễn Thị Mùa, who had since passed away. Olivia never got to meet her.

"I was emotional," Olivia recalled, "like in some way, there was a part of me back in Việt Nam." She could not understand her own feelings. "This is someone I'm not close to. I have no connection with her. The only connection I have is that we're related by blood." Olivia had never longed to be reunited with her birth family, yet at the same time, she said: "I remember feeling so sad, just like I missed my chance or opportunity to build a relationship."

Olivia tried to put herself in her mother's position, to understand why she had not written back right away. Perhaps, she reasoned, Keely did not think she was ready to know her birth family. Perhaps her mom worried about losing her own daughter. Olivia always looked up to her mother, and she loved the entire Solimene family so much it scared her. Her worst fear was losing them. "Sometimes I worry that if I were to connect with the birth family over there in Việt Nam, my mom would feel replaced," Olivia said. "And I would never want that."

Hà

Growing up in Việt Nam, I thought I had everything. I never thought I lacked anything. I grew up in poverty. But at a very young age, I did not worry about finances or money and all of that. Yeah, some days we went to bed without food in our bellies. I remember those days. Sometimes I look back to my life and I wish that parts of it was different. I wish that I had more food to eat.

But life in the countryside taught me a lot, it has shaped me, the way I think about the world, who I am. I grew up in this environment where everyone had the same life as me, so I didn't really compare my life to anybody else's.

Some days we didn't have electricity, so that's why I appreciate the light of the moon and the stars. If I had a TV, I would have stuck around watching TV and would not have explored the nature around me. If I lacked something, I explored something else.

I didn't have toys. If I did have toys, I wouldn't have been able to keep any of them because all of the storms and flooding would just take it all away, you know? And my parents would not have been able to afford toys for me. So I played with whatever I found around me, like trees and dust. I didn't mind playing with the dust.

And I think that I would never have had that kind of childhood if I wasn't living in my countryside with them, because, you know, I wouldn't be able to appreciate the moon the same, the stars, the sand, the trees, and the environment around me.

Now when I think about that, my mind is literally back in the countryside right now. I'm not going to lie, I love it.

NINETEEN

Storms

ONE EVENING IN 2007, nine-year-old Hà stayed awake past midnight listening to the wind and rain thrash her home. The weather pounded the planks and rattled the tin. It shook the leaves and seeped through the cracks.

To grow up in Khánh Đông is to know the uncertainty of storms. You learn to take shelter from the wet whiplashing, to steady yourself as the winds play a violent tug of war. Monsoons feed off imbalances. Warm land and cooler ocean. They behave like storms, though they're not technically classified as such. They can bring landslides, thunder, floods.

Typhoons are not born the same. They spiral over the ocean first, nourished by the moisture of warm water. A typhoon twirls itself an eye, its own witness. You cannot see inside. It does not always make landfall, but when it does, it forces you to pay attention. Both weather patterns barge in and disrupt. Uproot, then leave behind.

The rainy season was nearing an end, and until now their hardy home had held together, withstanding the water and whipping winds, emerging with fixable damage just as it had always done since Hà was a baby. But this furor was different than the rest—it did not want to let go. No one in Khánh Đông slept. The rain soaked the ground, turning Rô and Tuyết's living room to mud.

Normally during heavy monsoons or typhoons, neighbors and family members dragged their belongings to Rô and Tuyết's, since their home was on high ground. They would all wait it out together, hunkering down inside of the small space until the rain stopped and the water receded. Hà always enjoyed the extra company. It felt like a big party under her roof.

On this night, Hà's uncle and a cousin had already arrived with their belongings. Neighbors from lower down the path had come carting their things too. But Rô and Tuyết seemed extra nervous as the water poured in through the seams of the walls. They moved their possessions on top of tables and shelves. But the water rose to their knees. Then to their hips. It was getting too high, too fast. They could not stay.

Everyone splashed outside carrying bags of blankets, clothes, and mats, making their ascent higher up the hill as the rain welted their cheeks and drenched their hair. They stopped at a patch of damp dirt beneath the tall trees.

From there, Hà watched over her home under the light of the moon, the water continuing to rise. By 2:00 a.m., it surged higher, until Hà could see it lapping at their roof. Higher, until the roof was no longer visible. The water swallowed it all.

The villagers stayed awake as the sun rose and the storm began to weaken. By noon, the rain had stopped, and the mucky water started to retreat. Hà could see her roof again. But as the floods withdrew, she noticed the walls beginning to buckle. Down, down, down.

Hà watched her childhood home fold into itself, collapsing into a pile of soggy rubble. Later, they picked through the debris for anything they could salvage. There was nowhere in their old house to sit, nowhere to sleep. But at least they had survived. Hà would later learn that a neighbor who lived lower down the hill had drowned inside her house.

The typhoon had brought with it 130 mph winds. It triggered landslides and floods, destroying a hundred thousand homes. Some washed away completely, like paper boats beneath a barreling wave. At least seventy-seven people were reported dead or missing. Others were hurt by falling branches and hurling debris. Weeks after the typhoon, bodies continued to wash up. The region struggled to feed its homeless. Crops were destroyed. Cattle had drowned. Mosquitoes raged.

Tuyết and her brother constructed a tent from blankets, draped them over tree branches and pieces of wood. They searched for sheets of plastic to cover the blankets. They laid mats on the ground. They stashed all the clothes and items they could recover beneath tarps. Rô, Tuyết, and Hà slept huddled together under this makeshift tent.

It took several weeks, but the government gave money to families whose homes had been destroyed. Tuyết and Rô received around 10 million đồng. For two months, the family slept in the tent under the tree as Tuyết and her brother built a new, stronger home on the same plot. They painted the inside walls turquoise, a color that Hà saw as a tranquil ocean, a color of hope.

In that newly erected home, the family would celebrate Tết holidays with sticky rice filled with pork and mung beans and wrapped in banana leaves, fruit trays arranged on altars, and roasted duck, which Tuyết and Rô also raised on their land, though in less abundance than their chickens, which Hà learned to raise. Her family had at least ten chickens at a time, in different colors like brown, black, yellow, and red. Sometimes the mother hens gave birth to more chicks, and their coop grew to twenty-five.

In their yard, Rô and Tuyết built a wood and straw coop for the chickens, with a door that locked. Each evening around 5:00 p.m., they called the chickens back to the coop, using a "chi-chi-chi-chit" sound. They shut the birds inside to protect them from predators, like snakes. Each night they counted the eggs. The chickens would wake around 3:00 a.m., peeping and clucking. By 5:00 a.m., Hà would let the chickens out to run and peck in the yard. It was her job to clean the pen and count the eggs again. Sometimes, despite the locked door, the snakes crept in and snatched a few.

When Hà's family wanted more chickens, they let a few of the eggs hatch, but mostly they relied on the eggs for food. It was Hà's duty to collect the freshly laid ones. "I hated grabbing the eggs," she said. "I would think, 'Oh my God, the mother is going to hate me.'" It felt wrong to Hà, stealing a hen's unhatched baby chicks—she was convinced the mother knew exactly what was happening to her offspring and held it against her.

Sometimes, when Hà's family had no money to buy meat, they killed the chickens for food too. This disturbed and confused Hà, who learned while attending the local temple that humans should not kill their own animals because they are sentient beings with their own karma. They could have been humans, even relatives, in past lives. "If you have to kill your own chicken, you should ask another people to do that for you," as Hà explained it, but Rô and Tuyết broke those rules.

"Do you really think I am going to run around to the neighbors and ask them to kill our chicken for us?" Rô told her. "I'm just going to do it myself."

"I will never kill my chickens," Hà replied.

"You will when you have to take care of your own family," Tuyết said. "When you grow up, these are the kinds of things you will have to deal with."

To Hà, this small lesson imparted to her by her adoptive mother, with whom she shared no blood or DNA, taught her something about the sacrifices that mothers made, the choices they faced based on their life circumstances.

ONE DAY, HÀ's birth mother traveled from the city to the countryside of Khánh Đông to visit. Liên brought along her two youngest daughters, Hà's half siblings. Liên was now raising two girls with Quý, who had found work as a cyclo driver.

As Hà told it, she always knew the two girls were her half sisters, much like she always knew Liên was her biological mom, but there was emotional distance between them. On this occasion, Rô and Tuyết prepared chicken and rice. With Rô and Tuyết busy in the kitchen, Liên pulled Hà aside, told her to come with her outdoors. They stopped beneath a mango tree a few yards away from the house.

Liên spoke in a hushed tone. "I want you to know that I am your mom."

"I know that," Hà replied. Rô and Tuyết had never kept this information from her.

"I gave you to Rô and Tuyết because I was too poor to raise you myself."

Hà knew that too.

Hà noticed Liên's other daughters peeking outside, trying to get their mother's attention. Liên and Quý had also named their fourth daughter Hà—Phan Nữ Hồng Hà. The child would come to be known as Baby Hà. The older Hà never understood why Liên made this choice. The shared name bothered her, as if her mother had simply replaced one Hà with another.

Hà would explain years later, "Inside me, there is always a question: Why did you give me away? How can you love me if you gave me away? But when I grew up, I said, 'It is what it is. I cannot blame her for anything.'"

That same year of Liên's visit, Hà fell dangerously ill. She had not been that sick since she was an infant. No one knew what was wrong with her. It started with a cold. She developed a cough that lasted for months. She threw up, and her skin felt hot to the touch. She refused to eat. Even medicine prescribed from a doctor did not help.

Rô could not keep herself together, weeping with worry. Tuyết fretted, too, terrified that Hà would die. Tuyết thought they needed to try something else to cure her: she would take Hà to see a spiritual guide. Tuyết hoisted Hà on her back and ran frantically to the temple, where the spiritual guide, in a gray robe, was surrounded by statues of Buddha. Hà had darkness in her soul, the guide explained.

In a past life, Hà had been a female Buddhist monk. But she had died young, and this misfortune had followed Hà into the present life, which is why she was always sick, even from birth. The cycle of bad karma could be broken, the guide told them, through prayer and meditation. Hà could be released from the bad spirits because she had garnered good karma in her past life.

She held up a cup of water and a lotus flower near Hà's head, praying and blessing her. She told Tuyết to give Hà a mixture of fried oranges and honey. Tuyết and Rô fed Hà the remedy for one month and prayed over her. Rô put carnations and daisies on the altar, cleaning it regularly. Tuyết read from a prayer book every night. They pledged never to leave this child and asked that she not leave them either. Hà slowly got better; her good karma was restored.

Tuyết always worried, because the local school expected Hà to be able to count from one to one hundred and to read and write a long list of Vietnamese words and letters. She was concerned that Hà, who had not been enrolled in preschool, would soon fall behind. When Tuyết came home from working in the rice fields all day, she would sit at a small table alongside Hà. She handed her a notebook and a pencil and wrote a single word on the page. She told Hà to copy the word over and over, until the page was filled. Then she would turn the page and begin again with a new word, also having Hà practice the pronunciation.

Tuyết knew that Rô could not read or write, so this responsibility was left to her. Hà started out writing with her left hand, but Tuyết would hold her right hand, guiding her until she was able to write with it too. She tutored Hà like this every night for a year.

Some nights, Hà asked Tuyết to tell her stories. Tuyết's nighttime tales were not fables or mythical folk tales. They were pulled from the pages of real life.

"Why do you look like a boy?" Hà would remember asking Tuyết before bedtime.

Tuyết told her that she used to try to live like a person she is not. She explained that she had tried to date a man: "But I wasn't honoring my own feelings, my true feelings. I didn't even tell my family how I felt, how I felt different about my body."

Tuyết told Hà that one day she realized she wanted to be herself, even if others might not approve or understand. The two of them did not get into explicit discussions about being gay or love and relationships. "We did not talk about the LGBTQ community," Hà explained. Growing up in her small community in Việt Nam, she said these subjects were taboo.

Instead, she said, "Tuyết told me about her oldest brother, how she always looked up to him as the role model. She wanted to become like him. She changed from a girly girl to a person more like who she wanted to be. Like her brother." Without fully explaining the concept of gender identity to her daughter, Tuyết imparted a lesson about how she learned to live as herself, even if it felt like the world wanted to bend you into becoming someone else.

When Tuyết made the decision to adopt Hà, she committed to raising her with like values. She taught Hà how to rebuild when storms tore you down and how to have say over her life, no matter her karma.

TWENTY

The Fog

TOWARD THE END of those five years of Keely's detective work, Isabella, now ten, began to wonder what would happen if her mom actually found her twin. The thought of a child, whom Isabella did not know at all, dropping into the Solimene family and calling herself her sister, parachuting into the life that Isabella was still figuring out how to negotiate, unsettled her. She wasn't ready for such an intrusion.

Isabella had no desire to travel with her mom to wherever in the world she was always going. She wanted to stay back and play soccer and hang out with Olivia, and she wanted her mom to be with her, in Illinois, instead.

One day in 2008, Keely came into the bedroom that Isabella and Olivia shared; she seemed serious. Keely told Isabella she was going to Việt Nam again. She would bring two of Isabella's older sisters, Victoria and Arianna, on the philanthropy trip.

"I think I might find your twin this time," Isabella remembers Keely telling her. Keely waited for a response.

"Okay," Isabella replied. "Let me know if you find her."

THERE COMES A moment of awakening for some adoptees when they start to see beyond the tales of fate and fairy tales—a lightbulb moment in which they begin to stand outside of the familiar narratives of their lives and question everything.

This process, known in the adoptee community as "coming out of the fog," can feel terrifying and unsettling. Many who have experienced it also say the process is eventually liberating. Unlike chronological narratives that build off progression, the process of emerging from the fog is nonlinear, "a very convoluted, complex journey," said Lynelle Long, a Vietnamese adoptee who in 1998 founded InterCountry Adoptee Voices (ICAV), which has grown into a vast network of adoptees from around the world. Members share stories, recommendations for mental health services, and work to reform intercountry adoption practices.

"It's all so heavy, so deep, so intense," Long told me over a Zoom interview from her home in Australia. "It's not just about a woman giving up her children or losing her children." Rather, coming out of the fog involves simultaneously holding their adoptive family's love and well-meaning intentions alongside other truths that are much harder to digest, like how adoption can also cause trauma and rippling pain.

Transracial adoptee and sociocultural anthropologist Victoria DiMartile studies the social and economic forces of the adoption business and their effects on children and families. Children are not offered up for adoption in a vacuum, she explained. "They are available because of certain, very strategic political policies that have disenfranchised large swaths of Black and Brown communities, or have disproportionately incarcerated them, or have a history of child removal, such as Indigenous communities."

The dominant narratives of fate that many adoptees come to learn, DiMartile continued, "are designed to feed the adoption industry." Many of these fairy-tale themes were a product of the color-blind era, in which social workers advocated for total assimilation. "And what people don't know is that is a colonialist approach, a specific approach that is born from Indigenous communities, having their children removed and placed for adoption through the Indian adoption project."

But adoptees, already dealing with rejection from their birth families, may think to themselves, "If I go against the dominant narrative and I explore those more complex emotions, is there a possibility I will experience more rejection?" They might fear being cast out. So some adoptees will choose not to question, DiMartile said, because "it is too great a risk." They may think: "I can't go back to my birth family. I can't start over with my original script. On top of that, this is the family I love. This is the family with my memories, and my joy, my sadness, my growth. Am I willing to risk all of that?"

Coming out of the fog can be excruciating and painful. But when DiMartile went through it herself, she felt a release. "For most of your life, you haven't really had a vocabulary. You did not have the words to articulate whatever conflicting emotions were happening inside of you," she said. But when you find other adoptees with similar journeys and experiences who can "articulate the trauma, the loss, the grief, the confusion, you feel like somebody has cracked open a canyon inside of you, and you can breathe a little bit."

Many adoptees do not get to this phase of awareness until their twenties or later, when they leave for college or become more independent from their adoptive families, meet people from other marginalized groups, and have intimate relationships outside of their immediate family. "We also start realizing, 'Oh my God, I actually have difficulties in relationships,'" Long explained. "We really struggle with connection."

Some adoptees, Long told me, become too close to people, too quickly. Others hold people off, she said, because they are frightened of rejection. At this same point in their lives, adoptees might start to learn about adoption systems and to see the bigger picture that they're a part of. "It's not just our individual life. This is a global issue that has impacted hundreds and thousands of us around the world."

This diametrical reality holds true for many adoptees, Long said, who might come from loving homes with supportive parents and at the same time have struggled immensely or witnessed other adoptees suffer. There are high rates of depression and suicide within the adoptee community—reported suicide attempts are nearly four times as common among adoptees than those who are not adopted, according to a study in the journal *Pediatrics*. The system itself is not the rosy family picture that public relations campaigns portray. "We can love our adoptive parents but also have the challenging, difficult experiences," Long said. "And we need to uphold that there can be all these contradictory realities within our experience."

DiMartile also works to get hopeful adoptive parents to understand that when they adopt a child, it is not the first chapter of the story. "There are many previous chapters that do not simply include a family wanting to grow," she said. "And if they're going to advocate for their child's racial, cultural, and heritage-based identity, they uncomfortably have to be aware of that really dense and complex history, which is shaped by race class, intergenerational poverty, and the wars that the US have engaged in, which have often been a huge component leading to the influx of international adoptees coming from war-torn countries."

Adoptees, especially transracial and transnational, exist in this space of extraordinary collision. Fairy-tale adoption narratives don't leave room for trauma or grief, which can lead to mental health challenges, especially for adoptees who don't have the tools to navigate their conflicting emotions.

"You've got to be able to tolerate two very competing emotions," said Amanda L. Baden, a transnational adoptee from Hong Kong and a licensed psychologist and professor in the counseling program at Montclair State University who studies adoption. "You love your parent and might also feel anger at them for maybe not always doing what you needed. Those can be hard to hold at the same time for some folks; it takes a certain kind of emotional development to get there. It's challenging. A lot of transracial adoptees feel really mistreated by having parents who don't understand the impact of racism on their lives and the impact of being a person of color in our society."

Historically, there has also been a stigma associated with adoptees who chose to search for birth families, Baden explained. People

assumed adoptees who wanted to search for birth parents were malad-
justed, unhappy, or ungrateful. But with the popularity of TV shows
focusing on birth family reunions in the last decade, as well as DNA
search databases, and the stream of Disney movies and children's stories centering on a lost child's search for their parents, many came to
expect the same aspirations from every adoptee.

"With searches and reunions, you're walking into a complex pool of
everybody's traumatic emotions from the past," Long said, "which in
many cases they've never processed and never actually talked about nor
had any professional help to deal with."

Often those involved are immediately confronted with realities of
their own privilege or lack of it. Birth families may ask for money or
resources, and that can be hard for an adoptee to grasp. Long said it
may feel like, "You've rejected me and now you want money from me?"
Even if the adoptee is not in a position to offer money, their adoptive
families might be. This presents another delicate situation.

Historically, there has long been a narrow idea in the West about
adoption, which involves adhering to the structures of a nuclear family.
Adoptees have been pushing against that paradigm to expand notions
of family so that society understands it can include multiple parents
and kin from different places and backgrounds. But navigating the
sociological and economic differences can be confusing and challenging. Long added: "I always say to prospective parents, 'If you're going
to adopt a child, you better be prepared in decades to come—if they
reunite—to embrace that family as your own.'"

TWENTY-ONE

"I Got Her"

IN SEPTEMBER 2005, Tuyết Hồ, the owner of the dress shop in Việt Nam, traveled to America on vacation, stopping by the Solimenes' home in Barrington, where she stayed as a guest. The Solimenes sponsored her tourist visa and paid for her travel expenses. Tuyết Hồ went shopping with Keely for ingredients to make phở. It was chilly and rainy outside. Tuyết Hồ cooked in Keely's newly renovated kitchen, as Isabella and Olivia, seven and six, hovered near the broth, taking in the smells.

"I still want to find Isabella's twin so badly," Keely again expressed to Tuyết Hồ.

Tuyết Hồ would not forget how Keely described hearing Isabella crying from nightmares. She went on, "I think Isabella must miss her twin."

Tuyết Hồ returned to Việt Nam more determined to find the child and eventually went back to the director at the Center for Khánh Hoà Social Protection. But the director did not offer any more clues.

So Tuyết Hồ approached one of the workers instead. She knew the employee had been around since before the Solimenes adopted the girls and had cared for them both. Tuyết Hồ asked if she could please help. Did she know anything at all?

The woman looked hesitant. "Don't tell the director I am telling you anything," she said in a whisper.

The employee told Tuyết Hồ that in 1998 a mother came with twins. She gave one to the orphanage. The worker did not know what happened to the other child. "But the mother did come back to the orphanage over the years to visit and play with the daughter she left," the woman told Tuyết Hồ. "Sometimes she brought another child, a daughter of hers."

The child was younger than Isabella, the woman explained, and not the twin.

This little girl, the Solimene family would later realize, must have been one of the two daughters born later to Liên and Quý, half sisters to Isabella and Hà. "The mother had a physical disability," the worker told Tuyết Hồ. "She still lives in Nha Trang." The worker still spotted her around the city sometimes.

"Write down your address," the worker told Tuyết Hồ. "I will give it to the mother if I see her again."

Looking back today, Tuyết Hồ said she could not pinpoint when exactly a woman with a limp walked into her dress shop, but it was sometime between 2006 and 2007. Here is what she did know: This stranger said her name was Liên. And in 1998, she had given birth to twin girls.

"Will you take me to Hà's village?" Tuyết Hồ asked Liên.

Liên agreed to take her in a few days, but she said the child's parents, Rô and Tuyết, might be wary that Liên would try to take Hà from them.

IN 2007, LIÊN took Tuyết Hồ by motorbike, locating the couple in a home on a hill in Khánh Đông. Tuyết Hồ approached the women, with Liên by her side, introducing herself. "There is an American family," Tuyết Hồ said. "The mother is especially kind and wealthy. She adopted Hà's twin, and now the family wants to help Hà. They hope the sisters can one day meet."

Rô and Tuyết, as Tuyết Hồ would remember, looked at her and Liên firmly. "We do not want any help."

"Don't worry," Tuyết Hồ insisted. "I don't want to take Hà away from you. I have no right to do that. No one has a right to do that. But I want to find a way to help Hà, so she can study. This family will help her."

Rô and Tuyết told her again they did not want help.

"Hà is not home," Tuyết said. She was at the pagoda, studying Buddhism with the other children. But Liên knew how to find the pagoda. They got back on the motorbike.

When they arrived, the pagoda was filled with people, including probably one hundred children, all dressed alike in uniforms and practicing their Buddhist prayers and chants. Liên and Tuyết Hồ strolled through the crowd, searching face after face.

Liên spotted Hà and pointed her out.

Tuyết Hồ stopped and stared. She thought the child in front of her looked just like Isabella, whom she had spent time with recently in Illinois.

She pulled out her camera and took several photos. She handed the camera off to someone else, who snapped a photo of Liên and Tuyết Hồ together with Hà, who looked glum and confused.

Okay, I got her, Tuyết Hồ thought. She had finally found Isabella's twin.

TUYẾT HỒ EMAILED on October 3, 2007:

Dear Keely,

Finally, I visited the village where Loan's sister lives. It's impressed me when I saw her, she is exactly like Loan! She lives with 2 homo woman, very poor, but she goes to shool [sic], she is a good girl, good kid. Her neibourg [sic] and her mom told me. I took some photos with her, but I am so exciting write you, let you know first, then I'll send photos in next email. . . .

I talked with two ladies who take care of her. They seem nice people, take good care for her, she is like their princess, even [though] they are very poor. . . . Her name is Hong Hà, this is the name of one biggest river in the North. She is very cute.

Tuyết Hồ sent another message on November 2, 2007:

> As I told you this season is rainning [*sic*] season, flooding in that area, so people can not work, then they have no enough food and clothes to keep warm. I suggest if you could send some money (by western union is the fastest way) I would like to buy for them food and help money in control for her keep going to school. That'll be big help at the moment. . . . My business is still low cause season and also economic all over the going down. We keep praying and try to work hard as always.

Keely did send money for Tuyết Hồ to give to the family.

Two weeks later, Tuyết Hồ wrote to her again:

> I've been busy and so I went to visit Kin [*sic*] Loan sister during Tết and took pictures. . . . I gave them 100 usd, then save for next few month. I divide amount of money for 3 or 4 times to encourage her to study. I told her that is money come from your sister, she is very happy with that. She also think of Kim Loan and ask me when ever they can see each others?

Hà

Growing up, I loved being an only child. When I was acting bad, my mom would threaten me and tell me she would adopt another child if I did not behave. I would cry and tell her no! I did not want them to adopt another child. I did not want my parents to have to divide their attention for me with someone else.

I was curious about my twin. I knew she lived in America. But I did not want to go to America. I told myself I would not ever go to America. So I just thought then, I guess I will not ever meet my twin sister either.

TWENTY-TWO

Strangers in the Village

ON A MUGGY July afternoon in Khánh Đông in 2008, ten-year-old Hà spotted a white woman emerging from beyond the mango trees, with a small group trailing behind her. She carried a black backpack and wore a lemon-yellow T-shirt, white shorts, and sunglasses atop her head. Hà never saw white people in her village. She hid behind Rô at first. Tuyết and Rô smiled back at the stranger sweetly, suspiciously.

The woman had brought guests with her to Khánh Đông—including, she explained through a translator, two of her five daughters. Hà studied them. The two white daughters resembled the older woman. One wore a white tank top and a brown flowy skirt; a scarf was wrapped around her head of curly hair, its tail hanging loosely over her shoulder. The other girl wore a blue T-shirt and plaid shorts. The next guest, Tuyết Hồ served as interpreter. Tuyết Hồ explained to Rô, Tuyết, and Hà that the foreigners were from America.

Hà watched the smiling visitors who drifted past the beaded curtains hanging in the doorway into her family's newly built two-room dwelling. Tuyết's guitar hung on the wall. The foreigners snapped photographs: of the altar where Hà's family lit incense sticks and offered green bananas and rice to the ancestors, of their chicken with iridescent feathers, of her floor mat woven with sun-dried reeds, which Hà slept on each night alongside Rô and Tuyết. The red and gold Vietnamese flag that Hà tied to her clothes whenever she went to school hung above their sleeping area.

The older woman with a strange-sounding name, *Keely*, pulled out a silver bracelet, which she pressed into Hà's palm as a present.

"I bought a second matching silver bracelet," the woman explained through the dress-shop owner. "I am going to give it to your sister in America." It took Hà a moment to grasp the situation. It seemed this woman claimed to have information about her sister. Not just information. The woman claimed to *have* Hà's sister.

But why, Hà thought, had she not brought her sister along to Khánh Đông with her? Why had she left her behind in America? The stranger nodded as she watched Hà come to understand why she was here.

Keely repeated. "I know where your sister is." She would prove it.

Keely pulled a video camera from her backpack and pushed its buttons, scrolling through and stopping on footage of a girl with long black hair tossing around a ball with another girl. Both looked like they could be Vietnamese. The girl with the ball was Loan, the woman said. She called her *Isabella*.

Hà looked closely. Whatever her name, the girl looked somewhat like her. Taller, perhaps. She spoke in the same sounds of the Americans. Hà felt a twinge of excitement. *Could it be? Do you really have my sister?*

Hà sensed kindness in Keely's demeanor, but she didn't trust her, or the other visitors, and she could feel Tuyết and Rô's wariness too.

"Do you go to school?". Keely asked Hà.

Hà said she did.

Rô stood in front of Hà, like a shield. Tuyết touched Hà's shoulders. They watched as Hà nodded.

"Where is the school?"

It was a short walk down the main road.

"Can you take me there?"

They saw their daughter reach for Keely's hand.

Hà held it as they walked down the dirt path, onto the road where police sometimes paused to catch speeders, past palm fronds, cornfields, cud-chewing cows, power lines, and the local vendor who ground sugarcane into juice, past the piles of husks on the ground. Hà wore a striped plum-colored shirt bought from a shop about fifteen minutes from her village down the main road. Tuyết's brother, a soldier who lived in France, had given her the money.

They approached the school, a one-floor building atop a swath of green land, its yellow walls browning at the edges. When school was in session, Hà attended from noon to 5:00 p.m. Rô would sit on the side of the road where she sold bánh mì while waiting for Hà to be released so she could walk her home. Hà loved going to her school. She walked up to the open-air windows and curled her fingers around the turquoise bars. She peered inside.

Keely snapped photos of the rows of wooden desks and benches, enough to seat fifty or so children, the chalkboard, and the teacher's desk. A cow was tied with a rope to the front of the school, their friend, from whom Hà and the other kids drank milk during class breaks.

"Is there another school that you could attend?" Keely asked.

Hà told her yes, but it was too far to walk to, and she had no bike.

When they were done with the tour, Hà guided her back down the road, past a cluster of wooden tables under a tin canopy, where a neighbor sold a breakfast phở made from the broth of beef bones and sprinkled with basil.

On the way, Keely looked at Hà and said something. Hà waited for Tuyết Hồ's version: "Do you want to climb in my backpack and come back to America with me?"

Hà stared at them both, taken aback. She said firmly in Vietnamese: *No.*

Her defenses suddenly shot up. Hà wondered again if this American actually did have her sister.

Rô remembered once, many years ago, during the height of the baby-selling adoption scandals in Việt Nam, that a stranger came to their village, saying she could offer a lot of money for Hà, who was still very young. Enough money for Rô and Tuyết to buy a new home in the city. The person wanted to buy their baby. Rô and Tuyết said no, and not enough money in the world would change their minds. They would never give their child away.

"Do not speak to any strangers," Tuyết would always warn Hà. "Stay inside when we are not home."

These people from America did not seem like kidnappers. Still, Hà thought, why should she trust anything they said? The girl in the video just as easily could have been an unrelated person or some actor in an elaborate ploy to lure Hà away from her village, just as her parents always worried about. And though Hà had dreamed of finding her sister and bringing her to live with her in the village, she was not about to travel anywhere with a person she had only known for a few minutes, especially not to America. Besides, Rô and Tuyết would never allow it.

If the foreigners truly did know the whereabouts of Loan, they would have to bring her here, to Khánh Đông, to prove it.

Keely looked at her. "We're going to bring her back."

TWO WEEKS AFTER that visit, Tuyết Hồ came back to the village with a gift for Hà sent by the Americans, who had since returned to their country. It was a cake with red frosting, along with a bike, and a photo of Isabella with other members of the Solimene family. Tuyết Hồ said the treats were sent for Hà's birthday, which the Americans believed to be July 24—the same day as Isabella's. Tuyết Hồ explained to Hà's family that American birthdays involved cakes, presents, and parties. Hà had never celebrated her birthday.

Adoption paperwork, notoriously unreliable, recorded that the twins had different birthdays. Hà knew her official date of birth, on her government paperwork, had passed before the Americans ever came to Khánh Đông, twenty-two days before Isabella's, on July 2.

Hà did not care for the cake. It was too sweet. Nevertheless, Rô and Tuyết celebrated with a party, as Tuyết Hồ suggested, American-style. They invited neighbors, and the adults drank beer outside, while the kids drank soda. The power turned on that day, surprising everyone as it stayed on late into the evening.

Weeks passed. Then months. Hà turned eleven, then twelve.

She wore the silver bracelet that Keely had given her. Hà turned thirteen, and still no word from Keely or her twin sister. Tuyết Hồ also seemed to have disappeared.

One evening, Hà sat with Rô and Tuyết on their porch, admiring the moon. It was especially bright and beautiful.

"Why hasn't that woman come back yet?" Rô said. "I'm suspicious."

"What if it was a scam?" Tuyết told Hà. "I don't believe she has your sister."

Hà felt anger coming over her. *I'm not going to wait for them anymore. She was lying to us. It was some kind of prank.*

For the last three years, Hà had kept a photo of Isabella and the Solimenes tucked inside her school textbooks. That night, she rose from the porch and went inside the house to her desk. She found the photo and stuffed it inside the waistband of her pants. She walked back outside and told Tuyết and Rô, "I'm going for a bike ride."

She pedaled hard along the road, crying. *Why would you lie to me? If you don't have my sister, why would you say you would bring my sister back?*

Hà stopped near a ditch under the sugarcane trees. She pulled out the photo. She told herself she would not wait anymore. She would not let herself care about these strangers. She threw the photo into the ditch.

The rain will wash it away.

TWENTY-THREE

"They Love Her"

AS KEELY HEADED back to the United States after that first encounter with Hà in 2008, she received news that her seventy-eight-year-old father's health had taken a turn. He lived in Florida and was suffering from Parkinson's. He was not expected to live much longer.

She rerouted to Florida to join him, along with her siblings. The slow days that followed at his bedside allowed time for her to reflect. This was the man who taught her to "hold life's possessions with a loose grip," who wanted his daughter to know that human connections mattered more than money and things. Keely thought of the first time her dad met Isabella and Olivia. She had a picture of Isabella sitting on his lap, tugging curiously at the beard of her grandfather as he beamed. Keely remained at her father's side for over a week as his condition declined. On the tenth day, the nurses entered. "We think it's time," one of them said.

Keely stood up and went over to hold him. She leaned in and said, "I want to go with you."

He mustered a reply: "You can't."

He died after midnight on July 17, 2008.

For the last six years, she had spent so much time traveling. Now, she told herself, it was time to go home. When Keely returned to Barrington, her family needed her. There were children who needed her guidance. College moves to prepare for, elementary-school projects to complete, soccer practices, homework, family emergencies—her family needed every ounce of her.

Over the next year, Keely continued to send money to the dress-shop owner, Tuyết Hồ, trusting she would deliver it to Hà and her family. And Tuyết Hồ obliged, making the journey to the village every so often. But Keely felt the gesture was unwelcome. "We wanted to give them money," Keely said. "We wanted to do all kinds of things for them, but they didn't want it. They were very leery of us."

In 2009, Tuyết Hồ moved to Vancouver, British Columbia, to join a daughter who lived there. Tuyết Hồ was the key person who knew Hà's village and how to get in touch with Hà's parents. Though Rô and Tuyết had a phone in their home, Keely assumed there was no way to call them directly. Meanwhile, Keely's hopes to reunite Isabella and Hà remained in the back of her mind but fell behind other priorities. And another part of her did not want to press.

Six years earlier, Keely had lodged this idea of adopting Isabella's twin in her mind, ignoring the idea of any other mothers entirely. When she finally found Hà, she said, "it felt like I was looking at Isabella. Let's say I was in Việt Nam, and I wasn't looking for a twin, and I was just there, and I saw this child. Someone would've had to really impress upon me that that wasn't Isabella. The feeling was that strong."

But that day in the village, Keely also realized that "Hà is part of a family. These ladies. They love each other. She loves them. They love her." She went on, "Now I knew that Hà was in a loving home. It's poor, sure, but it's a loving home. I think back about that time, and I was feeling like who am I to go there with all my money and my ability to get a passport, and visa, and tickets, and rent cars, and who am I to go there and break this family up?"

She remembered that feeling of wanting to bring Hà home with her and at the same time noticing Tuyết and Rô's unease. "When I came back, I was just feeling like, 'Oh, wouldn't that have been just like a rich person? To think they could just go to Việt Nam and snatch this kid out of their home and bring her here?' You know, like who am I to think that I'm going to come in and save this little girl? She's so happy."

For the next three years, Keely put off the idea of a twin reunion. Isabella did not bring it up either. Keely had taken up reading books about the poverty-wealth gap, and she was especially influenced by *The Power of Half: One Family's Decision to Stop Taking and Start Giving Back*. One day, Mick came home with a new Porsche. She looked around at how they lived in Barrington. "The house just felt too big. The lifestyle there just felt too big."

Keely convinced Mick to sell their home. He returned the Porsche. His career was tied to Chicago, so they decided to buy a smaller, simpler house in Arlington Heights, about ten miles away. It was a more economically diverse place than Barrington, though not much more ethnically diverse (about 90 percent white at the time).

On moving day, two trucks showed up. The family packed necessities into one truck. Anything they did not need went into the other. The truck with the essentials went to their new home, and the truck with the extra stuff went to charities. They made more deliberate cost-cutting choices. When the kids were old enough to drive, the family would share two vehicles, a Jeep Wrangler and a Chevy Tahoe, and they would carpool. They would invest in modest wardrobes made of quality clothing that would last, not fast fashion.

Keely had been working with the UN Foundation since 2006. She also worked on antimalaria projects in Việt Nam. The foundation had recently formed an organization, Girl Up, to empower young women to engage in social change. Keely told her kids that Girl Up would train girls to be social justice leaders around the world, teaching them about gender equality and issues of health, safety, and education.

Isabella enrolled in the program and was selected to be a Girl Up ambassador in its inaugural year. A *PBS NewsHour* film crew recorded a segment featuring Girl Up and interviewed Isabella. The footage from August 2011 showed her in a blue soccer uniform, kicking around a ball. "Adopted at the age of four," the reporter said, "her Vietnamese mother gave birth to twin girls, couldn't afford both, and sent Isabella to an orphanage. Isabella has never met her identical twin sister still living in Vietnam, named Hà."

A spokeswoman from the UN Foundation talked about Isabella and the twin she had not yet met: "Very similar girls. If they had the same opportunity, they'd probably have the same trajectory, they'd both be going to UCLA, both be thinking about being doctors or having dreams. Sadly, the girl in Vietnam can't get there."

Keely watched the segment and felt her yearning to reunite the twins reignite. She reached out to the dress-shop owner again, and Tuyết Hồ told her she would contact her sister, Dung Hồ, who might be able to help her organize a reunion. Dung and Keely connected, and the Solimenes planned to meet her in Việt Nam the following month.

With reunion plans now under way again, "PBS wanted to join us," Keely recalled. "Mick was levelheaded. He's like no, let's not do that. He clearly had some wits about it. I did not. I would have brought a whole PBS crew."

Keely pictured a wonderful, tearful twin reunion, like the ones on television. "I thought it was going to be amazing."

TWENTY-FOUR

They Are Coming

IN 2011, A woman reached out to Rô and Tuyết. She told them her name was Dung Hồ, and she was the sister of the dressmaker. Tuyết Hồ now lived in Canada, but Dung had contacted Rô and Tuyết to relay a message to Hà: the American woman they had met in their village three years earlier was planning to return soon. "She is going to bring your sister back."

To Hà, this news seemed to come out of nowhere. *When I see her*, she thought, *I will believe it.* After that day when Keely and her daughters showed up to her village, Hà had not heard from them personally since.

A few days later, Dung paid Hà's family a visit. She gave Hà and her family 3 million đồng. "She told me to go learn English fast," Hà said. "Pay someone to teach me as fast as possible, so I can communicate." Hà's family hired an English teacher they already knew from a local school. In September, Dung called again and told the family to prepare to visit Nha Trang.

DUNG WAS A resourceful woman. In the past she had worked as a smuggler. This was when she was in her twenties, after the Fall of Sài Gòn. "The communist government didn't import or export anything," Dung explained. "Everything we would buy we used a ticket, a stamp. And from the stamp you can buy food."

She was referring to ration stamps used to purchase goods and groceries. Dung would smuggle anything she could—sugar, coffee, beans, medicine—from Nha Trang to Đà Nẵng, more than five hundred kilo-meters to the north. "I put in the bag and around my body," she said. "I tied it like I was pregnant."

Sometimes she bribed police to let her through. Other times, she got arrested and had to pay police to let her out. By 1990, Nha Trang was becoming a popular tourist spot for Europeans, and with that came the opening of hotels, which meant job opportunities for locals. Dung had learned French as a child, and that helped her get a job at the newly opened Evason Ana Mandara Nha Trang, the same hotel where Keely's family stayed when visiting during their adoptions. Dung left smug-gling behind and worked in the hotel business center, and the position helped her pay for her son's college education.

Another sister of Dung's got a job at a nearby hotel in Nha Trang, and Dung came by often. One day, a friend of her sister's told Dung he wanted her to meet an American named Dick McKenzie, who was stay-ing at the hotel. Dick moved to Việt Nam in 2004 after retiring from an administrative career at an Illinois college. Dick told the mutual friend that he wanted to do some humanitarian work, perhaps get connected with a nongovernmental organization.

Dung knew of a leprosy village he could visit if he wanted to get involved. She offered to show him the way. Dick drove the motorbike, with Dung seated behind him. It was a rough ride, but when it was over Dung told Dick, "You drive a motorbike pretty good."

"Does your husband drive too?" Dick asked.

Dung told him she did not have a husband.

Dick had been divorced three times before he met Dung in 2004, and he was two decades older than her. They married in 2005 and built a home together. Dick wrote emails to his former high school peers from the 1952 class at New Castle High in Pennsylvania, which were posted on a website. The online class newsletter reported that Dick moved to help the people of Việt Nam and that he had fallen in love with an "exotic" Vietnamese woman.

Dick had icy blue eyes and liver spots on his fleshy bald head. When I interviewed him at a beach cafe in Việt Nam, he wore shorts and a linen island shirt with jellyfish patterns. He carried an iPad and a book, *The Man from Beijing*, by Swedish writer Henning Mankell. His smile revealed a row of crooked bottom teeth and a silver cap on his left fang.

Dick told me all about his take on Vietnamese women: "You will see a beautiful, young Vietnamese girl married, in many cases, to an ugly old European or American." He continued: "It always puzzles me when a [Western] couple can come here and stay together, because nine times out of ten if they stay long enough, the man will get a Vietnamese girlfriend and dump his wife. Vietnamese girls are gorgeous, and they are very available."

When Dung first heard the story from her sister about the pair of twins born to a disenfranchised mother with a disability who lived in Nha Trang, it sounded familiar. She thought of a woman who had shown up to her church that same year, a stranger who needed help feeding her family. The woman had moved haltingly, as if injured, and told the congregation that she had given birth to twins but had to give them away. She had two more daughters and struggled to feed them. It was Liên.

By the time Liên showed up to the Protestant church in Nha Trang in 2011, Dung had already been a member for two decades. Liên explained that she wanted to become a Christian, and Dung empathized.

"At that time, the church helped a little bit," Dung recalled. "When people come, they share their real story; the church always helps with rice, providing something for poor people."

Dung learned that Liên had a husband who helped her, but "he was also poor and came to town to work as a bike taxi driver," Dung said. "He had to pay for taxi rent too. She always told me if she could get enough to raise her family, it would be okay."

When Tuyết Hồ asked her sister if she could look for Hà, Dung immediately thought of Liên and approached her at the next service. "My sister is the dressmaker Tuyết Hồ," Dung explained. "You might remember her, she was friends with the American family that had adopted your other twin."

Dung told Liên that the Americans wanted to find the Vietnamese twin again. Dung was convinced that a reunion of the girls could be good for Liên. "This US family might help support you too." Liên told Dung that her sister, Rô, was raising the child and that this "aunt loved Hà so much, and she had a good life. Their house is small, they don't have food enough, they don't have much clothes, but her aunt takes care of her good. She's lucky."

But Liên also cautioned about her sister's partner, Tuyết, "the girl-boyfriend," as Dung recalled—that Tuyết especially did not want her around meddling in their lives.

As Keely, Mick, and Isabella made plans to travel to Việt Nam for the girls' reunion, they wired $300 to Dung to deliver to Hà, Rô, and Tuyết. Dick emailed Keely with his own advice:

Dung got the money and Hà and her biological aunt and her foster mother came this morning to get it. Dung also gave her a lot of clothes, some pens and stationery from her church collection for poor people.

She is a darling girl, a bit shy but that's to be expected. . . .

This evening Dung explained to me her circumstances to communicate to you.

. . . She apparently lives a long distance from a good English teacher, about 28 kilometers. The English teaching at her school is not good. She is anxious to learn good English so she can talk to her sister. There will obviously be other benefits for her future as well. The cost of a motorbike taxi both ways and the English teacher is approximately $70.00 a month and she would go three days a week all year for a total of $840.00.

Here's the proposal that Dung asked me to make to you. If you would be able to add another $540.00 through the course

of the year to the $300.00, they would begin the English regi-
men. . . . If this is something you would entertain you could send
the money by wire to Dung and she would give it to them each
month while monitoring her English progress and overall school
effort.

Let me know how you feel about this and send me your tele-
phone number so we can talk.

Regards,

Dick and Dung

TWENTY-FIVE

Motion Sickness

ONE MORNING, Rô, Tuyết, and Hà awoke early. They ate rice for breakfast, then climbed onto a motorbike as the moon melted away and the sun began to lift its face. They would again make that familiar drive to Nha Trang. Hà took her seat in between Tuyết and Rô as usual, and they zipped past the rice paddies, shrines, cafes, and cows with russet hides. Today, Hà was nervous. She felt jittery and thrilled. She would meet Isabella for the first time since thirteen years ago, when they were babies.

They arrived at the address for Dick and Dung's home. From the outside, it was a nondescript location in an unremarkable alley. No stranger could have guessed that tucked beyond a set of gated doors beneath an arched entryway was a modern Mediterranean-style home.

Hà stepped inside. It was a villa unlike any in Khánh Đông. Under a sunroof, there was an indoor waterfall that trickled into a stone pool adorned with lotus plants. Dung had decorated the entire property with greenery and potted flowers. The sliding glass doors led to a living room with a ceiling fan, a sofa, two easy chairs, and a coffee table. The wall shelving, heavy with vases, was made of the same slate-colored stone as the waterfall. The kitchen had a stainless-steel refrigerator, a microwave, granite counters and backsplash, and wineglasses hanging from a built-in rack. The second floor of their home had another sitting room with a television, balcony, and wicker furniture bedecked by bright cushions.

Tuyết, Rô, and Hà waited awkwardly inside of Dick and Dung's home. The plan was to ride in a van to the airport to greet Isabella, Mick, and Keely. They would be arriving around 4:00 p.m., after lunch.

"Dung gave me some clothes," Hà recalled. "She told me to take off my clothes and put on this new one. I thought, 'I like my outfit.'" But Hà didn't argue.

Dick seemed polite enough, though Hà could not understand anything he said, but to Hà, something about Dung felt off putting. It was the way Dung looked at them, how she addressed Tuyết and Rô. Hà felt that Dung saw herself as better than them, like they were just poor people from the countryside, ignorant of the ways of the city and Westernized lifestyles. Dung informed them she would be their interpreter when the Americans arrived. She would help them.

Hà's unease heightened during the van ride. She had never ridden in a van, and the vehicle felt stuffy as it jerked around. She tried to look out of the windows and began to feel her head spin. All the excitement and suspense had made her exhausted. As the car jolted, she felt like throwing up. Her head throbbed.

Dung looked at her. Hà remembered Dung's words: "Do not show that sad or tired face. If they're not tired, you can't be tired."

Hà did not say anything, but she wondered, *How am I supposed to control my face if that is how I feel? All I want to do is lie down.* Yet Dung, this person who was not her mother, made her feel like she did not have permission to feel tired.

Hà leaned back against the seat. She wanted to meet her sister. She wanted it to be a happy experience. But so far this day did not feel happy. Rô and Tuyết suffered motion sickness too. When they arrived at the airport, Hà remembers Dung telling them, "You look like dead bodies."

Hà lay down on a row of airport seats. *I can't throw up,* she told herself.

"Your sister is coming from America, twenty-four hours traveling," Dung told her. "And you are acting like you are tired?"

TWENTY-SIX

The Cold

THIRTEEN-YEAR-OLD ISABELLA AWOKE in Hồ Chí Minh City in a hotel room with Keely and Mick that morning in 2011. The day before, they had flown to Hong Kong, then Việt Nam, landing after midnight. Isabella had the jitters throughout the first fifteen-hour flight. When they finally landed in Tân Sơn Nhất International Airport, her anxiety intensified. She could not wrap her mind around what she would encounter once she arrived in Nha Trang. Việt Nam felt vaguely familiar to her from the home videos she had watched over and over yet at the same time completely foreign.

As they boarded another flight the next afternoon to Nha Trang, Isabella tried to keep her nerves under control, she tried not to think too much about the sister she was about to meet.

It was a short flight, just forty-five minutes. Before she could finish a cup of water, the city had disappeared, and they were descending over the beaches of Nha Trang. The plane touched down and Isabella began to feel her nerves exploding into a panic attack.

Holy cow, she thought stepping off the small plane. *Baggage claim is right there, and I have zero time to think about this.*

She felt her head pounding, her body sweating. It seemed like she had swallowed a softball. Her dad would later write out a list of questions that she could ask Hà through the interpreter if she felt at a loss for words:

Do you have any pets?
How many kids are in your school?
What is your favorite subject?
Do you play sports?
Do you like to read?
What do you like to watch on TV?
Do you like Nike or Adidas?
Have you ever seen snow?

Yet in this moment Isabella felt like she could not speak at all. She didn't want to cry. She didn't want to jump for joy. She did not know how she was supposed to feel, though she had an idea of how everyone else expected her to react when she met her twin. *I don't know how I'm going to be able to do this.*

Her legs felt weak. "There they are!" she heard her mom's voice as they were retrieving their bags.

What? Isabella had figured she would have more time. She thought maybe they would drive somewhere else first, that she would have at least a few more minutes to mentally prepare for this meeting. But no, her sister was already here at the airport waiting for her, at the bottom of the steps. From baggage claim, Isabella glanced over. She could see her sister's silhouette. She was standing with a group of people.

Oh my gosh, they're right there.

Isabella tried not to look back again.

Then they were at the bottom of the stairs, and the group was moving closer. People were smiling and crying. There was an audience. A freelance photographer, who lived in Việt Nam, captured it all. He had met Keely during one of her trips to Việt Nam, and he joined the family in Sài Gòn before the reunion, boarding the flight to Nha Trang with them. Passersby in the airport could not help but notice the spectacle.

To Isabella, some of the people in the group with her twin looked like they were wearing pajamas. She recognized the style from the home videos, or was it a recollection from somewhere in the depths of her memory? Isabella couldn't think or see straight. She wanted to bolt out of the airport doors.

And then there was Hà. Standing in front of her in a tank top, her ponytail pulled up in a scrunchy, flanked by one woman in polka-dot pants and another who stood behind her in a golf shirt. Hà was crying and shaking. The woman in the polka-dot pants was weeping. Keely was too.

Isabella looked at her twin. Maybe Hà somewhat resembled her, but she looked unlike her at the same time. Hà's bangs swept to the right side, like her own, but Hà's were longer. Isabella wore braces. Hà had a smaller physical frame.

Hà hugged her, and Isabella felt her body go limp. Isabella might have said hi, but she couldn't be sure if the word even made it out of her mouth. She kept moving toward the doors.

Isabella's family had always called her an "ice princess" because she kept her emotions so bottled up. As she puts it, she was never "a touchy-feely person."

Isabella felt Hà grab her hand even as Isabella kept walking. Hà did not let go.

Isabella made it to the door, not looking back at her sister, as if she were pulling Hà behind her by the hand.

Years later, Isabella would reflect on her memories of that day. She would remember how uncomfortable it was. How her palms were sweaty. She would remember thinking that Hà must have noticed how awkward and uneasy she felt.

"I was just so resentful," Isabella recalled. "I was in denial about everything. The photographer was taking pictures, and I had to buck up, but I was mad." Hà seemed like this "very affectionate, loving, caring person. And I was just like, 'I don't want anything to do with you. I have Olivia.'"

The entire interaction made Isabella want to run away. She never did cry, but she felt guilty for how she behaved. She worried that she was hurting Hà's feelings by reacting so coldly, but Hà didn't shy away.

That entire day of their reunion, Isabella could barely look at Hà. She could not communicate without a translator. And she had no idea just how overwhelmed Hà was too.

"DON'T TOUCH ISABELLA!" Hà remembered Dung scolding her in Vietnamese after they all exited the airport. Hà recoiled, worried she had done something wrong. Dung warned Hà that Isabella did not want to hold hands, and she should have realized this and let go sooner. She warned Hà not to be so overly affectionate.

"It was overwhelming," Hà would later remember. "They hugged me and showed Rô and Tuyết respect. Nothing like Dung and Dick."

Hà felt confused. "I was happy to see my sister but other than that, I was so upset."

In the van, Isabella and Hà sat in a middle row side by side, looking out separate windows. Hà did not get too close again, except when they posed together for a photo.

When they arrived at the Sheraton Nha Trang Hotel & Spa, everyone loaded into an elevator. The doors closed, and the elevator shot up to the thirtieth-floor penthouse suite. Hà had never been in an elevator, and it moved so fast it frightened her.

The suite offered a sweeping view, and the families looked out over the entire city from the balcony. In the room, the Solimenes pulled a rectangular box out of their luggage and handed it to Hà. It was a laptop computer. They told her it was a gift that would enable her to talk over Skype. It was not yet set up, but the photographer had an iPad, which the girls used to type messages into Google Translate.

"How are you?"

"Fine."

"Are you tired?"

"Yes."

"Are you hungry?"

They decided to go out and get something to eat. The hotel restaurant offered a buffet with Western-style food, like pizza, pasta, and black beans. Rô, Tuyết, and Hà had never eaten such dishes. Throughout the Solimene family's visit, Hà found herself in the same predicament. "I have to figure out my food, and I have to figure out Tuyết's food, I have to figure out Rô's food," she would remember. "I don't even know what to get."

Hà tried pizza and scraped off the cheese. The Western food did not taste good and she left most of it on her plate. Dung again admonished her in Vietnamese. The Solimenes had no idea of the interaction unfolding before them.

Hà recalled Dung telling her: "Whatever you order, no matter if it's good or not, you have to eat it. Eat it all. You can't leave anything on the plate because that's rude. That isn't respectful. They order for you. They paid money. Why are you not eating it?"

Dung rebuked Rô and Tuyết for not eating too. At one point during the visit, Hà ordered a large banana smoothie. She could not finish it, she felt so full.

"Drink all of it," Dung told her.

Hà obeyed.

Later that night, she got sick. "Diarrhea," Hà said. "I got in the room and I was so tired. It was too much for my stomach . . . The next day when I woke up, I was still full from it."

Hà, Rô, and Tuyết learned when the guests asked "Are you hungry?" to just say no.

"We didn't feel happy at all," Hà recalled. "We loved to see Isabella, and we loved to see the family, but we were scared of going to eat."

At some point that first day, Hà realized that she, Rô, and Tuyết would sleep in the Sheraton penthouse suite overnight. Dung explained that the Solimenes had reserved it for them. Hà said Dung gathered up all the hotel shampoo, conditioner, body wash, and lotion and scooped them into her bag. Keely had given Rô and Tuyết each a scarf as a gift. One was vanilla-colored, the other darker. Dung asked if she could have one of the scarves. They gave her the dark one.

When Dung left, Rô, Tuyết, and Hà were alone in the room, which was freezing. The air conditioner felt like it was blasting so high. They had never relied on air-conditioning in the village and didn't know how to turn it off or that they could call the front desk to ask. None of them had ever stayed in a hotel. When they showered, they did so without soap, again not knowing they could call to ask for more. There was a king bed, but it was so cold that none of them slept that night.

"HOW ARE YOU feeling?" Isabella would remember her mom and dad asking her over and over again during the trip. They went to the beach with Hà, played soccer, walked around the city, shared meals and conversations translated through Dung. All the while, Isabella felt herself retreating inward.

"Why aren't you opening up to Hà?"

She dreaded that question. It made her feel ashamed of her behavior and feelings about this whole trip. She wanted to be there but also didn't. She wanted to know Hà but also didn't feel ready. The photographer captured an image of Isabella looking down glumly as Keely spoke with Hà inside of their car and another of the two girls on the balcony of the Sheraton, their backs to each other. He captured an image of the girls side by side in Hà's village, their faces veiled behind a bed net. He photographed them in matching Girl Up T-shirts, which Keely had brought for them both, and he snapped images of Tuyết sitting with her hands in her lap, looking off despondently in the distance. He captured an image of Keely and Mick talking seriously to Isabella, visibly distraught, as Hà stood off to the side in the background.

Dick and Dung accompanied them on some of these outings. Dung seemed nice, but Dick irked Isabella. At one point, they all went to the market in the city to buy a bicycle for Hà. Dung and Dick were fighting in English, but he still couldn't understand her. Dung stopped talking to him, so Dick ordered Isabella to act as a messenger between them.

Okay, this is really weird, Isabella thought. *Not into it*. But she could not communicate with Hà directly about Dung and Dick because everything they said to each other was communicated through Dung. "He never learned Vietnamese," Isabella said. "That was also weird to me. Getting married to this woman. Just for the sanity of your own self, you live in a country, your wife's country . . . I don't know, you would at least try to learn something. He gave zero crap. He used Google Translate for everything."

She asked Dick why he didn't speak Vietnamese.

"It's too hard," he replied.

Then again, Isabella told herself, who was she to question his lack of language? She had not tried hard to learn Vietnamese either. She wondered: Did everyone expect her to learn Vietnamese now that she had met her sister and traveled back to her birth country? Was she suddenly supposed to embrace being Vietnamese over American? The thought of it all stressed her out.

Olivia

People see me as a confident person. That's how I like to be perceived. That is what I share. But I was insecure internally. I can't always keep this mask on.

Being trapped in a white suburban area can really isolate you from what is out there in the world. I went to Catholic school. I wish I went to public. Honestly, I think about this, though. I wouldn't change anything. All the things I've experienced—negative, positive, neutral—made me who I am. Made me the woman I am.

Even though there was a breaking point, multiple breaking points actually, they showed me what strength is and what I can overcome.

TWENTY-SEVEN

The Night

THERE HAD BEEN a miscommunication. During the reunion trip orchestrated for Hà and Isabella, Olivia's family somehow received word that the Solimenes were coming to Việt Nam. They showed up in Nha Trang to meet them. The Solimenes were at the Center for Khánh Hoà Social Protection when Olivia's birth mother walked toward them, along with five of her other children and two of her sisters. They thought Olivia would be traveling with the Solimenes too. When they discovered Olivia had not come, the family began to weep hysterically.

"It was heartbreaking," Keely recalled. She felt overwhelming guilt, seeing their faces, how desperately they wanted to see Olivia. Keely thought back to a letter that had been mailed to her in 2006, five years ago now, from Olivia's grandmother.

My family has an aspiration: Can we keep a correspondence together?

Keely had not forgotten the words in that letter. In 2009, when Olivia was ten years old, and a year after Keely first met Hà, Tuyết, and Rô, she finally responded:

My most sincere apologies for not contacting you sooner. I am sending the enclosed photographs that were taken of Như at one-year intervals. Như turned three just before we adopted her. . . .
When she was little she loved balloons, bubble gum and bows

in her hair. She loved to blow bubbles and chase them around outside in the backyard.

She started school just after we arrived in the United States and loves to go to school. She is very smart and a very good girl in school.

Nhự loves sports, she swims, plays basketball and rides her bicycle like a little girl twice her age. Everyone is amazed at how athletic she is.

Nhự is a beautiful girl with a beautiful spirit. All of the children love her and she always makes sure she says hello to everyone she meets . . .

There is so much that I could say about Nhự. If there is anything that you would like to know about her, I would be happy to share with you. She is absolutely amazing and a real gift to this world.

Fondly, Keely Solimene

Keely had mailed the letter but never heard back.

Unexpectedly standing in front of Olivia's birth family now, two years after sending the letter, Keely looked for a person who might be Olivia's grandmother. But Nguyễn Thị Mùa, Keely was told, had recently passed away.

Keely looked at Olivia's mother, now sobbing before her. "I felt so guilty," Keely said. "It was just devastating."

The photographer who accompanied the Solimenes had an iPad. They could FaceTime Olivia.

MORE THAN EIGHTY-FIVE hundred miles away, as Isabella absorbed the reality of meeting her twin sister for the first time in Việt Nam, twelve-year-old Olivia was asleep in her bedroom in Illinois when a FaceTime call came in.

Arianna and Alexandra, Keely's two oldest daughters, were sleeping in the same room as Olivia when the phone rang around 2:00 a.m. Arianna answered.

Keely explained they were in a village with Olivia's birth mother and family. The birth family needed to see her.

Arianna pushed back at their mom for asking to wake up Olivia. "No, I'm not doing that. This is too emotional."

She didn't think it was right for Olivia to meet her birth family this way.

Keely asked Alexandra, who was next to Arianna, to please wake Olivia.

Alexandra didn't want to either. "This is going to traumatize her."

But Keely insisted. She seemed so distressed, and the birth family members in the background were in a state of total despair.

Arianna and Alexandra could hear the photographer in the background too. Mick got on the phone. "We need to do this," he told the girls.

He also seemed visibly upset, which was surprising, because their dad was not an overly emotional person.

"Her family traveled for hours to get here," he said. "They thought she was going to be here."

Alexandra later recalled the scene: "They were upset. My mom was upset. I think my mom was feeling this guilt and pressure. She didn't know what to do, and she was on the other side of the world. My mom was pleading with us."

Olivia felt herself being shaken awake by Alexandra, who had climbed up into her bunk bed. Arianna got into bed on the other side of Olivia. When Olivia opened her eyes, she saw both of her sisters with tears in their eyes.

"We're going to talk to your mom."

Olivia rolled over, thinking they meant *our mom*.

"She's with your birth family. They want to say hi to you."

Olivia buried her head in the pillow. *This cannot be happening.*

After a few seconds, Olivia took the phone. "What's up?"

"They have been looking for you."

The FaceTime camera panned over the scene. Keely and Mick were in a village in Việt Nam with Isabella. But there were a lot of other people there too. Vietnamese people, all crying.

"It's your birth family. They want to say hi to you."

Olivia saw her birth mother blowing kisses to her on the screen. Her mother, she learned in that moment, was deaf and nonverbal. She could only gesture and make faces. There were siblings and aunts, all crying so much that Olivia broke down too.

They stayed on screen for a while. "Hello?" Olivia said. "Hello?"

She didn't know what else to say. They could not understand her. She could not understand them. It all happened so fast. Then the call ended.

Arianna and Alexandra sat by Olivia, comforting her, stroking her hair. "I have a family in Việt Nam," Olivia said. "I need to go back. I need to visit them."

TWENTY-EIGHT

"Harder than This"

BEFORE THE SOLIMENES left Việt Nam, everyone gathered at the rooftop bar of the Sheraton, with its glittering view of Nha Trang, and menu of Long Island iced teas and mojitos, cheese platters, baguettes, and fries. Hà and Isabella listened as Keely and Mick presented an idea to Rô and Tuyết. Dung translated.

"What if Hà could attend a more elite private school in the city with their help?"

The Solimenes would pay for the tuition and housing. Tuyết, Rô, and Hà could move from their village to Nha Trang and live in a home owned by Dung's sister. It would be an opportunity for Hà to get a better education. It would also be an opportunity for Tuyết and Rô to live in the city.

By now, Tuyết and Rô had spent enough time with the Solimenes to see that they loved Isabella, and their love seemed to extend to Hà, which they understood was why they wanted to help her. Tuyết had always emphasized the value of education and convinced Rô that a top-tier school would be a gift. In her village, Hà excelled in literature and writing. But she never had a chance to master English, which a tuition-based school in the city would offer at a higher level than the ones in her village. It would open job opportunities for her.

Rô and Tuyết sometimes went two months in the countryside without steady work. But in Nha Trang, there were enough jobs to go around, and if they did not have to worry about paying for housing in the city, they could also save money.

Rô, Tuyết, and Hà returned to Khánh Đông, nervous but also excited by the possibilities. They packed up their belongings and paperwork. Two weeks later they moved to start their new lives together as a family in Nha Trang.

THE HOUSE THAT Dung's family owned near the beach was spacious, with a living room, a kitchen area, two bathrooms. To them, it actually felt too big for three people. The Solimenes sent money to cover the $250 monthly rent.

Tuyết took a job making bricks in a factory and Rô found work in a restaurant as a dishwasher. Their hours were sporadic, sometimes in the evening or overnight, which meant Hà would be home alone after school.

Hà started classes at a middle school, Trần Quốc Toản, where Dung's cousin was the principal. From the first day, Hà realized how different this new school would be from her education in Khánh Đông. There were about thirty students in her class, all from the city. When Hà showed up, they looked her up and down.

"Where did you come from?" one asked.

"Khánh Đông."

"I don't know that place."

"That doesn't mean it's not a place," Hà said, but it seemed to her as if they had already stereotyped her, putting her lower on the social ladder than them. "I'm a girl from the village, so I know nothing," Hà said. "The students think I'm not smart enough. I'm not smart like them."

Hà struggled to catch up to what her new classmates had already learned. She had to take twelve subjects in eighth grade, including English and geography. She would copy the notes her teacher wrote on the board, but when she tried to ask the teachers for help, she felt like they dismissed her or just did not have time. One teacher announced her low scores in front of the class. Students laughed at her.

"You are so stupid," one said to her. "Why don't you know this?"

Months passed and she did not make friends. Hà would come home sometimes to a big empty house and fix herself noodles and eat dinner alone. She would try to figure out her homework on her own.

Someone at the school suggested she get tutoring. "How can I get tutoring?" She did not know where to even begin; Rô and Tuyết were busy with work.

Hà remembered the monk who once told her about destiny: "You will become great, but only if you put the work into it." She thought of Tuyết's lessons about education, hard work, and sacrifice.

I can do it myself, Hà told herself. *There are a lot of things that are harder than this. If I cannot overcome this, I cannot overcome any problems in my life.*

ONE DAY IN Nha Trang, the next-door neighbor of Liên and Rô's sister came to pick up Hà. "You're going to see your dad today," he told her.

Six years earlier, Hà had told the neighbor that when she was six, Liên came to her village and said that her dad was dead. (Liên would not remember saying this years later, but Hà believed it was true for two years, until she met the neighbor.) The neighbor told Hà that her father was actually very much alive. "He's my brother," the man said. He explained that he saw his brother occasionally. Perhaps she would meet him one day.

On the day the neighbor came to pick up Hà, who was now fourteen, he explained it was the tenth anniversary of his father's death. Hà's grandfather. There would be a ceremony in his honor at their home, in a village forty-five minutes away from Nha Trang. Hà was surprised that the neighbor had invited her. She would never admit her excitement to Rô and Tuyết, but Hà had always wondered about her father, and now she would finally have the chance to talk to him.

Hà's grandparents' former home was near a rice field and next to a small river. The property was surrounded by mango trees and bamboo. Inside, an altar had been set up with a Buddha and a picture of her grandparents. The room was full of about twenty people, none of whom Hà had ever met, including several sisters of her uncle and father. But they seemed to know who she was. A man walked into the room. Everyone fell silent. Hà heard a woman gasp.

"She's your daughter," someone said to him, gesturing toward Hà. "She looks exactly like you when you were young."

Hà watched her dad look at her, then look away. He did not speak. The ceremony continued with chants and prayers. People watched as Hà sat next to her uncle. She tried to smile at the strangers. Finally, after a long time, her father came closer. He stood before Hà and looked into her eyes.

"You are not my daughter."

Hà did not know how to reply. "I am not asking you to be responsible for me," she said.

Hà had not expected him to tell her that he missed her or even loved her. She had not even expected a hug. But she also had not expected him to deny to her face that he was her father. He left the ceremony.

The neighbor apologized for her dad's reaction and for bringing her to the memorial. Her aunts and cousins frowned and hugged her, also feeling bad for her, but Hà would never come back to her grandparents' village. If she ever met those aunts or cousins again on the street, she would not even be able to recognize them.

After that day, she never saw her father again.

BACK IN NHA Trang, Hà did not reveal how miserable she was feeling. Not to Rô or Tuyết. Not to Keely, Mick, or Isabella, with whom she now regularly Skyped, always via Dung.

Each Sunday, Hà would go to Dick and Dung's house to spend an hour or longer speaking over the computer with the Solimenes. Hà could have called them from her own home on the computer that the Solimenes had given her as a gift, but Dung directed Hà to come to her house for each conversation so she could interpret. Some weeks, Hà did not feel like going. She had a stomachache. Other times, she told Dung she had other plans. "I have to go to the countryside." Rô and Tuyết had to take care of business or visit friends or family in Khánh Đông, and Hà wanted to go too.

"The Solimenes have been waiting for you for the whole week," Dung would reprimand her, reminding her of all the money the Solimenes were spending on her. So Hà would back down and go to Dick and Dung's after all.

But she would think to herself, *Why do I have to ask Dung for permission? Why is everything so under her control?*

Since Hà could not communicate directly yet with Isabella on Skype, they would make animal noises at each other. Other Solimene siblings would show up to the conversation. Often, Hà sat silent as Dung spoke. Sometimes Hà wondered why she was there at all if she could not really express herself. Hà would ask a question, but there were times that Dung ignored it and asked her own instead. Part of her felt like they wanted to monitor what she was saying. "Am I saying bad things? Or am I saying a nice thing about them?"

Hà wanted to tell Isabella and Keely about her life, without Dung as the filter. She wished she could ask questions in English herself, even "What are your plans this week?" or "How was your soccer game?" If she spoke better English, she thought, perhaps she would be able to tell Isabella that she had met their father. She got mad at herself for not learning the language faster.

Each month, Keely sent money for Hà's education and housing. Dick and Dung received and handled it. "I remember Dung only gave us the same exactly amount of money we needed for electricity, water, internet bills. No more than what the bill said. Which was very cheap. Less than $50 a month," Hà said. "I always went to Dung's house whenever we needed money because Rô and Tuyết refused to go. . . . If we needed something, Dung would be the one giving the money out." Hà felt humiliated asking for money, and she dreaded riding her bike to Dick and Dung's home to face them.

Hà did not know of the emails that Dick had sent to Keely offering his suggestions about Hà's needs. In one from September 2011, he wrote:

> I had suggested to Dung that we bring [Hà] here and let her work as a housekeeper and go to school in Nha Trang . . . but Dung is unwilling to try to ride herd on a budding teenage girl. . . . My ultimate suggestion is to do whatever you can afford to do to work toward Hà's getting to the U.S. as a student as soon as possible. Getting there as a student is far easier than her eventual application as the family member of a citizen (your daughter) which currently is taking around 10 years.

As Dick and Dung explained it, they tried to convince Keely to also give money to Liên, instead of spending so much to support Hà, Rô, and Tuyết. The Solimenes, Dick said years later, spent thousands of dollars "on these three people. Meanwhile, the birth mother is gradually starving to death. And Keely doesn't do a damn thing for her."

In truth, over the years, Keely and Mick did send Liên and her family money, but they did not offer to support her on the same financial level as Rô and Tuyết.

Dung tried to explain to Hà that she should help Liên, not disregard her. "When you grow up you will understand," Dung told her. "You are too young. You need to sympathize with your birth mother. She didn't do anything wrong. She couldn't do anything better. And that's why your aunt kept you."

Dung also complained about what she viewed as Hà's lack of discipline and studiousness. Dung said she offered to tutor Hà herself. "Sometimes she didn't come," Dung told me. "Sometimes she came too late. Sometimes she didn't talk English in the sentences I wrote to her. She didn't want to."

By midway through her first year of school in Nha Trang, Hà was failing. When everyone discovered she had fallen behind in her grades, the idea of tutoring became part of a group discussion. Keely and Mick offered to pay for one.

Dung complained about Hà not always participating when the Solimenes called.

"Sometimes when her sister talked to her, I translated to her. I'd write something to answer her. She didn't care," Dung said. "She didn't talk. She kept silent. So the conversation stopped."

FOR MONTHS, HÀ felt like she had been treated like a poor, uneducated village kid. But in 2012, Keely and Isabella returned to Nha Trang, along with Olivia and Victoria. Suddenly other students noticed a wealthy white woman with her American, English-speaking children treating Hà like a family member.

"You have an American mom?" a student asked.

Keely also gave Hà an iPhone 4. Hà's classmates gathered around to look at the device. None of them had one.

"I never knew your family was rich like that," a student said to her.

Hà noticed the same kids who had bullied her now wanting to hang out with her, but she had no interest in befriending them. *You never knew my background, and now you feel like you're my friend? Too late!*

TWENTY-NINE

Always Loan

AT SOME POINT during their 2012 Việt Nam trip, Isabella learned that she would meet her birth mother. Since Dick and Dung had befriended Liên, they encouraged the encounter and arranged for the reunion to happen at their home. Keely remembered how they prepared Isabella by listening to Vietnamese language tapes and making memory books of Isabella's life to give to Liên.

Isabella thought of how emotional Hà had been at the airport reunion and how she had not reciprocated the response. Isabella worried that her encounter with her mom would bring the same discomfort—tears, hugs, and prolonged, strained hand-holding. If Hà was so apt to touch Isabella, she imaged her birth mother would practically be on top of her.

When Liên came to their door, Isabella knew immediately it was her. Isabella, who wore white shorts and a gray Abercombie & Fitch T-shirt, smiled politely, revealing her braces. She looked at her first mother and saw hints of shared physical features.

Liên wore a turquoise, yellow, and blue dress. She was shorter than Isabella, and rounder, missing a few teeth. But she had the girls' same petite legs with strong calves, and despite the limp, Liên held herself up with shoulders raised, as both the twins did. Liên grabbed Isabella's arm and kissed her hands. Hà did not attend the meeting, but Lien's other two daughters, the twins' half sisters, joined them. They looked younger than Isabella and seemed nervous as the group went out to lunch and later visited Liên's home, where they all sat together in a group.

A man accompanied Liên. He had solid, muscled arms—Liên's husband, Quý. He started sobbing as he spoke through Dung, explaining that he blamed himself for Liên's decision to give the twins away. He told them he had encouraged Liên to do so and that he had felt guilty about it for the last thirteen years. He never thought they would see Isabella again. It was another would-be epic moment that, to Isabella, fell flat. She did not feel tears welling up. There was a performative nature to all of it, and if she could have pushed a button and fast-forwarded through the awkwardness, she would have.

But something else besides Quý's sentimentality and Liên's physical features struck Isabella: as other people in the room wept, Isabella saw Liên's eyes were dry, like hers. Isabella could sense Liên's restraint. She did not try to hang all over Isabella. She seemed almost partially removed from the drama unfolding before all of them. *Probably uncomfortable*, Isabella thought. She could relate.

Liên's lack of emotion made Isabella feel more at ease. *Okay, this is not so bad*, Isabella told herself. *I'm the same way.*

During the reunion, and throughout the entire trip in Việt Nam, Isabella also noticed how Liên, Quý, Rô, and Tuyết still referred to her by her Vietnamese name. Isabella would listen closely as they spoke to each other in Vietnamese, and she would catch them talking about her. Never Isabella. Always Loan.

Thinking of herself as Loan did not bother her for some reason, especially when Liên called her by that name. "It made me feel connected to her in some small way," she would later explain. "And connected to my past."

THERE WAS NEVER a clear plan, Keely said, from searching for Ha, to reunions, to everything that would happen after. "I completely relied on the universe to line up the chaos of this journey. And it was chaotic.

Confusing. And uncomfortable at times." She told me it was a journey of faith.

"Adoptive parents, though well meaning, are often fixers," psychologist and intercountry adoptee Amanda L. Baden told me during one of our interviews. "They tend to think, 'If I find every piece of the puzzle, then my child will be whole, and I can protect them.' But it just doesn't work that way."

The choice to look for birth families "should not be at the control of adoptive parents," according to Lynelle Long, founder of ICAV. It must be "completely adoptee led," because if the adoptee is not emotionally ready, any search, reunion, rejection, or failure to reunite can be detrimental. Long can see why adoptive parents want to facilitate the happy-ending story. "They think that's what their child is going to want, and that everything will be okay now, all the pain."

But what happens, Long added, if that parent and child discover the adoptee was actually stolen, sold, or abducted? What happens if they find out the birth families loved and wanted them and that if they had had the financial means, they would have raised the child on their own? What if the child discovers a birth family wants nothing to do with her? What if the child decides she wants nothing to do with her birth family, even though they have now reestablished this relationship?

Keely admitted she had not thought out the reunions "with everything in line, like psychological support or counselors available to talk to the kids to work through this. I stayed very much in touch with the kids as the process went on. But it wasn't like we had therapists they were talking to."

Years later, Keely would get a tattoo on her wrist, a series of disconnected dots, inspired by a 2005 Steve Jobs commencement speech, in which he said: "You can't connect the dots looking forward; you can only connect them looking backward. . . . You have to trust in something—your gut, destiny, life, karma, whatever."

THERE WAS SOMETHING else that Hà desperately wanted to discuss with Keely during her 2012 visit, without the interference of Dick or Dung. One night during the visit, Hà, Rô, and Tuyết joined Keely and Isabella for a meal at the Sheraton, and Dung was not there to interpret this time.

"Rô, Tuyết, and I had dealt with Dung so much," Hà said. "Dick, we didn't speak the same language, so we don't know what's going on in his head. But I couldn't deal with Dung's behavior anymore."

Hà was terrified to bring this up. How would the Solimenes react? How would this impact her relationship with Isabella? A waiter walked by who had spoken English to the Solimenes earlier.

"You need to tell them," Rô begged Hà. "It's now or never."

Hà had watched Dung belittle Rô and Tuyết before her eyes, speak to them like children. "I wanted to stand up for them so bad," Hà said. "I respect Rô and Tuyết so much at home. For them to come over here, for her to yell at them, I didn't want that. But didn't know how to stand up for myself. That upset me."

Hà motioned to the waiter and asked him to interpret for her. Through him, Hà explained to Keely how controlling Dick and Dung had been this past year. She told Keely that Dick and Dung never revealed exactly how much money the Solimenes had sent for them. Furthermore, she said, Rô and Tuyết no longer wanted to live in Dung's family's home. It was too big and expensive (they had raised the rent, which seemed suspicious even though Rô and Tuyết were not paying it themselves). They preferred to find a smaller, cheaper place in the city, one not under Dung's family's management. The couple, she told Keely, had not been kind.

"I think that Keely and Isabella could see it on my face," Hà said. "There was so much more that I wanted to tell them, but I couldn't say it, because I didn't speak English. They could see I was very frustrated, having anxiety." Hà worried that Keely would not believe her, that she would side with Dung and Dick instead.

She watched Keely's expression change. She could tell she was taking her concerns seriously. Keely agreed immediately to cut off business with Dick and Dung. She said Rô and Tuyết would no longer have to go through Dick and Dung for financial help. Keely would set up a bank account specifically for Hà, Tuyết, and Rô that they could access themselves.

"Ever since then, we didn't have to deal with Dung and Dick again," Hà recalled. "I thought, 'Oh my God, this is a relief. I don't have to see Dung and Dick anymore. I don't have to go over to her house every Sunday.'"

When Keely told Dick and Dung about the change of plans, the reaction was swift and harsh. Dick and Dung told Keely they believed that Rô and Tuyết were the greedy ones. Dung would later say that Tuyết seemed like a "gangster" and treated Liên "very badly, like dirt." Dung said, "The lesbian woman, she's mean. . . . She wanted to isolate the birth mother of Hà."

Dick had a harsher take. In one email to Keely, he wrote: "It has brought nothing but sadness since the early euphoria vanished with the realization of how devious the two women are. Frankly we do not have a high regard for Hà's integrity either."

After the Solimenes left Việt Nam in 2012, Keely Skyped with Hà, suggesting that she bring a bouquet of flowers to Dick and Dung as an act of goodwill, thanking them for what they had done on their behalf over the last year, despite the way it had ended.

Hà agreed to do so. She knocked on their door, flowers in her arms. Dick opened it, took one look at Hà, and slammed the door in her face.

THIRTY

"Where I Am From"

AFTER HER REUNION with Hà, and throughout middle school, Isabella stayed involved with the UN Foundation and Girl Up, trying to learn more about international issues. She read Mark Bowden's *The Killing of Osama bin Laden* and Nujood Ali's *I Am Nujood, Age 10 and Divorced*, about the author's child marriage in Yemen. She read the autobiography of Malala Yousafzai, the Pakistani activist who at fifteen survived being shot in the head by the Taliban.

Isabella chose these stories for the history and sociopolitical issues and fascinating people; she was hungry to learn about poverty, religion, the treatment of women globally, and international conflict. She got especially excited by an assignment to read Tim O'Brien's *The Things They Carried*, poring over the pages and coming to school ready to discuss passages in student small groups. Before reading *The Things They Carried*, Isabella's education on the war in Việt Nam in history classes had been confined to testable US classroom facts: the war started on November 1, 1955, after Hồ Chí Minh's communist government of North Việt Nam sought to reunify with South Việt Nam. Hồ Chí Minh launched a guerrilla war with supporters of the communist National Liberation Front, the Việt Cộng, against anticommunist Ngô Đình Diệm in South Việt Nam.

The United States came into the picture in March 1965 to curtail the spread of communism, but American troops withdrew in 1973, before the end of the war on April 30, 1975. The communists won, taking over

South Việt Nam. More than three million people were killed—more than fifty-eight thousand Americans perished, and more than half the dead were Vietnamese civilians. It was, until that point, America's longest involvement in any war.

Isabella knew enough to write a term paper. There was also the My Lai massacre, the antiwar movement, the Pentagon Papers, the Tết Offensive, the Gulf of Tonkin incident, the Paris Peace Accords, napalm, booby traps, and agent orange.

For Isabella, O'Brien's book had these complex characters and resonant scenes that lifted the war off the page and into her imagination. She especially wanted to discuss the portrayal of women in the book, like Mary Anne, first introduced as a soldier's girlfriend who left Việt Nam a soldier herself. But when she pulled out her copy alongside her classmates, she quickly realized that few seemed to have read it as closely or cared as much about what the author was writing. The conversation felt forced and flat. Isabella kept her most of her thoughts about the book to herself. She didn't want to seem overly eager or annoyingly bookish.

Outside of school, Isabella found it refreshing to be around other young women from Girl Up. They came from a variety of ethnic backgrounds and seemed as interested in world issues as she was. They went on retreats and worked on campaigns to tackle malaria. Isabella began taking part in speaking engagements during which she found herself talking more about her twin sister in Việt Nam.

Isabella had written her story in summary and told it before smaller audiences before. She remembered one event was televised. Isabella wore black pants and a Girl Up shirt. When she arrived and saw hundreds of people, many in business attire, she felt like she had not dressed up. She went through rounds of security checkpoints and received a badge for the events. The room was full, with at least a hundred people, including many journalists who had lined up with spotlights, cameras, and microphones in the front row.

Isabella stepped onto the stage and introduced herself.

"I haven't always had the name Isabella Solimene. Before I was adopted from an orphanage in Nha Trang, Việt Nam . . . my name was Nguyễn Khánh Kim Loan. I have a sister named Nguyễn Thị Hồng Hà. We are identical twins, but our lives have been very different. . . . Hà and I were separated at birth."

After her speech, an Asian American woman pulled her aside. "Are you aware you are mispronouncing your name?"

All this time, in one public speaking event after another, Isabella had been pronouncing it "Na-gu-yen."

The woman told Isabella it was actually pronounced "wen."

How could you be so stupid? Isabella thought to herself. *And on national television?* She had given this speech in front of other Asian Americans before. They must have known but didn't correct her. She was mortified.

Isabella felt like she was making missteps everywhere she went. In middle school, she had gotten used to being excluded from social circles. Kids at school did not invite her to weekend events, and some avoided her on campus, but by the time she reached Saint Viator High School, the alienation had gotten worse. Isabella became a punch line. Students even confused her with another Asian girl on campus. At one point, Isabella tried to join the Chinese Club, which was made up of students who were recent immigrants.

"I thought it was more like everyone would be able to join it, but it was like hardcore Chinese," she said. "They were not very welcoming. They were like, 'Wait a second. You don't speak Chinese?'" So she ended up not joining after all.

Isabella did join the freshman soccer team, but she was added late because she injured her ankle and was not recovered enough to play until the last two weeks of the season. A rumor spread. *Isabella thinks she's a better soccer player than she actually is. She thinks our team sucks.* Teammates from soccer did not speak to her.

In class one day, Isabella loosened an orthopedic walking boot she had been wearing ever since her injury. A girl walked up behind her and kicked her boot. She felt her ankle spasm. It hurt so badly she had to leave school early to go to the doctor. It turned out the kick had caused her Achilles tendon to tear, since her boot had not been on properly and her ankle was still so fragile from the previous sprain. Now it was tender and swollen again. It would take a year before her ankle fully recovered. Recovering mentally would take longer.

Another day, someone stole the iPad that Isabella was required to use for school. She figured someone swiped it from her bag. When she went to her classes, she could not participate and had to go to the dean's office.

"I really don't know where my iPad is. I swear it was in my backpack."

Administrators threatened: "If no one comes forward, everyone will get detentions."

Five girls finally admitted they had taken the iPad and stashed it in a locker.

But that was not the end of the bullying. Later that semester, Isabella realized her cell phone was missing. She searched all over campus before realizing she could track it down using the locations setting. She followed the signal on her laptop and found the phone in the yard of a stranger's house, presumably dumped there by a classmate. If Isabella could have counted all the students who bullied her, she estimated the number would have come close to fifty kids.

ONE DAY, DURING her freshman year, her literature teacher assigned a book called *Our America: Life and Death on the South Side of Chicago*, stories from the Ida B. Wells housing projects in Chicago, a place not far from her suburb but one probably no one in her school had ever seen up close. The teacher assigned the students to write a poem addressing the question: "Where are you from?" They would break into groups over two days and workshop the poems before submitting final drafts.

"I remember just feeling so like conflicted over what to write," Isabella recalled years later. In her heart, she had a poem. But she could not share her heart with her classmates. She sat in front of the fireplace in her living room and wrote it anyway.

> I am from a world of unique colors.
> I originate from a country with ancient pagodas
> From a region where peasant women wear conical hats
> a place where silk is valued like money
>
> The dishes we eat are exquisite
> A place where taste is divine and dry.
> The smells are strong and hold exotic herbs
> The spices are universal themes
>
> This is the birthplace of my home
> The waking sounds of a million motorbikes
> A feel of joy and connection when speaking to locals
> I am from a place that can only describe Nature's beauty
>
> Where I am from, I once worshipped the Buddha
> The belief and conception of man and world
> Today I am from a new world that changed me
> I love the sense of being a cosmopolitan woman
> I will never forget where I came from
> I am from the countryside of East Vietnam.

Isabella finished the poem and thought, *I can't go to that workshop tomorrow with this poem. I just can't.*

She quickly jotted down a completely different poem.

The new poem "sucked," she said years later. "It was nothing that I actually thought." She believed her classmates would never understand her original poem—they would never understand her. "I just wished that I could freely write whatever I want and not have to be judged, you know, to speak what I feel inside," Isabella said. "But I just knew so many students that had bullied me were in that class, and so many people in my class knew that they were bullying me, but they weren't doing anything about it. I wasn't friends with anyone. I sat by myself. I kept to myself. I read my books. I read the assignments. And that's how I survived."

She endured the next two days of workshopping with her fake poem. Then, when the deadline came, she submitted her original poem to the teacher instead. Her teacher wrote her an email, asking her to read it in front of the class and whether she could submit it to a national writing contest.

Isabella replied: "I'm not comfortable reading it."

First off, she reasoned, "no one's going to care. They don't care about me. And then second, I'll probably even get even more bullied for reading this."

"Can I read it to the class?" the teacher asked.

Everyone's going to know it was me. She told her no thanks.

When class resumed the next day, the teacher made an announcement: "There were quite a few of you who wrote great poems, but there was one person who wrote a phenomenal poem."

Isabella felt her heart pounding. The room was silent.

"That person knows who they are," the teacher continued. "And they know that this is getting submitted for the contest."

After class, Isabella heard students whispering, trying to guess who it could be. When she got home, she worried more. What if the poem made it far in the national contest? What if it was publicized? Then everyone would know it was her. *I should probably tell her something now rather than later.* She contacted her teacher.

"Thank you for recognizing my work," Isabella told her. She explained she didn't want any part of the contest and she was very uncomfortable with any attention. "I appreciate what you had to say. But I'm going to back out of this."

ISABELLA DECIDED NOT to return to Saint Viator after her freshman year. She didn't want to put up with the sneers and harassment. She transferred to another campus, Carmel Catholic High School, a forty-five-minute-drive away.

Meanwhile, Olivia had arrived as a freshman at Saint Viator. Since Olivia played varsity basketball, she ended up on the team with girls from Isabella's grade level. The same teenagers who had excluded Isabella seemed to like Olivia, inviting her to parties, hanging out with her on campus and on the weekends.

Isabella could ignore the mean girls. Tell herself they did not matter, not in this world that now felt much bigger than Saint Viator High, especially since she'd become part of Girl Up and traveled to Việt Nam. But when Olivia befriended some of the same girls who had bullied her, Isabella felt betrayed.

"I remember being very lonely and not feeling like I could confide in Olivia anymore," Isabella said. After years of birthday parties, backyard games, sharing a bedroom, and swapping secret theories about their birth families and the orphanage they came from, to her Olivia now seemed like a different person. "I hit a low," Isabella said. "I just wasn't able to relate to Olivia anymore."

AFTER ISABELLA TRANSFERRED out of Saint Viator High, she became part of a circle of girlfriends at Carmel Catholic High. Two of the girls, whom Isabella had known since elementary school in Barrington, also had been adopted, and their families all knew one another.

Life seemed to be getting better at her new school. Then the annual spring Turnabout dance came around, and Isabella decided to take a swig of alcohol before hanging out with the group. It was not a habit, but she thought it might help her relax, especially since social situations gave her such anxiety. When she joined her friends, who were not into drinking, they told her they could smell the alcohol on her breath. One of them blew up at Isabella and threatened to tell her soccer coach.

After that, the group stopped inviting her to hang out.

"What are you doing this weekend?" her mom would ask.

"I have no idea," Isabella would reply. No one had called her in weeks. Her brief social life at Carmel Catholic High fizzled.

Everyone had heard that Isabella got "extremely drunk at Turnabout." Isabella said that was simply not true. She had taken a drink of liquor around 3:00 p.m., but the dance was not until five hours later. More false rumors spread, including one about Isabella's parents getting divorced.

At one point, one of the girls invited Isabella to lunch and then a soccer match after a half day at school. Isabella was happy to be included. When lunchtime rolled around, she called their cell phones to find out where they wanted to meet for lunch, but no one answered.

She called again. One girl finally picked up and told Isabella they had already gone to the soccer game. Isabella drove forty-five minutes to the game and paid the entrance fee to get in, but she couldn't find the girls. She tried calling again. When Isabella finally did reach one of them, she learned they had already left. "I never hung out with those girls again, not a single day of my entire time there." *I need to do something*, she told herself. *I can't go back.*

"Junior year, I was fed up," Isabella said. "I was very, truly lonely, because I would go to school and then I'd come home, and I wouldn't do anything. I didn't even play soccer that year. I was so uncomfortable with everyone at my school."

Isabella talked to her parents about it all, the alcohol, the broken friendships and bullies, the loneliness. It was decided. She would not return to Carmel Catholic High. Isabella would homeschool for the rest of her high school career instead.

THIRTY-ONE

"Be with Us"

A YEAR AFTER that FaceTime call with her family in Việt Nam, Olivia agreed to travel to her birth country with Keely and reunite with all of them. Victoria and Isabella came too. Olivia would remember how her family's entire community from Xã Vạn Thắng came out to greet her when she arrived at the village—neighbors, shop owners, children. How the crowds parted as she walked toward her family's home, as if she were an NBA star. How the strangers trailed her as she made her way to her birth family's home. How the crying Vietnamese faces from FaceTime morphed into real people she could feel and touch.

She would remember how they kissed her, their tears wiping against her cheeks. How her birth mother squeezed her and gestured toward her older sister, a girl who looked a lot like Olivia, named Ngà. The very sister whose name stayed on Olivia's tongue for so long when she was a child.

There were other siblings, too, and they ran up and hugged her. Olivia did not know their names, but she hugged them back. She realized these siblings had been raised by their family members, together. To Olivia, this not only felt confusing, but devastating.

She spotted a ball in the dirt and picked it up, trying to show her family members how to play basketball. Her birth mother dribbled surprisingly well. They spent the warm afternoon together, holding hands much of the time.

At the end of the day, her family asked through a translator, "Would you stay overnight and be with us?"

The idea of spending the night in this village she did not know, in a home so drastically different from hers in Illinois, scared her. To sleep on the ground in one room, side by side with people who were family but still strangers to her. She could not speak their language; she was thirteen years old. The Solimenes were the only people she felt safe with.

"No, I'm sorry," Olivia said. She looked at Keely. Olivia felt affection for her birth mother and siblings and aunts, but, she thought, *I want to be with my mom, the one who has taken care of me all of these years. I'm more comfortable with my mom. I love her so much.*

Olivia was satisfied that she had come, but she didn't want to stay overnight.

OLIVIA WOULD RETURN to the United States and try to put this experience behind her. She would begin freshman year at Saint Viator High and embrace her place within the social scene. She did not want to go back to Việt Nam, at least not any time soon, or to stay in touch with her birth family via Skype or Facebook either. As much as she could feel that they loved her, Olivia still felt like she never received a satisfying answer to the one question that haunted her: *Why did you give me up?*

Three months after this emotional visit, she woke up in Illinois and thought to herself, *This is my life, right here in America. I've got to accept it.* She thought of her Vietnamese family members, how she should feel guilty because they were poor, and she was not, but she told herself, *I don't owe them anything, and they don't owe anything to me either. They gave me up. I want to focus on my life.*

Olivia wanted to love her birth family without feeling weighed down by obligations to them, to be an American teenager without burdens or constant pangs of guilt, thinking of what her birth siblings didn't have.

They were not her responsibility, at least not at this point in her life. She was still just a kid herself.

OLIVIA COULD FEEL her interests drifting from Isabella's. She would walk into a room and see Isabella watching a documentary or a film with subtitles. Olivia preferred comedies or shows like *Grey's Anatomy*, *One Tree Hill*, and *Friday Night Lights*.

In class, Olivia would act like a goofball, throwing paper airplanes and cracking jokes, though still respectful of teachers. She found history and social science class discussions about World War I, World War II, the Holocaust, and the Civil War fascinating. She remembered learning about the war in Việt Nam. Every time the teacher said, "Việt Nam," the students looked at Olivia humorously, as if she had more information to offer.

Olivia replied with a joke, "Yup, that's me. Thank you," then would add with a smile, "Sorry, I'm still trying to learn myself."

"Should I go out tonight?" Olivia would ask her mom. "Or should I hang out with Isabella?"

She felt bad leaving Isabella behind. *We're family, and here I am going out with friends.*

At one point, when Isabella was still in the same school, Keely told Olivia, "You know, kids are giving Isabella a hard time." Olivia had noticed that some who said hi to her would ignore Isabella, even if she was standing right next to her. She didn't know how to react. "Like, do I say hi to them? Do I be nice to them?"

Olivia felt bad. It wasn't right for kids to treat Isabella this way, but she also didn't know how to deal with the situation.

"So I kept saying hi to them," Olivia explained. "I didn't realize how badly it hurt Isabella, for her to see that I'm still cool with these people."

Olivia was still navigating her own identity, racially, sexually. It had been two years since Olivia came out to Keely, admitting her crush on a classmate. Most of her peers still did not know.

"Are you going to be mad at me if I don't like boys?" Olivia said when she was in sixth grade.

"I just sort of played it off a little bit," Keely told me. "I might have said something like, 'You don't have to really think about that right now. Think about what you want to be when you grow up.' She was processing it. I was processing it."

For Olivia, processing felt more like suppressing.

"People saw this external shield of me," Olivia explained. "Like this is who I am, but they didn't really see the person inside. I realized this isn't who I want to be. But I kept going, another three years of being someone that I'm not. And I'm so ashamed of myself for that."

Olivia had figured out—on the outside—how to exist by assimilating. But, she acknowledged, "I honestly think Isabella had it the worst, and that's the saddest part."

THIRTY-TWO

Goodbye

HÀ GRADUATED FROM the middle school and enrolled in iSCHOOL in Nha Trang for high school, a private, bilingual campus with native English-speaking teachers. She no longer found herself being bullied for not knowing enough or for being a girl from the countryside. By now, students either assumed she had money because she had an iPhone and could afford tuition of 36 million đồng a year, or they heard from their peers that she had wealthy American family members. Whatever the reason, Hà got the impression that the students believed she was rich, and she never again had problems with kids being mean.

While she was at iSCHOOL, Keely planted another idea in Hà's mind: What if she tried to apply for a visa to come to the United States? She could enroll in an American high school, and it would be an opportunity to spend time with her sister. Hà and Isabella talked over the computer regularly, but the conversations had nothing to do with the bullying both had experienced, or their loneliness. They were mostly still surface level: "How is school?" or "What are you doing this weekend?"

Perhaps Hà could one day even attend a college in America, Keely suggested. Keely offered to send a packet of immigration paperwork for her to fill out. Then Hà would have to travel by bus to Hồ Chí Minh City to be interviewed by a US Embassy official.

Hà went along with the idea, and Rô and Tuyết did not object. But the truth was, when they started the visa application process, she, Rô, and Tuyết didn't really know what they were getting themselves into. They didn't know how quickly Hà could end up in the States if it did actually get approved. They didn't even know if getting a visa would guarantee that she would go. Hà told herself that filling out the paperwork was just a chance at one day getting an American education.

When Hà received the packet of forms by FedEx, she filled out every page and carted the packet along on the overnight Friday bus to the US Embassy in Hồ Chí Minh City, accompanied by Rô. When they arrived Saturday afternoon, Hà and Rô checked into a motel. They had never taken family vacations, so the trip to a city that Hà had never been to before was a lovely weekend getaway. They enjoyed lunch together and strolled around the city, exploring.

When Hà arrived at the front of the embassy the next morning, she was amazed at the long the line of people—it looked like a thousand.

It began to dawn on her how badly some people wanted to go to America. She waited for hours in line, documents in hand. When she finally made it to the window, the embassy employee sorted through her documents, then handed them back to her. She had missed one of the necessary forms.

Denied.

Hà texted Keely with the news. Keely told her it was okay, that they would try again. And they did. Over and over again.

Every few months, Hà would receive more packets of documents from Keely, who also sent money to cover the bus fare and motel. Hà would fill out the pages and ride overnight to Hồ Chí Minh City with Rô. They would get to have more lunches out and leisurely time together. Then Hà would stand in line for hours with hundreds of others. She would watch person after person before her get rejected, finally make it to a window herself, only to get denied again.

Sometimes it was because of another missing document.

"What document?" Hà asked. "Can you please tell me so I can tell my guardian?"

The agent replied, "I can't say."

Sometimes Hà made it past the first window into the interview. She sat in front of the agent and tried her best to speak only in English, explaining how she met the Solimene family, how she had a twin sister in the United States. By the end of the interview, the response was always the same:

Denied.

The reasons varied. Once, the embassy official spoke to her in English, but she replied in Vietnamese. "Oh, this one is going to America, and she doesn't even know how to speak English?"

Denied.

Or the agent would look at her grades and say she was not a strong enough student.

Denied.

Or he looked at her family name, Nguyễn, and questioned why she had not taken Tuyết's family name, Trần, if Tuyết was indeed her legal guardian. He told her to go back to her village and get more documents. Other times, the agent expressed suspicions that she would never want to return to Việt Nam. *Denied.* Each time Hà was met with rejection from the US Embassy, she became determined to come back and prove the agents wrong. She had not felt any burning desire to go to America when she started this visa application process, but with each denial, she felt herself wanting it more. *Who are these agents to tell me no?* Hà thought. *I have done nothing illegal. How can they tell me I do not deserve this?*

These past three years, Hà had worked hard to catch up with other students who had spent their whole lives in better schools. She had endured bullying. She had left the village she loved, convincing Rô and Tuyết to do the same—all for her, so she could have a shot at a more successful future. Hà had already surpassed Tuyết's sixth grade education. She told herself she could be the first in her family to go to college, the first not to have to work in the sugarcane fields or rice paddies, or babysit, or wash dishes, or clean wealthy people's homes. She could be a teacher, or a psychologist, or a businesswoman. *I am going to learn English,* she told herself. *I am going to come back stronger. I deserve this visa. I am going to go to the US. I am going to be with my sister.*

For her next trip to the US Embassy, Keely sent extra money for Hà and told her to go shopping with Rô to find a nice outfit. If she came to the interview looking professional and studious, perhaps that might sway the agent in her favor. Hà and Rô bought a polo shirt and khakis in Nha Trang; they packed the outfit and again boarded the overnight bus.

Using her iPhone, Hà sought out advice about the interview process: "What should I say to the US Consulate?" She arrived at her interview feeling confident in her new clothes. She answered the agent's questions honestly, trying her best to respond in English.

At the end of the interview, she received the verdict.

Denied.

Hà returned to the hotel with Rô feeling disappointed in herself.

She texted Keely. "I got rejected again."

This time when Keely replied, she offered a new idea: "Maybe you need to go to a school with a better English program."

Keely found two schools in Hồ Chí Minh City: the American School and the Australian International School. Both had excellent English programs.

"Keely thinks I need to go to Sài Gòn for a better English school," Hà told Rô. But enrolling meant she would have to move to a place that was a nine-hour bus ride away.

Rô burst into tears. She immediately called Tuyết.

"You have to talk to Hà," she told Tuyết. "Keely says she should move to Sài Gòn."

Rô handed the phone to Hà.

"Who are you going to live with in Sài Gòn?" Tuyết demanded. She and Rô had found jobs, and they were not going to move away from Nha Trang.

"Who is going to cook breakfast, lunch, and dinner for you?" Hà also felt scared. *Tuyết is right*, she thought. *Who am I going to live with?*

KEELY FLEW TO Việt Nam a few weeks later. She met Hà, Rô, and Tuyết in Nha Trang and boarded an airplane to Tân Sơn Nhất International Airport with Hà. Rô and Tuyết had never been on a plane and took the overnight bus to meet them instead. It was Hà's first time flying. She remembered as a child in Khánh Đông peering into the sky to watch airplanes and wondering how they carried people. Now she realized how big the inside of the aircraft was. She looked out the window and realized she was inside the clouds.

When they all arrived, Keely introduced them to Joy, the daughter of the woman who ran the adoption agency that first connected the Solimenes to Isabella and Olivia, and the same woman who helped Keely search for Hà a decade earlier.

Joy, who was born in Việt Nam but adopted to the United States, had returned to Hồ Chí Minh City as an adult and was raising her own daughter, Bella, six years younger than Hà, who was now seventeen. Joy offered to let Hà live with her while she attended school—she had been accepted to the Australian International School. Hà babysat Bella in appreciation for Joy's offer of room and board. She did not know that Keely and Mick were paying Joy around $10,000 to house her and another $30,000 for schooling.

Tuyết and Rô stayed the first night with Hà at Joy's. Keely flew back to the United States, and Tuyết had to take the bus back to Nha Trang to work the next day. Joy had asked if Rô might be able to stay for an extra week because her housekeeper had to take time off. Could Rô help around the house? Rô agreed, mainly to spend those last days with Hà.

Tuyết did not eat the night before she left. She barely spoke. Her face looked heavy with worry, and Hà could tell she was upset, but unlike Rô, Tuyết rarely cried. Hà and Rô walked her to the taxi, which would take her to the bus terminal.

"Be well," Tuyết told Hà. Hà would not cry. But by the time she got back to Joy's house, Rô was already on the phone with Tuyết. The couple talked all night as Tuyết rode the bus back to Nha Trang, lamenting about how sad they were that Hà was moving to Sài Gòn. Hà felt herself getting angry. Why were they making such a big deal of this?

"I don't understand why you need to talk to Tuyết," she said. "Get off the phone and go to sleep. I have school tomorrow."

FROM THE MOMENT Hà walked onto the campus of the Australian International School, she knew the experience would change her forever. All the teachers and students spoke impeccable English. The place had an academic atmosphere rooted in intensive language-building that surpassed anything Hà had experienced in her two previous private schools.

She thought: *I know this will place will push me so hard to learn English.* She would become proficient, and it would be hard for the US Embassy to deny her a visa next time. When school ended that week, Hà avoided going back to Joy's. She knew Rô would be leaving on the bus to Nha Trang. Hà had promised she would take Rô to the bus station by 7:30 p.m., but she didn't want to deal with another goodbye. She called Rô.

"She was crying already," Hà would recall years later. "My heart felt so heavy."

"Where are you?" Rô said. "Why are you home yet? I'm about to leave."

"I know I said I would take you to the bus," Hà replied. "Can you take a taxi to the bus station instead?" She offered to call the taxi for her.

Rô began yelling and crying. "Are you kidding me? I'm leaving. You can't say goodbye to me?"

"Okay, okay," Hà replied. She would come back to see her off.

When she got to Joy's house, Rô cried all the way from the door out to the street. "Please take care of yourself."

Hà hailed Rô a taxi, and as soon as she shut the car door, she turned around and ran back to the building.

"I ran like somebody was chasing me, like I was on a mission," Hà later recalled. "I didn't want to see the taxi driving away. I didn't even look back. I sat inside for like thirty minutes. I was like, 'Oh my God, what did I just do? I could have taken her to the bus. Why didn't I do that? Why didn't I spend every last minute with her?'"

Hà felt like she was breaking. "This tightening in my chest, you know, like when you hold your crying in, like it's squeezing it tight in your belly."

No sooner did Rô board the bus than she called Hà's cell phone, still crying. "Don't go out with boys."

"Okay, don't worry," Hà replied. "I promise. I will be back in two weeks. I will come back." The truth was, she would not actually be able to visit again for a month.

What Rô said next stung: "I never prepared myself for this day that I would have to let you go. I never thought that you would want to go this quickly. I never prepared myself to not be with you."

Looking back on the moment, Hà would realize the jumble of emotions she was feeling too. Her whole life with them, she had never even slept a night without either Rô or Tuyết, except once during a storm, when Tuyết could not immediately make it back to the village.

"I was hurting inside. I was so sad," Hà said. "I didn't prepare myself either. I didn't even think, 'I will never live with Tuyết or Rô again.' That was the first time in my life I had ever said goodbye to Rô and Tuyết. I wanted to cry, and I wanted to tell Rô and Tuyết, 'You know what? I'm scared. I want this education so bad. But I also want to be with you guys. I can't have both. I can't have Rô and Tuyết and go to the Australian International School. So I sacrifice Rô and Tuyết. I'm sorry. I have to say goodbye.'"

Hà

Some people, they believe in God. They say, "Oh, I'm just going to let God decide whatever happens to me. God has a plan for me."

Of course, God has plans for everyone. But are you willing to work with this plan? Or will you just sit there and let God decide what the plan is?

I apply this back to my own beliefs in Buddhism. My family in Việt Nam, we do not think of Buddha as a god, or like Jesus. But if we did ask Buddha for blessings, would I really want to sit around and pray to Buddha and say, "I need to be successful?" Would I say, "I need to have good karma"? But then I don't actually have to do anything about it myself?

If I just go home and pray to the Buddha, then all of a sudden, is the Buddha going to do everything in his power to give me a good life, just because I'm a good person?

I totally believe that I have blessings. I would never forget about that. I have been blessed my whole life from the minute that I was born to now.

But I also do think that a lot of what happens in my life is in my control, in my choices, in my decision-making.

THIRTY-THREE

"I Will Come Back"

AT THE NEW school, Hà's English improved. She studied Vietnamese literature, information technology, algebra, design technology, art, music, physical education—all taught in English. She began to research America: its presidents and the number of states, its democratic system and history. She began to fantasize about what it would be like to live there. To become closer to Isabella. When they spoke over the computer, it was still mostly small talk. Never "I can't wait to see you" or "I can't wait to live with you." They didn't feel comfortable with each other like that. But maybe, Hà told herself, one day they would.

Not only did she speak English all day at school, from 8:00 a.m. to 4:00 p.m., but when she got home, Joy spoke only English. Since Joy had been raised in the United States, she often cooked American food, like tacos with onions, which Hà despised, and she gave Hà Cheerios with milk for breakfast every day, which she didn't care for either. Hà would leave Joy's house and buy sticky rice from a street vendor on her way to school.

Hà was homesick, but she didn't tell anyone. She didn't want Joy, Keely, Mick, Isabella, Rô, or Tuyết to think she was not strong enough to handle this. Twice a week, Hà would take Joy's daughter to her dance class and wait for two hours until it was over, then drive her home on a motorbike, which Joy allowed her to use. Hà enjoyed Bella's company, and the two girls spoke to each other in Vietnamese. Joy was strict and had high expectations, but not like Dick and Dung. Hà got the feeling that Joy really did want her to succeed.

Joy took Hà to the US Embassy for her next interview in April 2016. Hà was prepared with her package of signed documents. She told herself she would not speak one word of Vietnamese in the interview—she would prove to the agent that she had mastered English. This time, Hà also brought a letter from a lawyer from Baker & McKenzie, a firm that the Solimenes had hired:

Ms. Nguyen has convincingly expressed to us that she has no intention of staying permanently in the U.S. She views Vietnam as a place of promise, but realizes that English is becoming indispensable to gaining success in an increasingly internationally-oriented world. . . .

Upon approval of her visa and subsequent enrollment at Saint Viator High School, measures have been put into place to ensure Ms. Nguyen's success in the school environment. The attached letter from Saint Viator High School shows that the school is aware of the English issue and the school has arranged accommodations in an English language environment to accelerate Ms. Nguyen's learning through immersion.

Joy waited for her at the coffee shop across the street while an embassy agent took Hà into a private room.

"You again?" he said.

"I know, I'm here all the time."

"After carefully going over your documents, I know how much you want this. I know how hard you are working," he said. "You are going to come back here after your education, right?"

"Yes," Hà assured him. "I'm going to receive the best education and then come back to Việt Nam and help my country."

"I am sorry," he continued, "for rejecting you for the last year and a half."

"It's okay," Hà said. Her heart sank. She knew what was coming next. *Denied.*

The agent took Hà's passport.

"I will mail this back to you," he said, "with your US visa in it."

Hà looked at the agent. He was grinning. She could not believe it. He had just approved her.

Hà bolted out of the embassy. It was raining, and she raced across the street to tell Joy but did not look out for traffic. A car swerved to avoid hitting her. *Is this even real?* Hà asked herself. She spotted Joy.

"I got my visa!"

Joy began to cry.

Hà called Tuyết, who was at work. "I have good news," Hà said. "They accepted my documents."

"You did it!" Tuyết said.

Hà called Rô.

"Finally," Rô said. Hà wasn't sure Rô or Tuyết really knew what it meant for her to receive her visa. She could barely grasp what would come next herself.

Hà called Keely next, who yelped in excitement.

Joy took Hà shopping. They bought grapefruits and flowers, and when they got back to Joy's home, Hà arranged the fruit and flowers on the altar in front of the big Buddha statue.

Hà lighted incense and prayed. *Thank you so much for helping me through all of this. Thank you. I finally got accepted.*

TWO MÒNTHS LATER, Hà finished her last class of the academic year at the Australian International School. She bid farewell to her teachers and left on the bus for Nha Trang that evening. Joy gave her $500, from the Solimenes. "Take this money and throw a party," she said. She wanted Hà to tell everyone that she was going to America.

When Hà got to Nha Trang, she went grocery shopping for her party and invited everyone she knew. Family members and friends traveled from Khánh Đông. They cooked spring rolls, Vietnamese curry, pork, and duck. Even Liên showed up.

"What is the party for?" Liên asked.

"I'm going to the US," Hà told her.

"When are you leaving?"

"In a week."

"Be safe. Take care of yourself," Liên told her. To Hà, this was classic Liên. Stoic. "Call me when you get to US," she said. "With Loan."

Hà packed her clothes, English schoolbooks, and all the Vietnamese foods she could fit into a suitcase and a backpack. She would take a bus back to Sài Gòn and then catch a flight with Joy and Bella, who would accompany her to Chicago.

Rô and Tuyết had asked to go to the airport to see her off in Sài Gòn, but Hà said no. She would rather say goodbye in Nha Trang.

The bus would leave by 10:00 p.m. the next day. Hà could not sleep all night. *Oh my God*, Hà thought. *This is going to be my last time sleeping here for a long time. What will my life look like after this? Where will I sleep? What am I going to eat? What if I'm homesick? How am I going to talk to people? What am I getting myself into?*

She did not voice any of these concerns to Rô or Tuyết; she didn't want them to worry even more. Hà couldn't believe how much she had changed these last three years. She was about to embark on an unimaginable adventure, and for the first time in her young adult life, her twin sister would be by her side. Hà never knew she could be this courageous. She told herself she was going to change her life—Rô and Tuyết's lives—with her American education.

"Some people think that I just got to come to the United States, that I was lucky. I don't think that," Hà said. "The Solimenes worked hard to get me here, especially Keely's planning. Besides being lucky, I had to work hard for myself. I had to get an education. I'm proud of everything I did."

Rô woke up the next morning crying. She continued to weep all day.

At the bus station, Hà turned to her parents and saw that Tuyết was crying this time too. The only times Hà had seen Tuyết cry was when she was mad at her. When Hà behaved badly as a child, Rô would spank her rear end, but Tuyết didn't. Instead, Tuyết cried out of anger or disappointment. Hà had never seen Tuyết cry out of sadness.

The bus pulled up, and Hà turned to hug them both.

"Please don't be sad. I will be fine. I promise. I will be fine."

They squeezed her hard.

Hà turned and boarded the bus.

Do not look back, she told herself.

Hà found her seat and removed her shoes. She could see Rô and Tuyết out of the corner of her eye, waving and crying, but she would not look at them.

"I didn't want to cry," she would later remember. "That image of Rô and Tuyết standing there waving goodbye, if I looked at them, it would stick in my head forever."

This is not forever, Hà told herself. *This is a normal goodbye. I will come back. Don't look back.*

The bus rolled away, until Rô and Tuyết were no longer in sight and Hà felt it was finally safe to look out of the window. Hà felt her cell phone buzzing. It was Rô. She picked up, but Rô did not speak; she just sobbed into the phone.

Hà said she had to go, and Rô called back.

Hà hung up again. She turned off her phone.

Before she had left their home in Nha Trang, Hà told Rô and Tuyết to look inside of their notebook when they got home. She had left a letter. "Read it after I leave." In it, Hà had written:

Thank you so much for taking care of me the last 17 years. I'm grateful to have you in my life. I won't ever forget all the memories we've had together. I promise I will take care of myself. I promise I will be a good student. I promise I will try my hardest. I promise I will come back. I promise I will take care of you until the day you die.

RÔ AND TUYẾT would find the letter once at home. But they would never open it. To do so would be to accept her goodbye.

PART THREE

THIRTY-FOUR

America

TO PREPARE FOR Hà's arrival, the Solimenes went shopping at Mitsuwa, a Japanese marketplace in Arlington Heights that had a small selection of Vietnamese food. They bought moon pies and other treats, as well as the family's first rice cooker. They bought balloons and bouquets of flowers.

Keely, Mick, Will, Victoria, Olivia, and Isabella piled into the Chevy Tahoe to head to Chicago's O'Hare airport. Arianna and Alexandra took the train. They met up at the appointed waiting area before Hà's flight was set to land at 7:00 p.m. The arrival time came and went. The monitors showed the flight had landed, but an hour later there was still no sign of Hà. Another hour went by. Still no Hà.

Keely called Joy's cell phone but did not get an answer. Had Hà even made it on the flight? The crowds of people waiting at the same terminal began to thin. The sliding doors opened and closed, opened and closed. Strangers exited.

It grew dark outside. Four hours had now passed.

Keely's cell phone rang.

"Hi, Mrs. Solimene." It was a man's voice. He said he was from immigration. "We were just wondering, What are you doing this evening?"

"I'm at O'Hare airport," Keely said. She told him she was waiting for someone traveling from Việt Nam. She gave him Hà's full name.

"Well, I have her here," he said. "She doesn't have the right documents."

The man told Keely that four people were going to be deported. Hà could be the fifth. "We're going to have to deport her too. The next flight is at 2:00 a.m."

ON THE OTHER side of the sliding doors, a frightened Hà was negotiating with the immigration officials. Inside the sterile room, it felt like she was going through the US Embassy interviews all over again. She felt like she was being scrutinized and watched. Hà paid attention as the agents interrogated others. When one got to her, he asked: "Why do you want to study in the US?"

Hà once again explained how she had met her twin sister, who was raised by an American family. She pulled out her packet of papers, the legal documents, lawyer's letter, transcripts.

"You missed one document," he said.

"What document? Can you please tell me so I can tell my guardian?"

"I can't."

Déjà vu.

"Find the phone number for your guardian," he said.

Hà watched the agent dial Keely and listened as he explained the situation. It was June. The school year did not begin until the fall. Hà knew that Keely was explaining to him that she was already enrolled in summer school—she was signed up to take a geography class starting that week. Keely had the paperwork to prove it, a letter from the school principal who approved Hà's admittance.

After he hung up, he handed back Hà's passport. She'll never be sure if she actually was missing a required document or if it had all been an elaborate test to see if she was lying about her twin, her schooling, or her American guardians.

"I'm going to send someone to your house," he warned. "If I see you're not going to school, I'm sorry, I will have to send you back."

A few minutes later, he let her through to baggage claim.

WHEN THE SLIDING doors opened, Hà emerged in jeans and a red and white striped sweatshirt. Olivia ran up to her first, cheering and crying while hugging her, a reaction that surprised everyone. Isabella, in glasses, jean shorts, and a flowy cardigan, embraced Hà tightly. It was a calmer reunion and considerably warmer than the first. One by one, Hà went through the Solimene train of hugs.

Hà climbed into the Tahoe with everyone else, but she was silent on the twenty-minute ride back to Arlington Heights as the Solimenes tried to make conversation. When they got to the house, the Solimenes' two dogs did not bark as they might have with strangers. Instead, they jumped on Hà lovingly, licking her. She fell for them immediately and nuzzled them back.

Hà saw the spread of Vietnamese foods laid out on the granite island in the kitchen. She smiled and pulled out the snacks she'd brought too. She had packed one suitcase full of clothes. The other was completely stuffed with shrimp chips, dried jackfruit, ginger candy.

Hà was too exhausted to socialize. Isabella showed her their room, a loft, on the top floor of the three-story house. It was past midnight in Illinois and 1:00 p.m. the next day in Việt Nam. Hà thanked her sister, lay down on a bed, and swiftly fell asleep. She would not wake up for another twelve hours.

WHEN ISABELLA ROSE the next morning, Hà was still sleeping. *Here we are*, she thought, *seventeen years old, and for the first time since infancy, we're roommates.* Isabella felt an immediate responsibility to look out for Hà. When she woke up, Isabella drove her to the Asian marketplace to see if there was any other food she might want to pick up before starting her geography class.

As the weeks passed, Isabella drove Hà to eat at American restaurants. Hà frowned at onion rings, Mexican food, and anything with cheese. At first, she always chose chicken fingers if she saw them on the menu but quickly got bored with that selection. So Isabella drove her to Chicago, where there were more Vietnamese food options.

In July, they would turn eighteen. There was still the unsettled matter of their birthdays. Hà's fell on July 2; Isabella's, July 24. No one could explain why the mismatch occurred. The sisters would continue to mark their individual birthdays on different days.

In the fall, Isabella homeschooled to finish her senior year, occasionally showing up to Saint Viator High to pick up course packets, not staying long on campus. Hà was a year behind Isabella academically and started her junior year at Saint Viator High, in Olivia's class.

Isabella drove Hà to shops to buy warm clothes as the weather cooled. The first time it snowed in Illinois that winter, Hà darted outside in a sweatshirt and shorts.

"Where's Hà?" Isabella yelled from inside.

"I'm right here!" Hà answered, scooping up a handful of snowflakes with her fingers.

Sometimes Isabella felt *too* responsible for Hà, like she needed too much hand-holding. She relied on Isabella for rides everywhere, for occasional translations, for academic advice, especially since she would soon be applying for colleges too. It was, at times, exasperating.

"I was going through a really tough time in high school," Isabella remembered years later. "She came the year that I decided to homeschool, a really difficult part of my life. I definitely ignored her a lot because I was going through things. I kind of thought that her timing of coming here was horrible."

Hà and Isabella shared a room but did not talk much to each other. "We would be in the car together for like thirty minutes and we didn't even say a word to each other," Hà said. The sisters would drive somewhere and listen to music in silence. "It's like when you are uncomfortable, and you just don't have anything to say."

If Isabella had continued going to the Carmel high school forty-five minutes away, she would not have seen Hà much; their schedules would have been so mismatched. Still, in those quiet, uneasy times together, they gradually did get to know each other. They realized they both liked to cook. They would make grocery runs at random hours to pick up baskets full of ingredients and come home giggling, experimenting in the kitchen for hours.

When Isabella first learned that Hà would be moving in with them, she had worried most about Olivia. "She doesn't want to feel like she's being replaced."

Olivia also did not love the idea of Hà being around all the time. It took months for her to be open to her presence in the Solimene home. "For a long time, I just thought it was just going to be me and Isabella," Olivia said. "When Hà came into the picture, it was a difficult adjustment for me." Olivia felt irritated by Hà, but it took her a while to figure out why.

Eventually, Olivia realized, Hà's presence made her think of her own family in Việt Nam. "It just brought back the memories and just the feelings that 'Oh crap, I have a family back in Việt Nam, and so does Isabella.'"

This would likely be Olivia and Isabella's last year living together in the same state for a long time, with Isabella headed to college soon. Olivia missed the relationship they used to have.

"I didn't want anyone to take away Isabella," she explained later. "Because she's been with me since I was like three years old. It's a special thing we have." Olivia added: "I just didn't want Isabella to love Hà more."

Isabella felt the strain between them too. She told Olivia one day, "I miss coming to you and confiding in you about small little things that I get frustrated about." Most of all, she told her, "I miss *you*."

This vulnerability pulled them closer.

For her eighteenth birthday, Isabella got a tattoo of the date she and Olivia were adopted—July 15, 2002—written in roman numerals on her right wrist. When Olivia turned eighteen, she got the same tattoo on her left wrist.

WHILE ISABELLA HELPED Hà navigate life off campus, Olivia gained Hà as a classmate at Saint Viator. Olivia felt like she had been assigned a new sister, who followed her around campus and needed help with everything. The situation bothered her.

Midway through Hà's first year at Saint Viator High, Olivia told her mom, "This isn't working." Olivia's friends did not fully understand Hà's relationship to her.

"Is that Isabella?" schoolmates would ask over and over again.

"No," Olivia said, sighing. "It's Hà."

There was a small cohort of international students at the school, mostly recent immigrants and exchange students from China. Photos of members of the Chinese Students Association were displayed in a glass case in a main hallway, along with photos of international students from Russia and Korea, and the lone student from Việt Nam: Hà.

Over the years, Olivia had gotten used to her friends and classmates poking fun at international students.

"They are weird looking," some would say.

Olivia would roll her eyes.

"They smell."

"They can't do sports."

"They eat weird food."

"You eat Chinese food all the time," Olivia would snap back, annoyed.

Olivia had long straddled the high school's social dividing lines. The international students considered Olivia an honorary member. She didn't like it when her other friends turned into mean girls, but lately, the jabs had been hitting too close to home.

One day, Olivia overheard her friends making fun of Hà.

"Why does she speak that way?"

"Something smells," one said.

"It's Hà's lunch," another replied, and the other girls laughed.

She pulled the girl aside. "Some people like certain kinds of foods.

That's not cool. She can eat whatever she wants. She's part of our lunch table. People have different backgrounds, different ethnicities. It doesn't give you the right make them seem like they're nothing."

"She's an international student," the girl told Olivia. "She can't even understand what we're saying."

"Yeah, she can," Olivia said. "She can understand. Stop being a bitch."

"It's a joke."

"Sometimes you joke about this stuff a lot," Olivia said. "So check yourself."

Olivia had always regretted not sticking up for Isabella in those earlier years of school. "It was hard," Olivia would later recall. "Because if I didn't have Hà with me, this wouldn't be happening. I wouldn't be fighting with my friends. But, then again, Hà was here. And she's my sister too now. You can't disrespect her like that."

Something surprising was beginning to happen for Olivia. As she got to know Hà, she began to realize how nurturing she was. Isabella and Hà cooked for her. Olivia discovered that Hà loved comedies. Growing up in her village, the only show Hà had ever watched as a kid was the *Tom and Jerry* cartoon on a neighbor's television. In Illinois, Hà would curl up with Olivia and Victoria and watch movies like *Bad Moms*, or *Sisters*, with Amy Poehler and Tina Fey, and they'd all crack up together, giving them jokes and reference points to share. They tore through *The Hunger Games* together, as well as all the Harry Potter movies.

It didn't happen right away. But the bond among all three of the girls was strengthening, their triangle fortifying.

"I really love Hà," Olivia said one day. She counted Hà as her sister. "She's part of the family. I will do anything to protect her."

THIRTY-FIVE

"We're Still Here"

BY THE SPRING of 2017, Isabella had finished homeschooling, graduating with her high school diploma. She decided to take a gap year. It gave her more time with Hà and Olivia, both of whom would be heading off to college themselves in a year. Isabella also signed up for a study abroad program to spend three months in Nepal starting in February of 2018.

But by the summer of 2017, her family started to hear reports that thousands of transnational adoptees who came to the United States as children were at risk of discovering they were not American citizens, even though their parents thought they had filled out the proper paperwork. Many of these adoptees had since grown up, obtaining drivers' licenses, even starting families of their own. Yet it turned out they had not been provided the citizenship they had been promised and believed they already had.

The Child Citizenship Act (nicknamed the Delahunt bill after Representative William Delahunt of Massachusetts, the adoptive father of a daughter born in Việt Nam) was enacted in Congress in 2001, allowing most transnational adoptees to receive citizenship. But the law applied only to adoptees who were eighteen years or younger as of 2001, when it went into effect. It did not cover adoptees who were already, or would soon be, adults.

The federal government has not made data available to confirm how many adoptees are living without citizenship, though the National

Council for Adoption estimates that 15,000 to 18,000 intercountry adoptees have found themselves in this precarious position as adults, some even facing deportation. The Adoptee Rights Campaign, an advocacy group, puts that number higher, estimating that between 2015 and 2033 the total population of adoptees with uncertain immigration status will reach between 32,000 to 64,000. Taneka Jennings, a Chicago-based founding member and campaign manager for Adoptees for Justice, told me that the Korean government reports that there are 18,603 intercountry adoptees who have not yet been naturalized in the United States. And that's only adoptees from South Korea.

Some adoption attorneys and agencies misinformed or neglected to follow up adequately with families to ensure they had the knowledge and resources to secure citizenship for their children, and the US government failed to update laws to prevent this predicament. In some cases, adoptive parents withholding citizenship was an intentional choice. Jennings, who is also an intercountry adoptee from Korea, emphasized that the children should not be held responsible for other people's failures to finalize their immigration paperwork.

In 2017, as Keely began looking into Olivia and Isabella's cases, she discovered their permanent resident cards had expired in 2012. "They were valid only for 10 years, from 2002 to 2012," Keely said. "I just thought that meant they were here now as citizens."

In fact, Isabella and Olivia were not US citizens after all.

FOR DECADES, THE issue of adoptee citizenship had flown under the radar, but awareness started to spread as adoptees over the last twenty years became adults and increasingly began to connect to one another. From lawmakers to parents, "nobody was thinking about it, to be honest, which really goes to show how broken our immigration and adoption systems are," said Jennings. The law has traditionally focused on the needs of the adoptive parents, but the children became afterthoughts. "As soon as we were adopted into all this, it was like, 'All right, our job is done,'" she said. "The adoptive parents were looking to complete their families. And that's it. We were not being thought of. I could tell you, even in my own adoption, I didn't have social workers come check on me to make sure that the home environment was good, to make sure that I was being loved, taking care of, or that my citizenship was secured. None of that happened."

In the wake of the September 11 terrorist attacks, as Muslim and immigrant communities came under surveillance, the country began to see waves deportations of people from the United States, including Vietnamese refugees and Asian adoptees. By 2015–16, the mainstream media outlets began paying attention to the tragic stories of Korean adoptees Adam Crapser and Phillip Clay, both of whom realized they were not US citizens and were eventually deported.

Adam's first mother, Kwon Pil-ju, had relinquished her three children in South Korea after struggling to provide for them when their father left. Adam was adopted at age three, along with his sister, by a US couple who abused him. He and his sister were split up and sent into foster care, where he was eventually adopted into another family, which brutalized him even more. This second set of adoptive parents were convicted of the abuse in 1992. Meanwhile, Adam became homeless and dropped out of high school. At sixteen, he was convicted for burglary.

Twenty-three years later, when Adam was thirty-nine, married with three kids, and living in Vancouver, Washington, agents from US Immigration and Customs Enforcement (ICE) showed up to his door seeking to send him to South Korea, a country he did not know. Not even able to fluently speak Korean, he was deported in 2016.

Phillip Clay was adopted from an orphanage in South Korea when he was eight years old, then raised by an American family in Pennsylvania. As an adult, he struggled with mental illness and substance abuse and had a few run-ins with the law, sometimes for stealing bicycles. In 2012, he was deported to South Korea, where he spent the next five years struggling to survive. He endured homelessness and received no mental health services. In 2017, at age forty-two, Phillip jumped off the fourteenth floor of an apartment building, killing himself.

Adam and Phillip galvanized many adoptees around the world, challenging "the dominant notion of adoption as rescue or inherently a 'better life,' as the US adoption system continuously failed," wrote Emma Wexler (now Jade Wexler), a transnational adoptee from Việt Nam, in her 212-page honors thesis for Brown University in 2020. Wexler, who is a year older than Isabella and Hà, was adopted from an orphanage in northern Việt Nam in 1998 and raised by a white Jewish single mother in the United States. Adam and Phillip's stories "require transnational/racial Asian American adoptees to confront the tenuous nature of their adjacent privilege from their white US citizen parents," Wexler wrote, "and serve as a wake-up call to the ways in which well-intentioned colorblind assimilation do not protect transnational Asian American adoptees."

Wexler, who previously served as a member of Adoptees for Justice, added: "Adoptees are not taught to see themselves as immigrants." Those who are not citizens must go through a naturalization process, which can cost hundreds or even thousands of dollars, especially if hiring an attorney (many of whom are not familiar with the complexities of adoptive immigration law), another barrier for some adoptees who do not have the resources or whose parents decide they don't want to help.

The Adoptee Citizenship Act of 2021, spearheaded by groups such as Adoptees for Justice, would amend the Child Citizenship Act of 2000, extending citizenship automatically to all intercountry adoptees. Previous versions of the bill have been introduced in Congress year after year, and stalled. "We just want to get an inclusive bill passed in Congress, with bipartisan support," Jennings told me in the fall of 2021. "This is not an issue of Republicans or Democrats. It's an issue of human rights and civil rights that we can all agree on."

On February 4, 2022, the US House of Representatives passed the Adoptee Citizenship Act. It was tacked on as an amendment to another bill, America COMPETES, which aims to increase competitiveness with China. The Senate had already passed the COMPETES act the previous year. Next, the House and Senate would negotiate to decide which amendments would remain as part of the final bill to pass in Congress. It was not a clear victory for adoptees. Despite the efforts, Congress ultimately failed to pass the Adoptee Citizenship Act in 2022. Adoptees for Justice and other groups are now working to reintroduce the bill.

LYNELLE LONG, FOUNDER of ICAV, a worldwide network that she launched in 1998, the year Isabella and Hà were born, was adopted from Việt Nam in 1973 at five months old. She has spent more than two decades advocating for adoptee rights, speaking before government agencies, and creating adoptee initiatives, including a powerful educational video series designed to help doctors, teachers, and mental health professionals better understand and support the experiences of intercountry adoptees.

In the mid-2000s, the field of critical adoption studies began to emerge, led by scholars like Kim Park Nelson, who wrote that the discipline "seeks to complicate current views of adoption, family, and kinship. Instead of understanding adoption as a solution to a social problem or as a procedure that requires 'best practices,' it understands adoption as a complex set of cultures, processes, exchanges, relationships, losses, and gains. Critical adoption studies recognizes adoptee identities as layered, intersectional, and complicated."

In the series that Long spearheaded, intercountry adoptees from Brazil, Colombia, Ethiopia, Haiti, South Korea, Sri Lanka, and Taiwan tell their own stories, like how difficult it can be to celebrate a birthday and what it is like living with the fear of being rejected again. "If your own flesh and blood can give you away, who is to say these parents that have adopted you wouldn't, if they found some reason they didn't want you anymore?" said an adoptee from Ethiopia named Meseret.

Others spoke of searching, or choosing not to search, for biological parents. "Sure, you may find your biological parents and reconnect and maybe even have a really healthy positive relationship," said Kimberley, an intercountry adoptee from South Korea. "But feeling whole as a person, as an adoptee . . . I think it's more about finding peace with your story and integrating the adoption with who you are."

The adoptees in the videos, Long noted, demonstrate that it is possible to experience the challenges and trauma of relinquishment and adoption and lead a positive, healthy life. But having the right kind of support and community is crucial. "There are all of these issues that make adoption complex that people need to wrap their heads around and start to have conversations about," Long told me. Looking at US policies, "I just can't understand the mentality of a country that continues to adopt so many in but won't even look after the ones who don't have automatic citizenship and won't make sure that that the legislation gets pushed through as a priority."

A growing group of scholars, including many who are also adoptees themselves, are shifting the focus to adoptees and birth parents, and away from then-dominant perspectives of the adoptive parents, publishing in academic journals and organizing conferences. In recent years, adoptees have continued to build their own communities, largely online, while raising their own political consciousness, also publishing memoirs, novels, and poetry; writing blogs; and creating documentary films. "We've started to unpack and rebuild our own narratives to understand what were the historical political forces that resulted in our own adoptions and immigration stories," Jennings told me. This has led some adoptees to want to try to fix some of the injustices or issues they think need to change in adoption and immigration systems, including other groups such as Adoptees United, Network of Politicized Adoptees, Yeondae, Adoptee Rights Campaign, and Adoptee Voices Rising.

Rebecca Kinney, a professor of critical ethnic studies and American studies at Bowling Green State University and an adoptee from Korea, pointed out to me that the struggle to obtain US citizenship and practices to exclude Asians from the immigration policies are deeply entwined with the very fabric of the history of Asians in America. In 1790, the Supreme Court passed a prohibition against naturalization for Asians because they were considered "not white." Yet by the mid-1860s, after the Thirteenth Amendment abolished slavery, the United States began to witness a rise in immigration from China, specifically men who came to work as low-wage laborers as miners and on railroads. This led to a fierce and violent domestic backlash. In 1875, the Page Act was approved, blocking the migration of any people lawmakers deemed undesirable from "China, Japan, or any Oriental country" and specifically forbidding Chinese women from migrating to the United States to start families with Chinese men already living and working in the country.

By 1882, the Chinese Exclusion Act barred all immigration from China, preventing Chinese residents already in America from attaining citizenship. In 1907–8, President Theodore Roosevelt attempted to avoid offending Japan, a rising global power, by negotiating a pact. The Gentlemen's Agreement between the two countries denied passports to Japanese laborers wanting to come to the United States, and Japan acknowledged that America had a right to exclude Japanese citizens, including those who also held passports from other countries, like Canada.

Then came the Immigration Act of 1924, which employed ruthless national origins quotas to end most legal immigration to the United States, followed by the 1929 Undesirable Aliens Act, which criminalized undocumented immigrants. Continuing the longstanding pattern of racial exclusion of Asians, Congress began the process of granting the Philippines independence in 1934, only to turn around and restrict Filipino immigration to the United States.

Kinney told me about the case of Takao Ozawa, who applied for citizenship in 1914 and was rejected because of his race. At the time, Ozawa had been living in the United States for twenty years, graduating from high school in Berkeley, California, studying at University of California, educating his children in American schools, and attending American churches. "The Supreme Court said, 'No, you're not a white man,'" Kinney said. "Asians in the United States have long made arguments for proximity to whiteness, not because necessarily they wanted to be white, but because of the legal, social, cultural, and political power that whiteness has held, and continues to hold, in the United States."

I interviewed Kinney as she was completing research as a Fulbright Scholar. Her project focuses on adult South Korean adoptees returning to their birth country to build communities. She told me that these US cases are important to learning about how "we come to historicize and understand who legally belongs to the country or is able to be part of the country."

There are more than two hundred thousand Korean adoptees living throughout the United States and Europe. They began forming communities in the 1980s, as documented by cultural anthropologist Eleana Kim. Some adoptees have also become involved in single-mother advocacy groups in South Korea and in Việt Nam, as well as in fights for stricter adoption criteria and efforts to access original birth records, improve treatment of birth mothers and adoptees, and increase domestic adoptions in Asia. Numbers of transnational adoptees from Việt Nam are smaller than those from China and Korea, though many have also connected to advocacy groups and become involved in online social spaces, activism, and academic scholarship.

In the United States, domestic adoptees have also campaigned for access to their original birth certificates, open adoptions, and the rights of first parents. After Donald Trump's 2016 election, horrifying images of children separated from their birth parents at the US-Mexico border spread across the media, magnifying discussions of family separations and immigrant rights. Amid the turmoil, outcries ensued as Americans sought to adopt these children, echoing US reactions to adoptions following natural disasters, like the 2010 earthquake in Haiti. Some adoptees, according to Wexler, saw their own trauma and loss mirrored within these stories.

The period proved transformative, especially for transracial and transnational adoptees, many of whom grew up in predominantly white areas, cut off from others like them. In recent years, they have become increasingly connected through private social media groups and other online spaces. "This 'new wave' of adoptee activism," Wexler wrote, "is based in a sense of universal adoptee peoplehood—that adoptees are made and not born—linking the experiences of adoptees fighting for their manifold rights across the world."

In 2019, Long was invited to represent ICAV at The Hague, for a conference on illicit practices in intercountry adoption. She was also a guest speaker in 2020 at the US Department of State for the Intercountry Adoption Symposium, and again a year later for an adoptee town hall, which invited transnational adoptees from Russia, Korea, China, India, Paraguay, Ethiopia, Peru, Iran, and other countries to share their personal experiences. "We had over a hundred intercountry adoptees join a virtual teleconference with the Department of State. And they all talked about the complexities of adoption, the ups, the downs, the good, the bad. The really hard stuff."

Long said governments, agencies, and adoptive parents must stop being blind to the problems within adoption systems "so that they don't perpetuate the same mistakes." Take care of the ones who are already adopted before bringing more in, she said. Make sure they have citizenship, mental health services, and other forms of support.

"You do get to a certain part in your journey where you've kind of reconciled the individual emotional, personal story, you've come to terms with that," Long said. "But then, because you're so awakened to the big global picture, for some people now you can't help but feel compelled to want to try and make a difference and change it."

KEELY SUBMITTED THE required paperwork on the girls' behalf. It took a month to hear back from immigration services, along with a few thousand dollars for both applications and the associated legal assistance.

Isabella had no idea if her planned trip to Nepal would happen, but she quickly realized this moment was about much more than a passport. "It made me take a step back, and say, 'Well, I feel like I'm part of this American dream. I'm here. I've been here,'" Isabella said. "It made me really think about all these people, outside of myself, who were affected by these policies."

After six months of confusion, anxiety, and waiting, Isabella and Olivia were notified that their cases had been cleared. They were among the lucky ones. Some adoptees have delayed going to college or feared even going through the process of naturalizing at all. Isabella and Olivia were required to show up at an immigration office to take the oath of citizenship on October 18, 2017.

Isabella, Olivia, Hà, and Keely gathered for the swearing-in ceremony at a crowded and chaotic US Citizenship and Immigration Services headquarters in Chicago. When they arrived, the building was filled with people from all ethnicities, ages, backgrounds. The room felt electric and eager but also on edge.

Officials took Isabella and Olivia's passports and green cards. The girls joined the group of soon-to-be citizens, away from Hà and Keely. Olivia felt a sense of worry rushing over her.

From the moment she found out she did not have US citizenship, "it was so scary," Olivia recalled. "I was freaking out, like, 'Oh my God, is ICE going to break our door and take us away?'" The thought of being separated from her family and the only life she had known terrified and upset her.

"I'm adopted from Việt Nam—isn't that enough to meet your American standards?" she said. "This family took me in. I've been here all my life. It just hit me instantly: 'Oh, I'm not from here. But I've grown up here, and I have a family here.' Again, it just points to the fact that I'm different, and the government, the policies, just make it harder to show them that we're people. We've lived here all our lives. Why can't you just see that?" Olivia continued, "I'm going through the systems that *you've* built . . . What else do you want me to do?"

At the US Citizenship and Immigration Services building, Hà and Keely watched from afar as Isabella and Olivia raised their right hands beneath an American flag and repeated the oath with the other candidates: "I hereby declare, on oath, that I absolutely and entirely renounce and abjure all allegiance and fidelity to any foreign prince, potentate, state, or sovereignty, of whom or which I have heretofore been a subject or citizen; that I will support and defend the Constitution and laws of the United States of America against all enemies, foreign and domestic; that I will bear true faith and allegiance to the same . . ."

In the aftermath of the ceremony, Olivia, Isabella, and Hà felt like the experience cemented their trinity. Drawn together by the moment, they decided to get matching triangle tattoos. They came up with the idea and drove straight to the tattoo parlor. Each triangle represented one of them, each of the nine tips representing the members of the Solimene family through which they were connected. They drove to the tattoo parlor, ODESZA lyrics blaring from the car speakers: "I'm never gonna leave your side."

"We just thought, in that moment, nothing can break us," Isabella said. "If something does happen, like if we can't be citizens for some reason, we will still be sisters at the end of this."

"It was a defining moment," said Olivia. "We were like, 'Fuck the government. We're still here, bitches.'"

THIRTY-SIX

Switched

IN ARLINGTON HEIGHTS, Hà put a tremendous amount of pressure on herself to do well academically in her new school. She watched Olivia, such a diligent student with a perfect 4.0 grade point average, come home each night and immediately do her homework for hours until it was time to go to bed. Hà tried to emulate Olivia's work ethic.

"When I first came here, I said, 'Oh my gosh, I have so much homework. It's unreal,'" Hà said. "I took seven classes. When I came home, I put my backpack down and I hit the study table. I did my homework. It took me seven hours, from 3:00 to 10:00 p.m."

For six months, she kept up that habit. Still, she failed her American literature class after her first semester. "I was so embarrassed that I failed. I got a 69," she said. "The teacher said if you get under 70, you fail the class."

So she tried even harder the next semester. She remembers reading *The Great Gatsby*, studying the book to prepare for her test, which included a written essay. "I got used to the time management, my homework. I told myself I have to work hard. And my grade went up. From 69, it went up to 96. I was so happy."

IN MAY 2018, Hà and Olivia graduated from Saint Viator High, as Isabella and the rest of the Solimenes gathered in the stands cheering. Hà beamed in her navy cap and gown. Olivia followed, smiling and waving like a celebrity. Olivia had accepted a basketball scholarship to DePauw University in Greencastle, Indiana. "I'm proud of myself," Olivia said. "I'm proud of Hà. I can't believe we made it."

Hà's senior year transcript showed As in literature and composition, computer application, geography, comparative government and politics, modern world history, biology, social studies, geometry, and environmental science classes. She only wished Tuyết and Rô could also have seen her receive her diploma at the graduation ceremony.

Hà had been offered a spot as a freshman at the University of Colorado Boulder. With her status as a college student, she could remain in the United States, though she knew she would have to return to Việt Nam once she completed her education.

And Hà would not be alone at college that fall. Isabella had also been accepted at Boulder and planned to attend with her sister.

IN FEBRUARY OF 2018, before starting her freshman year of college, Isabella traveled on her own to Nepal. She joined eleven strangers, all college age, for the three-month trip. Immediately her social anxiety and self-consciousness kicked in. She thought of all the difficult times she had in middle and high school and wasn't sure she could socialize with this entirely new group of people. She was the only person of color on the trip.

Right away in Nepal, two individuals in the class challenged Isabella's thinking. These two students held passionate beliefs about culture, gender sexuality, feminism. They told stories of struggling with their own identities and explained why they preferred gender-neutral pronouns. Isabella could relate to their experiences of feeling alienated. At the same time, she found the conversations intimidating. She didn't know if she might inadvertently offend someone because of all that she did not know and had not been exposed to.

"One of my instructors had dreads," Isabella recalled. "He's British, and he married a Nepali woman." That instructor, as Isabella learned, gave these same students a "bad vibe."

Isabella asked why.

They disapproved of his dreadlocks: "That's cultural appropriation."

Isabella had never heard the term before. The two students explained it referred to members of one culture adopting or claiming parts of someone else's culture.

Isabella had been assigned a host family in Kathmandu, Nepal's capital. Every morning she woke up, and her host mother, whom Isabella called "Mamu," blessed her and put a red tikka dot on her forehead.

"Married women get the red dot right here," Isabella later explained, as she understood it through her host mom. "And since I'm not married, I get the powder and then they pushed it up. So I wore one almost every day."

One day, one of the same students pulled Isabella aside. "You're culturally appropriating this country."

Isabella forced herself to think about this with an open mind. Her host mom had initiated the idea of the tikka for her. Isabella meant to wear it only as a sign of respect. But she also thought about how the idea related to her own Vietnamese culture. "Especially if you were raised not in the culture," Isabella said. "When I come to Việt Nam, I don't wear the áo dài. I don't wear the conical hat. But I do see non-Vietnamese people who do it here. I see Russians, for instance, that'll be drunk on a cyclo wearing a conical hat."

Isabella tried to imagine herself acting like the Russians on the cyclo or marching around proclaiming to be a champion of all things Vietnamese. "I think, in a way," she concluded, "I could culturally appropriate my own culture."

This whole discussion made Isabella recall her friendship with Mirelle, back when she was in elementary school, and how much that friendship influenced her. How much Mirelle helped her love learning about Indian culture—love that transformed into her passion for learning about the Middle East, and now Nepal. She thought about how Mirelle's family faced discrimination after 9/11 because they were

Brown. "She didn't have many friends. And now I understand why I was her only friend," Isabella said. "Because the people that I went to school with, they were not very open minded."

Yet Isabella also thought about how she had always felt drawn to Indian culture and lately Nepali culture too. She could actually speak more Nepali than Vietnamese. "Is that dissing my own culture?" She was still figuring all this out for herself.

Her experience in Nepal was incredibly challenging. In Kathmandu, she got attacked and bitten by a dog and had to get rabies shots. She recovered enough to play soccer but then sprained her ankle. She ended up staying at another host family's home in a village called Chaukati, in the plains of Nepal, about two and a half hours outside the city of Bahrabise, while the rest of the class went on a twenty-one-day trek through the Himalayan mountains without her.

The Chaukati house was made of brick on the outside and mud on the inside, with a tin roof. Isabella slept on a bed with a mat and blankets atop wooden planks. It had a small kitchen connected to the main room, but oftentimes Isabella couldn't sit inside when her host family cooked over the fire because there was no ventilation for the smoke.

When Isabella woke up in the morning, animals ran through the house. "Chickens, goats, birds, dogs, cats, and occasionally a cow would stand in the entry," she said. "I laughed because they were like my roommates."

She drew water from a big black basin with a pipe that brought in and recycled river water. "We used that water to clean dishes, wash our hands and feet, clothes, and refill the squatty potty bucket." Isabella went twelve days without a shower. Often, the electricity in the village was turned off around 7:30 p.m. "Sometimes it would come back on," Isabella said, but it was the rainy season, and "if it rained all night, it wouldn't. I had a headlight as well as a flashlight."

Isabella did a lot of thinking and journaling. She had brought only one book on the trip, given to her by Keely, *Option B: Facing Adversity,*

Building Resilience, and Finding Joy, by Sheryl Sandberg. She read it over and over again, often by flashlight: "Resilience comes from deep within us and from support outside us."

At some points, Isabella felt desperate to go home. She looked at the photos she had displayed in a glass cabinet near her bed. There was one of her and Olivia; one of her dad, mom, and Victoria; one with Will and with all the Solimene siblings. There was a photo of her standing next to Hà during one of her trips to Việt Nam. Hà wore a yellow polo-style shirt and jeans and Isabella wore a black polo-style shirt and jean shorts, holding a yellow suitcase in her left hand. Mirror images that did not match.

One day in Nepal, Isabella woke up, the animals strolling around her bed as usual, and thought of how confident she had been to explore Nepal on her own, forcing herself to talk to local shopkeepers and residents in their language, even when they laughed if she got it wrong. She realized how happy she was there, despite how much of the trip had not gone as planned. She didn't know it then, but she would come back the next year, and the year after that.

She thought of her Solimene family members on the other side of the world. Her twin, who grew up in conditions much like what she was now experiencing for the first time in Nepal, was in Illinois, probably enjoying Netflix and hot water. It felt strange to think that the environmental realities they knew as children had, briefly, switched.

BACK IN AMERICA, as roommates, the sisters sometimes shared TikTok videos with each other. In one clip, Isabella watched as a TikToker reenacted a scene on the playground. It reminded her of when she was a kid wanting to go down the slide, but some kid at the end purposely blocked the way.

Isabella showed the clip to Hà, and said: "Oh my God, this is so relatable. This happened to me all the time. It was always the same girl."

Hà watched it, confused. "What is relatable?"

"You never tried to go down the slide and some kid was blocking it?" Isabella said.

"No, we didn't have slides," Hà told her. "I would get bullied if someone took my rocks."

This only reminded Isabella of how completely different their lives were growing up and how deeply that shaped who each of them had become.

"We have some similarities," Isabella told me. "But we are so different. I mean, sometimes I forget that Hà and I are twins."

Isabella

I think about my own personal experience with environment and intelligence—it's hard because I see how Hà grew up. It's hard to even compare.

I think there is a great depth of intelligence that comes from an education, and there is also a depth of intelligence that comes from your environment. And it differs based on where you are living in the world, and what kind of education you're getting, and where you're getting that education. Let's say you have that capacity for educational intelligence, but what if you just didn't have the opportunity?

THIRTY-SEVEN

Powerful Marks

IN THE 1960S, the adoption agency Louise Wise Services in New York intentionally placed twins and a set of triplets in different homes with differing socioeconomic situations—at the request of psychologists who would conduct home visits with them for research. As captured in the 2018 film *Three Identical Strangers*, the adoptive families involved did not know that the children were triplets, much less that they had been separated. Their identities were erased and whittled down to data points, their individualities probed, their differences dissected, all in the pursuit of research.

In the decades since eugenics, Nazi twin experiments, and Louise Wise scandals, scientists engaging in adoption or twin studies have tried to distance themselves from the field's abhorrent past while still conducting experiments that they contend shed important light on human behavior and development. Nancy Segal, the Cal State Fullerton twin researcher I met, has engaged with these touchy topics for decades. Her 2021 book, *Deliberately Divided,* investigated Louise Wise and the psychiatrists Viola Bernard and Peter Neubauer, who separated the twins and triplets to track their development, including the three brothers in the documentary.

Despite this troubling history of twin science, researchers like Segal still contend that twins provide a valuable model for studying the power of nature and nurture. "You have to talk about difficult research topics or progress is never made. If you don't talk about them, then mistakes and missteps can be repeated," Segal said in one interview. "I do think these twins' stories make us more sensitive to the whole research process, what's behind it, and whether we take part in research or not. You have to put the welfare of participants ahead of your own personal research interests. What is legally within bounds is not always morally acceptable."

Identical twins (also known as monozygotic twins) come from a single egg that splits in two and shares 100 percent of the roughly twenty thousand genes that make up an individual. Fraternal twins (also known as dizygotic twins) come from two different eggs and share around 50 percent of their genes. They are about as genetically similar as biological siblings who are not multiples.

Segal contends that twins who are reared apart continue to be particularly relevant case studies. Since 1922, there have been at least 1,894 cases of sets of twins reared apart. Today, there are more documented cases of twins separated at birth and later reunited than ever before, largely because the internet has helped connect them.

By comparing how closely identical and fraternal twins resemble each other in traits, researchers try to parse out just how many traits—physical, intellectual, and behavioral—may be due to genes. Their findings rely on correlations. If identical twins tend to share more similar IQ scores than fraternal twins or more similar scores than nonbiological siblings who share family, educational values, and practices, this suggests to many scientists that genes influence intelligence.

Twin and adoption studies have long given fuel to scientists who posit genes have a guiding hand in nearly every aspect of our lives. These conclusions cast doubt on our notions of just how much control we think we harbor over our personal choices, like who we marry, or whether we divorce, or our political or religious inclinations. Criminal behavior, smoking, anorexia, and drug addiction, according to scientists drawing from decades of twin studies, all have genetic underpinnings.

But genes alone have never been sufficient in explaining the whole story.

ENVIRONMENT, SCIENTISTS ACKNOWLEDGE, remains a wild card. Twins may share many environments—a room, a religion, a family. But for today's twin researchers, understanding "non-shared environments" matters. In life, a non-shared environment "could be a college course. A great teacher. A trauma," Segal said. "Say one twin took an exotic trip around the world, or one twin had a terrible disease, or won the lottery, or had an accident. It's those unshared experiences that affect behavior."

Non-shared experiences can also exist in the womb, as with slight differences in placenta size, umbilical cords, or fetus positioning. Some studies of twin newborns have shown that intrauterine and postnatal environments also lead to differences in gene expression, and some of these divergent patterns are detectable at birth.

My own identical twin boys always seemed to want to push each other away in the womb, constantly angling, elbowing, kicking, and shifting around, searching for more comfort in such a crowded space. One was born with a strawberry-shaped birthmark on his left ankle. The other, a thick birthmark resembling an em dash on the back of his right thigh. When they were babies, one had a hair whorl that swooped to the right. The other's swooped left. Without those defining markers—for the first six months of their lives especially—my husband and I might have mixed them up and never straightened out the mistake.

In utero, they shared a placenta (but not umbilical cords). In life, they've shared bottles, beds, diets, babysitters, common colds. Now preschoolers, it is no longer hard for us to tell our sons apart. There are subtle physical differences that those in our household can clearly see, but others cannot. Personality differences prove their not-sameness even more.

As a toddler, one was adventurous, daring—the first to nosedive off a sofa, the first to fall down a set of stairs. He also crawled, stood, cruised, and walked first. He hollered and cried when we left the room.

Our other boy has always been a keen observer. He could be laser focused, able to spend thirty minutes trying to click together a buckle as his brother marched around with chest puffed, in need of constant movement and entertainment.

As preschoolers, one brother is all heart and emotion, quick to cuddle, and also to raise a fist. The other is sparing with his affection, and his rage. The one who loved buckles now shows a keen interest in reading. The other would quickly put down a book to instead jump off a bunk bed. They wrestle, bicker, and endlessly play together. They annoy each other but always find their way back to each other. When I enrolled them in day care, a teacher told me how one refused to nap, pacing around the room as the other kids dozed off, finally finding his way to his brother's side and snuggling up next to him, a comforting mechanism to fall asleep.

I long wondered: What was going on inside my body, and in their shared environment, that may have influenced their different personalities in their first year of life? I now know that two identical strands of DNA can begin turning into two unique strands in the womb.

Researchers now understand that some differences in identical twins can also be traced to how each sibling's genes are expressed (or turned on and off), and it involves considering the environment and its impact on the genes themselves. A lifetime of experiences and habits, like exercise, sleep, trauma, stress, disease, and diet, have all shown effects on these marks, which can impact how genes awaken or go silent.

These microscopic genetic variations—known as epigenetic marks, or chemical groups that attach to DNA molecules but do not alter the gene sequence—can lead to radical differences in a person's health, personality, or appearance, even in twins with the same DNA. Whether a gene is active or not can depend on chemical compounds that click onto the DNA structure, toggling the gene's on-off switch (think of it as a biological lock and key). They can be clicked into place, and they can also be undone.

For twins raised together in similar settings who share the same genetic profiles, it isn't surprising that one's illness could befall the other, like identical twin girls both diagnosed with a rare leukemia at three months old, or identical twin brothers who received ALS (amyotrophic lateral sclerosis) diagnoses within weeks of each other, or the tragic story of identical teen boys who developed a deadly form of liver cirrhosis (one survived and his twin did not).

In 2020, Cynthia and Michelle Racanati contracted COVID-19 at the same time. The identical twin sisters lived together and worked as medical assistants at the same Iowa hospital. Cynthia's symptoms were mild. But Michelle was put on a ventilator. She did not survive.

In late 2021, Hà received a positive COVID-19 test. At the time, she and Isabella shared a bedroom and hung out together regularly before the diagnosis. Hà quarantined after the results, and Isabella did not test positive.

By comparing differing gene expressions in identical twins, researchers are beginning to better understand a variety of conditions. Rare pairs have "discordant" diagnoses (in which one has a disease, but the other does not), and this may help physicians determine risk factors and possible hyper-targeted treatments for diabetes, autism, schizophrenia, cerebral palsy, thyroid disease, cancer, ALS, and now COVID-19. Today, it is widely accepted that there is a genetic and epigenetic component to all human disease and disorders.

But scientists also now understand that genes and environment are not mutually exclusive. Wiring alone is an insufficient explanation, and there is so much they still do not know and cannot explain. What they can finally agree upon is this: "Nature and nurture work in concert," as Segal explained it, "affecting every measurable human trait."

THIRTY-EIGHT

Similar Scars

"WHAT IF ONE day you woke up and found out you had a twin?" asked Robin Roberts of *Good Morning America* one morning in 2017. Keely, like millions of viewers, would tune into the clip, which was shared widely online. The Sister Sledge song "We Are Family" played in the studio as Roberts set up the story: "Two ten-year-old girls got the surprise of a lifetime when they discovered they had a twin living across the country."

Roberts was referring to a pair of identical twins separated at birth, Audrey Doering and Gracie Rainsberry. These girls had been born in China; Audrey was adopted by a Wisconsin family, and Gracie by a family in Washington State, when they were a year old. Audrey's mother had recently discovered that her daughter had a twin after coming across a photo of the two young sisters together as toddlers, sitting together on a woman's lap and wearing matching outfits. She tracked down Gracie's adoptive family through Facebook not long after.

"Now they are about to meet in person for the first time," Roberts said as the audience applauded. Keely, at home in Illinois, watched the screen with anticipation. The camera flashed to side-by-side stills of Audrey in a Green Bay Packers T-shirt and Gracie in a blue Nike jersey, then to the live footage of both girls in separate wings of the ABC studios waving to the camera with their adoptive families behind them. Audrey and Gracie had talked beforehand on FaceTime and planned to dress alike—rose-colored tunics, black leggings, and black boots—for their first nonvirtual encounter.

The first twin came on stage to greet Roberts.

"Audrey, are you ready? You want to do this?" Roberts said. "Stand right here."

The studio fell quiet as Roberts darted out of the frame and left Audrey alone, a tiny child trembling on a national stage, smoothing her hair and adjusting her glasses nervously. "All right, Gracie. Come on out and meet your sister."

The door slid open and there was Gracie. Both hugged quickly, then pulled back, shaking as they simultaneously wiped tears from beneath black-rimmed glasses.

"I can't tell who is who now," said cohost Michael Strahan, adding that he was a father of twin girls himself.

Roberts turned to the professor sitting in the audience. It was twin researcher Nancy Segal, who had a front-row seat. She had worked with the pair in her research and helped coordinate the live reunion with GMA producers.

"This is a lot. This is an adjustment," Roberts said to Segal. "You were okay with them coming on TV and doing it like this?" It was as if she was anticipating disapproval that she would receive from viewers. More than thirty thousand commenters would post responses to the video on YouTube. Many wrote tearful and gushing responses, like "The adoptive parents are so amazing. Love is so amazing."

Others commented on their apparent similarities assessed over just a few minutes of watching: "They both wear glasses. Both say [the] word 'overwhelming.' Both cry the same way hands over face exactly the same and even sit the same way. Wow."

But others expressed outrage over the reunion: "While I'm glad the parents have reconnected these girls, it's disturbing that these young girls are paraded around in front of a camera for what is a complex and should be private moment," wrote one.

"This should NEVER have been done on live television," another posted. "Those girls are too young."

In the studio, Roberts told the audience, "We want to make everybody sure that this was okay."

Segal, wearing a blazer the same color as the twins' tunics, added, "The twin relationship, the twin bond, is a very strong one. So I think it was very important that these girls meet at this particular time when they have their whole lives ahead of them."

She then revealed the results of their DNA test, which she had also facilitated, proving they were identical. The audience cheered. Segal smiled.

In February 2017, Keely watched Segal on a different television segment, this one from CBS News. It featured three pairs of identical twins born in China, separated at birth, and raised by adoptive families. At the time, they were among eighteen twin sets born in China participating in Segal's study. "What we find with twins raised apart is they are as alike in personality as twins raised together," Segal told Erin Moriarty of *48 Hours*.

Keely looked for Segal's contact information. She sent the professor an introductory email. Keely wanted to tell her about Isabella and Hà.

AFTER KEELY REACHED out to Segal, the professor recommended a testing clinic, where Hà and Isabella could send in their DNA samples. The researcher called them personally to reveal the news: indeed, they were identical.

It wasn't a surprise, but it was affirming. Isabella and Hà agreed to more tests—intellectual and physical comparisons, interviews about their memories of growing up. They talked of how they had both endured injuries in similar places, at the same ages. For Isabella, it was in 2011, when she tore the labrum in her right shoulder during a soccer game. Hà also injured her right shoulder in 2011 in Việt Nam. "I just remember that I fell. It was so embarrassing. I went up into the hills, because we have a lot of rocks," Hà said. "My family said, 'You cannot run.' But I just ran up there and fell in the hills."

Hà had to go to the hospital, where a doctor said her shoulder was fractured. She still has a scar from the fall. "It's just a coincidence," Hà told me over lunch at a Vietnamese restaurant in Illinois one afternoon.

"It would be a stretch to say it's a twin thing," Isabella added, sitting next to Hà.

At one point, though, the girls did their own comparison of marks on their skin.

"We have similar scars in similar places," Isabella said. "Different little nicks and moles all over our bodies."

Isabella wears glasses every day; she's nearsighted. Hà has experienced eye problems, too, but did not go to an eye doctor in Việt Nam until 2013.

"For an entire year, I was trying to look at the board in class and I could not see. I could not write down the notes," Hà said. She did get glasses but stopped wearing them. She explained that Tuyết always thought that wearing glasses made your eyes get bigger, so Hà went to a doctor and got medicine. She rubbed it on her eyes every day for three months.

"Then I had to put hot water on my hands and rub with my eyes," Hà said. "I kept taking the medicine every night before I went to bed. I was able to fix my eyes, because in Việt Nam we have different kinds of medicine."

"Herbal?" asked Isabella.

"Yeah, different ideas of treatment."

"In Việt Nam, when I get a stomachache, my mom just goes out and gets some ginger roots. If she doesn't have ginger leaves, she gets mint. Then she just puts it in fire and lets it get hot. Then she puts it on my stomach, and I don't get sick again."

You don't have to be a scientist to know that growing up in such contrasting environments inevitably affects how Isabella and Hà interpret and experience the world. Hà loves phở. It took Isabella a while to develop a taste for it. Hà plays volleyball but, unlike Isabella, has never been a soccer buff. Both are impatient, nurturing, and kind to a fault. Both grew up biting their nails. Both were social loners until they came to know each other; they don't need a lot of friends but cherish the special ones they have.

Both also know that despite sharing the same genes, they are not at all the same.

Hà

The idea of fate, to me, is very blurry. With Isabella and I, Liên brought two of us to the orphanage, but then I was so sick and I had to come home. But Isabella stayed. Is that fate?

To think that fate could have separated us, and then made us go through what we went through, only then to reunite. That's a beautiful story to think about it, that it was always meant to be, because of fate.

But I truly believe that we have the power in our hands to change everything. Not the past. But the present and the future. We have the power to make things happen. And that's why I don't let fate decide what I do. I don't just say, "Whatever will be will be."

The whole thing about us meeting, and how I came here, I think that it has a lot to do with choices. In our story, destiny played a really big role. Obviously, Keely had to find me. She made choices for Isabella and I to reunite.

I also made choices to come to the United States. I've had to work hard so that I could be here.

So it's a little bit of both. Fate and free will. A little bit of both.

THIRTY-NINE

Unspoken

PROFESSOR SEGAL WOULD eventually release a study in the *Journal of Experimental Child Psychology* that incorporated some of the data drawn from intelligence tests on Isabella and Hà, as well as other twin pairs that were raised apart.

Additional tests on personality and behavior had not yet been processed and examined due to COVID-19 and other delays, but for the IQ study, Segal and her colleagues examined fifteen identical (monozygotic) and seven fraternal (dizygotic) twin pairs from countries around the world who had been separated at birth. Segal compared the findings with data from her previous studies on Chinese twins adopted together and virtual twins (nonbiological siblings who are close in age and raised in the same household).

The IQ scores of virtual twins, who share no DNA, turned out to be the least alike. "I found that the similarities in IQ, of course, were the highest in the twins raised together," Segal told me. "There were significant differences in the twins raised apart." But many of the participants, she added, were young kids. "I suspect that as they get older, their IQ scores will converge." She based this hypothesis on previous studies that have shown that twins raised together, identical and fraternal, tend to have increasingly similar intelligence scores as they are tracked year by year, finally stabilizing at a similar score into adulthood.

"The logical idea is that we become less like our twin over time, because of environmental effects," Segal said. "But in fact, you may become more alike." You might think of it as becoming more like yourself, she told me. "It's kind of counterintuitive. But that's what the data show."

Hà and Isabella scored ten points apart on the intelligence tests, which Segal said was a slightly wide gap for identical twins, reared together or apart. She attributed that to their different educational settings growing up. She hopes this will be the first in a series of tests comparing some of the same sets of reared-apart, reared-together, and nonbiological same-age adopted pairs over time.

IQ tests, however, are imperfect measures, with cultural bias toward the environments in which they were developed—specifically white, Western societies. In 1984, James Flynn, an intelligence researcher, showed how American IQs had been rising at a rate of about three points a decade, which indicated that environment mattered to test results. Over the years, studies have shown that IQ scores can change dramatically with shifts in family, work, parenting, and schooling. Other critics point out that it is impossible to control for environmental effects on intelligence in IQ comparison tests. Genes have an impact, but intelligence is not a fixed trait.

Environmental variables are influenced by more variables. Genes interact with other genes, which also mingle with their environments. Biological and behavioral patterns upon infinitesimal patterns. Not to mention the unpredictable and undeniable role of chance.

Spontaneous, unpredictable variations can also occur among all cells, and all people, including between monozygotic twins. New research shows that identical twins do not share exactly the same (roughly estimated) twenty thousand genes after all. Mutations occur as early as the embryo formation stage, and these gene variations can look different for each twin in a pair. Even at birth, identical twins have begun to develop distinctness due to epigenetic marks, shifts, and chance.

Segal once described identical twins to me as "variations on the same theme," which made me think about how literary interpretations can be so contrasting depending on the reader's life experiences and influences. A few sentences can never sum it all up. Just as genes won't either. Sometimes it can feel bewildering to try to wrap our minds around multiple truths at once, to embrace that we are a product of our biological makeup but also may have wiggle room to alter parts of ourselves. To accept that fate and free will are not incongruent. Or that you can have a good life, a blessed life, which is at the same time a traumatic and painfully difficult one.

Separated at birth and leading diametrically different lives, Isabella and Hà took years to finally feel a twin bond. Each grew up feeling alienated from their peers, only to find one of the most profound connections of their lives in each other. There may be a genetic attraction, a feeling of familiarity. But their bond also took deliberate, intentional work. Hà learned a new language, a new culture. Isabella learned to let a stranger in.

"We think we know who we are," wrote the journalist Lawrence Wright in his 1997 book on twins. "We become the people we choose to be; this is the premise of free will." Suppose, then, we meet our "doppelganger," who is fundamentally similar to ourselves despite living a different life with different experiences?

"Isn't there a sense of loss?" he wrote. "A loss not only of identity but of purpose?"

With Isabella, Hà, and Olivia, it is impossible to disentangle how fate intertwined within millions of choices and chances. All their mothers, whether biological or adoptive, made life-altering decisions about their daughters. To relinquish rights to a child. To take in a child. Decisions influenced by social inequalities, individual assumptions, and love. Choices that, as little girls, the sisters themselves had no say in. In their lives, chance and circumstance found entry points within a genetic pattern. Human choice slipped in to make its powerful mark.

Throughout her life, Hà did not forget the monks who told her, *You created good karma for yourself when you were a monk, but you did not get to use it, because you passed away so young. So, in this life, you will be able to use those blessings.*

ONE NIGHT IN 2017, together in their bedroom, Isabella told Hà about how she had been bullied. How hard it all was for her. Before that, Hà had always thought her sister had a perfect life in America. "But I was wrong," Hà said. "She opened her heart to me that night. And I opened my heart to her. It hurt me so much to hear about what she had been through. I told her about how hard it was for me in school in Việt Nam and about how I was bullied too. We stayed up all night long talking."

That conversation, Hà said, changed everything. "It saved our relationship. I have never had a best friend before. I always wondered what it is like to have a best friend. Isabella and I stay up late, cracking each other up until one in the morning. I love being around Isabella. We are more than best friends."

For Isabella, she did not know that Hà, at this point in their lives, would become a person she deeply needed. "I've had many moments since Hà has been here, where I'll be really upset and I don't tell her why," Isabella told me. "She can just sense that I'm not doing well. Or that I'm going through something."

Hà will say to Isabella: "Hey, I know you haven't told me much. But I know what you're going through. I can see it. I can feel it. I'm here for you."

For Isabella, her twin sister's compassion and understanding has lifted her up. For most of her life, she struggled to express her emotions. Her parents told her she never cried as a kid. She never caused trouble. She was stoic. Olivia was always there for her, but she was also going through so many complicated and confusing experiences of her own. Rather than discuss any of it, they both endured to survive.

"Hà has helped me a lot in my life to be a little bit more emotionally present," Isabella said. "She has allowed me to grow in an environment that is a safe space. I have always felt like she's had my back. She has never picked on me or pointed out certain things about me that I feel really vulnerable about in the different spaces, like how sometimes I feel unsafe to express different emotions. She has always understood that."

It is hard for Isabella to express her love for people. "I don't really say it out loud," she explained. "But Hà and I have this special relationship. Our love has definitely developed, and I don't tell her all the time. We don't talk about it all the time. But it is in our heads and hearts. I know it. I feel it."

Isabella

From the beginning, even when we were just little babies growing in the womb, I think we were always meant to be together. Siblings are meant to be together. That is your connection to your past life as well, and connection to your ancestral history.

So I think, from the very, very beginning, we were always meant to be together in life as siblings, as sisters. We were always predestined to be together.

But the little stuff, and the big stuff that happened in between, I don't think that was fate.

I think that all came down to decisions, and how our environment played out, and the people in our lives, who all made certain choices.

FORTY

Grandma

IN 2017, ISABELLA returned to Việt Nam with Hà, who by now had been living in the United States for a year. They were going with Keely to renew Hà's visa. In Illinois, Isabella had often felt frustrated that Hà was so dependent on her for daily tasks. But in Việt Nam, their roles reversed, something Isabella was aware of the moment she stepped off the plane. "It actually just lifted the responsibility off my shoulders," she said. "Everything was out of my control."

Hà scheduled the bus from the airport to the hotel, took them to the market, called the cabs. She translated for them everywhere they went, explaining Vietnamese customs. "It's fun to let her have that control," Isabella said, "because she doesn't have that in Illinois. But I'm totally dependent on her when I'm in Việt Nam."

One night, Hà pulled up on a motorbike to meet Isabella at the hotel. She told Isabella to hop on the back. Hà was going to give her a tour of the city. It was exhilarating for Isabella, cruising down the bumpy roads at 30 mph, zipping through neighborhoods and city streets. Hà drove Isabella down a dirt road that went straight through someone's home as a family ate their dinner. "The road literally was in the middle of their living room," Isabella said. Hà later told her that she had heard their father had once lived in that home.

The twins rode around Nha Trang late into the night, their long hair blowing from beneath helmets, Isabella holding on to Hà's waist, thinking about how far they had come since that reunion day in the airport when they were thirteen. They cruised across the giant Trần Phú bridge in Nha Trang. The city sparkled. On the bridge, they stopped and stared at the view, standing under the radiant moon, breathing in this place where eighteen years ago they had been pulled apart from each other. "It was," Isabella said, "one of the best times of my entire life."

Hà also took Isabella to meet their eighty-one-year-old grandmother, Nguyễn Thị Thanh, for the first time. As they rolled up to the home in Nha Trang, Isabella was surprised to see that Thanh's legs were thin as walking sticks, her left foot missing a toe. Thanh had lost her ability to walk a long time ago, and she had no wheelchair. Instead, she picked up each leg with both hands, adjusting her position before dragging herself along the floor with her arms, all the way onto the porch to greet them.

ISABELLA AND HÀ again returned to Việt Nam in 2018, when they were nineteen. This time, they allowed me to accompany them on the ten-day trip, along with their other Solimene family members. The sisters invited me with them one evening as they paid another visit to their grandmother. We rode in a cab, with Rô in the front seat, the moon half-shrouded by clouds. It looked like a birthmark in the sky, uneven and golden hued, a fuzzy crescent with its edges reaching upward. "There it is," Hà said that evening, staring at her old friend.

She had seen the moon now from different angles, countries, time zones. She had come to know that the moon itself is always the same, not the source of light it seems to be, but a reflection of it. Some see it as pure white. Others see it speckled in black. There are days when it seems to glisten gold. But in reality, it is gray. Full, crescent, waning. It can be all this at once, because everyone sees the same phases of the moon; it just looks different depending on where you are standing, depending on which angle you view it from.

The cab stopped in an alley. There were no streetlights, but the family home where their grandmother lived with relatives was illuminated by a large television playing in the living room. Rô led the girls down a long hallway into a humid kitchen where incense burned. There on the floor, next to the stove, lay Thanh on a straw mat.

Hà hugged their grandmother, leaning in close to her ear to say hello, since she had trouble hearing. Thanh looked at her with brown eyes that seemed layered in a film of bluish violet. At first, the woman seemed confused when she saw Isabella, who wore a navy USA T-shirt and denim cutoffs. Then she understood. It was the twins. She reached for Isabella and hugged her too.

This spot in the kitchen where Thanh slept day and night, she explained, was the same spot where one of her sons had died. She had stayed with him through his last breaths. And now as she lay here, Thanh said, she felt close to him still. It was hard for her to talk much more. Her voice came out as throaty rattle. The girls sat silently with her instead. They rubbed her legs, Hà on one side, Isabella on the other.

I watched as their grandmother took Hà's right hand into her palms and pulled it to her lips, kissing her fingers. Then she reached over and grabbed Isabella's right hand, kissing it and pressing it to her check. It was clearly painful for their grandmother to sit upright, so the girls adjusted her pillows, alternating a turquoise one and a purple one beneath her neck to prop her head up. They took turns cradling her head in their laps, stroking her hair. She breathed heavily, looked up at the ceiling, then closed her eyes.

Everyone sat in silence. Isabella and Hà stayed like this, comforting their grandmother for a long time until they realized how late it was. They had to go.

"Don't cry, Grandma," Hà told her.

"Okay," she said. "I will not cry."

Thanh squeezed both girls' hands. She made them promise to come back.

We climbed back into the cab, still parked outside.

"Hà," Isabella said as it drove off, "am I going to be able to see her again? Or is this it?"

Isabella would be leaving Việt Nam tomorrow, but Hà would stay longer to visit with Rô and Tuyết before returning to Illinois for college. No one knew that a worldwide pandemic would eventually interrupt any hopes they may have had to travel overseas again in the coming years.

In that moment, Hà didn't have an answer.

Olivia

People don't understand the position I'm in and what goes on in my mind. I'm not a bad person for not wanting to see the people that gave me up.

There are moments when I'm in bed, and I look through pictures and I think, Maybe I do want to go back; or maybe I want to go back, but not see my birth family. Like I want to go back and experience a culture that I was born in. I want to learn more about the country or about the culture.

I wish I wasn't exposed at such a young age. I wish that I decided on my own terms about when I wanted to go back to Việt Nam or when I wanted to meet my birth family. Here I am, being woken up in the middle of the night, and you can't really say no to that when they're already on the phone. Obviously, I can't change the past. And I'm feeling it right now in the present, and I don't know where I'm going to be in the future.

I feel like in the past, at such a young age, I was pressured to feel some sort of way. And that took its toll on me. Now I'm realizing, "Hey, this is the truth I want to live in. And this is my truth. I'm trying to be as honest as I can be."

FORTY-ONE

Where It Feels Safe

BEFORE WE LEFT Việt Nam in 2018, the Solimenes rented a van to visit Olivia's birth family. Olivia woke up feeling anxious, her right leg shaking like it does before a big basketball game. On the hour-long van ride, Olivia stayed mostly quiet in her seat, wearing a red shirt that looked like it had a Patagonia logo on it but read SAIGONIA. She listened to Maroon 5 in her earbuds.

As the van pulled up to the village of Xã Vạn Thắng, Olivia immediately spotted her mom wearing a green plaid shirt and leopard-print brown leggings; next to her was Olivia's aunt, who wore an orange face mask and straw sun hat. It was obvious the women were sisters, and although both were shorter than Olivia, they also resembled her.

"Oh God," Olivia mumbled. Her nerves were going crazy now. She stepped out of the van and put her best game face on. She smiled. A little boy, Olivia's brother, jumped up and down with excitement, waving his arms. Her birth mom ran to her and hugged her, holding Olivia's arms and taking her hand, guiding her to their home as she wiped her eyes.

A little girl in a red and white Minnie Mouse–style dress darted up to her and grabbed her hand, along with two boys. Olivia recognized the children, her biological siblings.

"Như did not come back for so long," said one of Olivia's aunts through an interpreter.

Her aunt explained that Olivia's mother had eight children. That came as a surprise to Olivia, who thought there were only six.

"Where are the two we've never heard of?" Olivia asked.

"An orphanage."

"Why are they giving them . . ." Olivia stuttered, upset. "Why are they giving us up?"

"She was suffering," the translator said. "She could not keep them."

Her aunt reminded the visitors of how Olivia's grandmother "had been waiting until the day she died to see her again." Olivia's aunt explained that her grandmother passed away because of a traffic accident while riding a motorbike.

Olivia listened, straight-faced. Each visit brought new, harder-to-process information.

In that moment, Keely again remembered the letter she received from Nguyễn Thị Mùa.

In some days in the future, can all your family come back Việt Nam to visit the old place? And we meet together?

Two days earlier on this trip, Keely had learned a devastating new piece of the story: Olivia's grandmother never received the letter that Keely had taken three years to send.

While visiting Liên's house with Isabella and Hà the day before, Keely found out her letter somehow ended up in the wrong home—Liên and Quý's home. Liên had pulled the letter addressed to Olivia's grandmother out of a stack of photos. Keely shrieked when she saw it, recognizing the words she wrote: *When she was little she loved balloons, bubble gum and bows in her hair. She loved to blow bubbles and chase them around outside in the backyard.*

It had been given mistakenly to Liên, probably via one of the adoption facilitators.

Keely realized Olivia's grandmother died not only without ever seeing her granddaughter again but also without ever reading the letter.

"I am so sorry," Keely said to Olivia's aunt, her eyes welling up. She asked the interpreter to please relay this: "I am so sad that happened."

They went inside and Olivia's aunt explained that her mother gave birth to her on the bedroom floor. A midwife, along with one of her birth mom's sisters, remained by her side for the two-hour birth.

Olivia looked at her birth mother, who seemed to be trying to read lips in both Vietnamese and, impossibly, English. Olivia stepped closer, nervously, and wrapped her arms around her birth mom. They embraced briefly, smiling the same way, with lips tightly pursed.

Keely said softly to Olivia: "She loves you, honey."

Again, they asked her to spend the night. Again, Olivia declined.

The next day, Olivia told me about saying goodbye: "Seeing my older sister cry. It was too sad," she said. "I looked at my sister, and I'm like 'Oh my God.' Driving away, I'm thinking, 'This is why I don't like to come back.'"

After returning from Việt Nam, Olivia told me she remembered when she was in middle school how Keely would play audio recordings of Vietnamese language lessons while they rode together in the car. She was trying to help Isabella and her learn how to speak the language. "It was very hard," Olivia said. "I couldn't do it." Learning Vietnamese made Olivia question what it was all for. Most of her life, no matter what was going on in the world outside or who else wanted to be a part of hers, Olivia had always felt safest at home.

Olivia thought of how when she was younger she sometimes felt panicked when riding in cars. Her heart raced, and her breathing felt labored. Her mom would grab her hand and squeeze. She calmed Olivia, telling her to look out the window and "breathe in and out."

Five years after her sudden iPad reunion, the very idea of continuing to return to Việt Nam, of interacting with her family there, of weaving in other relatives and another mother, threw Olivia's sense of security into a tailspin. She would eventually suspend her Facebook account, partly so she would not be expected to communicate with her family in Việt Nam.

"My birth mother wants to hold on to me, but I want to hold on to my mom, Keely," Olivia said. "It's already hard, and I have one family. I can't handle two."

FORTY-TWO

Climb Out

IN THE LATE summer of 2018, Isabella and Hà flew to Colorado to begin the school year at the University of Colorado, Boulder. Isabella had been assigned to a dorm, and Hà would live in a shared apartment with three other freshmen, a twenty-minute walk from Isabella's. Hà chose psychology as her major; Isabella, international studies.

Keely accompanied them around the campus and town before classes started, staying for five days as they got settled. She took them shopping at Target for home decor and school supplies and attended a campus orientation for parents.

They strolled the streets of Boulder, ate at restaurants, visited art shops, and came across a Nepali store filled with Buddha statues and tapestries. Keely bought a rose-colored tapestry for Hà to hang on her wall. Isabella had brought along a world map for her dorm room, as well as prayer flags she'd brought back from Nepal.

Every evening, there was a long lineup of student festivities, then fraternity parties and pregame parties, before students headed to bars. Her dormmates told Isabella about the various events, offering to get Isabella into a bar, even though she wasn't twenty-one. Isabella declined.

"A lot of people had warned us," Isabella said. "It's a big party school."

Isabella spent that first week trying to picture herself on this campus for the next four years in the middle of the intense social scene. "I'm sure there are people at Boulder that go there and nail their heads in books, and they're fine," Isabella said. It wasn't that she didn't want to socialize; it just depended on how well she clicked with the people she met. She was still working through her social anxieties and didn't always feel at ease or even safe around new people. So far, she did not feel comfortable in Boulder, even with Hà by her side. She passed on opportunities to go to most of the social events, staying back with her mom and Hà instead.

"We're so boring," Isabella said.

Hà didn't feel right in Boulder either. She didn't care for the fraternity or bar scene but told herself she could handle this campus life, after all the different schools she had already experienced. "I felt scared for myself. But I didn't say anything to Isabella. I thought maybe Isabella didn't have the same feelings as me."

Keely left campus to board her flight back to Illinois on a Wednesday evening; Isabella and Hà were set to start classes the following Monday. After Keely left, Isabella and Hà made pasta with vegetables at Hà's apartment. Isabella stretched out on Hà's bed. There were more parties happening that night. Neither of them wanted to go.

Although Isabella and Hà had both decided on Boulder, they had also been accepted to another campus, Lake Forest College, a private liberal arts institution in Illinois, thirty miles north of Chicago. Sixty-two percent of the classes at Lake Forest had fewer than twenty students. And the kicker: Lake Forest had also offered both girls partial scholarships. But they had selected Boulder instead because it seemed like it might give more of that traditional big-college life experience. Keely and Mick would cover both of their Boulder college costs.

Now, it felt like they may have made the wrong choice. That some of their classes could have up to one hundred students seemed more intimidating now that they were actually here.

Isabella sat with her laptop while Hà was cooking in the kitchen. She found herself on the Lake Forest college website, checking its calendar. Lake Forest classes had not yet started. *We still have time.*

"Why are you looking at the Lake Forest calendar?" Hà said, walking back into the room holding a bowl of pasta.

"You're gonna kill me when I say this, but I don't think I want to go here. I want to go home. I want to go to Lake Forest."

Hà looked at her sister with relief. "Me too."

Isabella was surprised, though not completely.

But how were they going to tell Keely and Mick? And how were they going to get back to Illinois?

Keely texted them from the airport. Her flight was delayed.

The girls walked outside and took their shoes off, wading in a creek behind the apartment as the sun set.

They had to tell her.

"What should we say?"

"You should say it."

"No, you should say it."

Isabella dialed her number. It rang twice. She hung up.

They finally got ahold of her as she was boarding. "We don't want to be here. We changed our minds."

"What's wrong?"

They told her the school didn't feel like it was the right fit.

Her flight was taking off. Keely said they would talk more when she landed.

Isabella sent an email to Lake Forest admissions, asking if their college acceptances and scholarships were still available. They waited to hear back.

By the next afternoon, a reply came: "Your scholarships are still valid."

Isabella and Hà looked at each other. "Okay. Go, go, go!"

They had to withdraw from Boulder. They had to pack all their stuff. They would rent a Suburban and drive to Illinois, make it back in time to enroll in classes at Lake Forest, and do all this on their own, before Keely and Mick even fully realized what was happening.

The girls loaded everything they could into the Suburban in the middle of the night. "All of our clothes, bags, backpacks, shoes, everything we had sent there," Isabella said. "Bedding, pillows, down comforters, a tall lamp."

Isabella's roommate was out. She had texted Isabella, "I'm at the Sigma Chi party. Come to the party!"

"I was like 'peace out,'" Isabella said. "'I'm leaving.'"

The girls left town before their roommates woke up.

Isabella drove seventeen hours straight, since Hà did not have her license.

They turned up the music to stay awake: Hindi songs, Vietnamese songs, YouTube artists, EDM, country, pop.

They listened to *The Greatest Showman* soundtrack. Hà fell asleep. Isabella switched the music. "The Fighter," by Keith Urban, played several times.

They made it to Iowa. "Conrad," by Ben Howard started. The lyrics beckoned them to climb out: "Out to where you see, curl of the world."

In a few weeks, they would begin their freshmen year at Lake Forest College. Hà knew that her visa was still set to expire when her education in the United States came to an end. She hoped to attend graduate school but knew that returning to Việt Nam to live and work one day was on the horizon. Isabella still yearned to live in the Middle East or to return to Nepal. They would not always be by each other's side.

But for now, on this empty road to Illinois, they crossed state lines together. The sun set and the moon brightened, and the sisters moved forward in tandem.

EPILOGUE

IN THE FALL of 2018, Olivia enrolled in DePauw University in Indiana to play on the basketball team and major in economics. But after her first year at DePauw, she transferred to DePaul University in Chicago. Olivia decided that playing basketball while balancing an intense college class load was too much for her. She also wanted to be in her home state of Illinois, close to the Solimenes, studying without a commitment to a sports team.

"Are you sure?" Keely and Mick asked.

"I want to do this," Olivia told her parents, standing her ground.

They supported her.

At DePaul, Olivia met and fell in love with a fellow student, who would become her long-term girlfriend. Olivia's partner came along with her to family birthdays and dinners and regularly hung around with her the house.

"She's part of the family," Keely told Olivia one day. "I love her as my own."

These words deeply resonated with her. Olivia felt seen.

"In terms of my sexuality, one hundred percent I feel confident in who I am," Olivia said. "I feel like I can be open." Coming into her own Asian American racial identity has been harder. Olivia has started connecting to transnational adoptee groups to have more of these conversations with people who may be able to relate.

Hà and Isabella began classes at Lake Forest College together. Hà majored in sociology and anthropology. Isabella majored in international relations and Islamic world studies, with a focus on Arabic. Midway into their college careers, COVID-19 shut down the world. Keely and Mick had sold their home, thinking they would have an empty nest, and moved into an upscale apartment in the city. Hà, Isabella, and Olivia all ended up in that apartment, too, taking classes online.

During a class taken during the height of the US presidential elections, the professor called on Isabella: "What do you think about the rhetoric behind Donald Trump calling it the China virus?"

I don't know, Isabella thought. *Don't ask me, ask the white kid.*

Then another student came on screen and said, "What? It came from China."

Isabella sighed.

A few months later, Isabella and Hà took a stroll together in downtown Chicago, when an angry, belligerent man began yelling at them both: "China, China, China, Chinese, Chinese. Kung fu, kung fu, coronavirus." Followed by more racist slurs. "Hà has never really had that happen to her in America," Isabella said. "It was really scary."

Isabella told her sister, "Ignore him as much as you can. Walk away from him."

She felt helpless in that moment. "It really took me back to high school when people would say things to me. And I would just freeze like, 'What do I do? How do I act?' I've always asked myself, 'Why didn't I just say something?'"

On the street that day, Isabella could sense Hà's fear and she felt an urge to protect and stand up for her sister. *Should I say something to him?* Isabella turned around and noticed the man was white and using a walker. She realized he was following them.

"I can just take him out if you need me to," Isabella told Hà. She was willing and ready to fight this man if she had to.

"I felt so much rage that I haven't felt in so long," Isabella later told me. "I also felt this great sense of responsibility to walk Hà through what had just happened. She was so traumatized by it. And so was I."

There were bystanders around them. But they didn't say or do anything. Isabella wanted to teach Hà. To guide and protect her in this painful American moment.

"I did my best," Isabella said. "But I can't shield her."

BOTH OF LIÊN and Quý's daughters had since given birth to babies themselves. Quý had provided for Liên and their two daughters, as well as for his grandchildren, with the money earned from driving the cyclo.

When the COVID pandemic first started to spread across the globe in 2020, pleas from Liên for money had grown ever more constant. The family in America sent money to Liên and Isabella and Hà's half sisters.

Then one afternoon in October 2020, Isabella and Hà received news that Liên's husband, Quý, had been in a motorbike collision. His internal injuries were severe; he would not survive.

Hà always knew that she would help take care of Rô and Tuyết once she finished her education and settled on a career. This was never a question. "But in the back of my mind," Hà told me, "I have always told myself that if I make enough money, I will take care of Liên too."

But after Quý's death, the family's pleas for financial assistance became increasingly dire. Isabella and Hà felt intense anxiety over it all: how to balance figuring out their own futures and careers while also worrying about supporting the family of their first mother.

There are ethical trade-offs to social mobility, according to Jennifer Morton, philosopher and professor at the University of Pennsylvania. "Why are these costs ethical?" she wrote in *Moving Up without Losing Your Way*. "Quite simply because they involve aspects of what, for most of us, count as essential elements of a good life. Family, friendship, and community." The traditional narrative of upward mobility in the United States praises resilience and determination, according to

Morton, but does not prepare people for emotional, psychological, and ethical challenges along the way "or how their success may come at the expense of their relationships with family and friends, their connection to their communities, and their sense of who they are and what matters to them."

The path upward, according to Morton, is so much more complicated than simply moving away from your family. Attaining a degree and a job, receiving a higher income, being in proximity to privilege— all of it involves a constant negotiation over "the distance between the community into which he or she was born and the one into which he or she seeks entry."

Those who venture out might have a chance to help their families or communities financially. Their personal choices are a response to a system of societal and global inequities. But often those obligations to family take hold before a person has started college or found a well-paying job. As young adults, they might already feel the pull of immediate family needs for assistance with childcare, medical care, and bills back home. Those pressures and feelings of responsibility, Morton noted, never go away. With adoptees, these responsibilities can be all the more complex and traumatic.

Hà and Isabella both know that, for as long as they live, they will be Liên's primary lifeline to economic stability, as well as their half sisters' and now their sisters' kids.

"Recently," Hà said, "Liên told me that Isabella and I are her only hope."

RÔ AND TUYẾT still live in Nha Trang. Rô found work as a child caregiver; Tuyết, in carpentry at a furniture shop. Rô and Tuyết appreciated the money sent by the Solimenes over the years. But by 2020 they were taking care of their living expenses on their own. Rô and Tuyết spoke regularly by video calls to Hà and spent many months terrified that she would catch COVID in America. During one of those calls,

Tuyết and Rô told Hà they noticed her skin had gotten darker. Hà had been biking outside during the pandemic. "In Việt Nam, people are scared of getting dark," Hà explained, "because . . . they think that dark skin is for people that are low income. So they have bad mentality about it."

Over the years, Rô and Tuyết had let go of their daughter a little more each year, allowing her to become the person she wanted to be. They were proud of her accomplishments, her education. They supported her choices for her future. Every so often, they tried to coax her back. "Do not forget you are Vietnamese," Tuyết often told Hà.

Keely has developed an abiding respect for Rô and Tuyết, as women, as mothers. On visits to Nha Trang, Keely is welcomed into their home with hugs; Rô cooks bánh xèo with shrimp and fish sauce. Keely also keeps in touch with Olivia's family, though Olivia still does not encourage or welcome the relationship. Keely's interactions with Liên are less frequent, their relationship tenuous.

Keely founded a shoe company that raises money through sales to send portable solar suitcases to off-the-grid medical clinics in countries with high infant and maternal mortality rates. Through a partnership with the organization We Care Solar, the solar energy helps power medical and surgical lighting and medical devices.

She named the shoe company Bella | Ha.

OLIVIA CHANGED HER major from economics to sports communication, to "undecided," to public relations and advertising, to marketing, to finance, and, finally, to sports business with a sports communication minor. "So this is my sixth major," Olivia told me. It will take one more year to complete, but she feels confident she made the right choice. "I'm sticking with it." She got a part-time job with the Chicago Cubs in guest services, as well as an internship with the Chicago Sky, a WNBA team. Olivia graduated in December 2022 and plans to continue working to promote and support women's sports.

Hà and Isabella graduated in 2022. As Hà contemplated next steps, Isabella made plans to take the US Department of State Foreign Service Officer Test to become a counselor or diplomat in Qatar, Afghanistan, or Pakistan.

Olivia had come to rely on her older twin sisters. "They take care of me emotionally and physically," she said. Olivia didn't want that to change, but she knew it would one day. Hà would eventually return to Việt Nam, and Isabella would likely go to the Middle East. "I'm always going to be a supportive sister," Olivia said. "But for me, I want to be close to home."

For Hà, it is particularly hard to imagine splitting from the twin sister she lived without for so long. She told Isabella, "If you find that job that is perfect for you in the Middle East, go. I'm not going to hold you back. I'm not going to pull out our story and say, 'Hey, remember we were separated at birth? Don't go.'"

Instead, Hà will tell her sister to follow her instincts. Create her own destiny. "I know she will say the same to me," Hà added. "And I know we will always find a way to come back to each other."

NOTES ON SOURCES

I INTERVIEWED OLIVIA, Isabella, and Hà, along with their constellations of family members, over five years, between 2016 and 2021. The sisters, who were eighteen and nineteen when we began speaking, graciously allowed me to travel with them to Việt Nam, introducing me to first families and adoptive ones. We spent hundreds of hours getting to know each other, and my conversations with these young women have been among the most meaningful and memorable of my career. Each of them taught me about themselves and the world in which we live, as well as my place in it.

Reporting about adoption involves extra awareness of your own positionality in the story, and close attention to the sensitivities of the real people who often have complicated and traumatic feelings they might still be working to understand.

Over the years, I walked each sister through her story multiple times, also reading their stories aloud to them, fact-checking, making sure each was comfortable with what she shared and periodically asking if she was sure she was open to having these parts of her journey in a book at all. At the time, each explained to me, in her own way, that she was sharing her life for others who might be able to relate, or for herself, out of a sense of pride in what she had overcome, or for those who know her personally but might never have really heard or seen her in her entirety. I came to know each of them as incredibly self-aware, brave, and resilient young women.

After going through fact-checking, Keely expressed upset over my conversations with Isabella, Olivia, and Hà about various issues that she saw as dark and negative, including race, identity, adoption trauma, and the difficulty of reunion. After the book went into production, Keely wrote to me: "In a world where there is so much tension and divide you could have told a story of love and inclusivity with difficult moments that were very real, but instead you have told a controversial, complex and ugly story with rare beautiful moments."

In writing this book, I learned more about adoption, twin science, and identity than I ever knew when I began my interviews. I tried my best to capture that complexity and context while honoring the various truths and holding empathy for everyone involved. I came to understand that in telling a story involving adoption, it was my responsibility to help readers understand its history as a system, especially when it comes to families, race, religion, class, and economics.

In a 2020 "Red Table Talk," Angela Tucker, a Black woman who was adopted and raised by white parents, said: "For me to talk about transracial adoption honestly is to hurt somebody." This is the burden and conflict that exists for adoptees in sharing their truths. The sisters bravely stood by the joyful and painful parts of their stories, while also maintaining their deep love and appreciation for all of their family members. The Solimene family can handle it, Isabella told me at the end of the fact-checking process. Their foundation remains strong, their devotion to one another unbreakable. "We still love each other as much as we did the day this family was established."

During the reporting, I witnessed some of the events portrayed, but I also reconstructed scenes from interviews, drawing from people's memories and stories passed down to them. In addition, I relied on videos, photos, social media posts, adoption records, letters, and other archival sources. Quotes and dialogue are captured, recorded, or rendered from their recollections.

In the notes that follow, I cite each chapter's primary sources, as well as reporting techniques used and supplementary or suggested additional readings. Sources document not just the boldface key phrases but also the sentences, and sometimes the paragraphs or topical sections, that follow those phrases. A bibliography section contains a number of secondary references and sources not listed in the endnotes and recommendations for further research or reading.

Prologue: Three Triangles

3 **the field of genetics has throughout history** Robert Plomin, *Blueprint: How DNA Makes Us Who We Are* (Cambridge, MA: MIT Press, 2018).

4 **There is a difference between fate** The difference between fate and destiny can be explored more in Richard W. Bargdill, "Fate and Destiny: Some Historical Distinctions between the Concepts," *Journal of Theoretical and Philosophical Psychology* 26, nos. 1–2 (2006): 205–20, who wrote:

Fate is a concept that acknowledges there are many aspects to our lives that we do not choose and do not control. There are events that happen to us by accident, by chance, and without our intention. Our lives are shaped by these events, these givens, and by the people who are in charge of our early development. Much of the psychological tone of our lives is already in place by the time that we become aware of our possibilities. We fade into being and our story is already begun by the time we have grabbed hold of the pen and understand how to write our own life. (000)

In contrast:

Destiny is to see into the future by evaluating the immature elements that are already present in our past. Destiny is a projection of those elements into the future; so that should one achieve their destiny at some unknown time, what is recognized is that these now mature structures have come together in an ideal alignment. To know one's destiny is to have some insight into what one could be by envisioning what one already is. But one's destiny will not be achieved without care, effort and deliberate choices. (000)

4 **Among the Sepik people** Brigitta Hauser-Schäublin, "The Track of the Triangle: Form and Meaning in the Sepik, Papua New Guinea," *Pacific Studies* 17, no. 3 (September 1994): 133–41.

4 **the theory of racial triangulation** Claire Jean Kim, "The Racial Triangulation of Asian Americans," *Politics & Society* 27, no. 1 (March 1999): 105–38.

4 **Model minority stereotypes** Elizabeth Raleigh, *Selling Transracial Adoption* (Philadelphia: Temple University Press, 2017). See also SunAh M. Laybourn, "Adopting the Model Minority Myth: Korean Adoption as a Racial Project," *Social Problems* 68, no. 1 (February 2021): 118–35.

5 **Within the adoption community** Amanda L. Baden, Judith L. Gibbons, Samantha L. Wilson, and Hollee McGinnis, "International Adoption: Counseling and the Adoption Triad," *Adoption Quarterly* 16, nos. 3–4 (2013): 218–37. See also Arthur D. Sorosky, Annette Baran, and Reuben Pannor, *The Adoption Triangle: The Effects of the Sealed Record on Adoptees, Birth Parents, and Adoptive Parents* (Garden City, NY: Anchor Press, 1978).

5 **But today, some prefer the term** Margaret D. Jacobs, "From Triangles to Stars: How Indigenous Adoptions Expand the Adoption Triad," *Adoption & Culture* 6, no. 1 (2018): 162–81; and Jenny Heijun Wills, Tobias Hübinette, and Indigo Willing, eds., *Adoption and Multiculturalism Europe, the Americas, and the Pacific* (Ann Arbor: University of Michigan Press, 2020).

Chapter One: 1998

9 **The babies are crying** Liên's point of view is reconstructed and drawn from interviews with her, translated by Khuyên Tưởng Thị Tú.

11 **That day at the Center** Letter, written in 1998, provided by the Solimene family.

12 **As at least one version goes** In-person interviews with Hà, Rô, and Tuyết in 2017; phone interviews in 2019 and 2020.

Chapter Two: Hà

14 **Nguyễn Thị Hồng Hà grew up** Hà's sections are based on interviews with her, as well as Rô and Tuyết's memories of Hà's childhood and visit to the orphanage. I also visited the village of Khánh Đông, accompanied by Hà and her family.

17 **They passed rice paddies** This description comes from Hà's memories, as well as videos I took and notes I made while tracing the roads they traveled from Khánh Đông to the Center for Khánh Hoà Social Protection.

Chapter Three: Loan and Như

21 **Nearly everything that Isabella Solimene remembers** This chapter is rendered from interviews with Isabella and Keely and home videos and photos from the orphanage, the hotel, and Nha Trang that the Solimene family shared with me. Dialogue is reconstructed and quoted from the video footage.

Chapter Four: The Baby Lifts

26 **On April 4, 1975, a windowless** More detailed reconstructions of the plane crash are found here: Dana Sachs, *Life We Were Given: Operation Babylift, International Adoption, and the Children of War in Vietnam* (Boston: Beacon Press), chap. 5; and Rosemary Taylor and Wende Grant, *Orphans of War: Work with the Abandoned Children of Vietnam, 1967–1975* (New York: HarperCollins, 1988).

26 **President Gerald Ford had recently allocated** Gerald Ford, *A Time to Heal: The Autobiography of Gerald R. Ford* (New York: Harper & Row, 1979), 252.

27 **The lead of a story** Malcolm Browne, "A Deep Bitterness toward U.S.," *New York Times*, April 5, 1975.

27 **"Our mission of mercy will continue"** Office of the White House Press Secretary, The White House Statement by the President, April 4, 1975, *Operation Babylift* exhibit, Gerald R. Ford Presidential Library and Museum, https://www.fordlibrarymuseum. gov/museum/exhibits/babylift/documents/.

27 **"When can I go home?"** Sachs, *Life We Were Given*, chap. 7.

27 **"The children would be happier"** Statement on the Immorality of Bringing South Vietnamese Orphans to the United States, April 4, 1975, Viola W. Bernard Papers, Box 62, Folder 8, Archives and Special Collections, Augustus C. Long Library, Columbia University, New York; available digitally via Adoption History Project, Department of History, University of Oregon, Eugene, https://pages.uoregon.edu/adoption/archive/ SIBSVOUS.htm.

27 **"Last Friday morning"** *New York Times*, April 7, 1975; available digitally via Adoption History Project, Department of History, University of Oregon, Eugene, https://darkwing.uoregon.edu/~adoption/archive/NYTOBad.htm. See also Fox Butterfield, "Orphans of Vietnam: One Last Agonizing Issue," *New York Times*, April 13, 1975, https://www.nytimes.com/1975/04/13/archives/orphans-of-vietnam-one-last-agonizing-issue.html.

27 **Many Americans, including protesters** Allison Varzally, *Children of Reunion: Vietnamese Adoptions and the Politics of Family Migrations* (Chapel Hill: University of North Carolina Press), chap. 1. See also Ayako Sahara, "Theater of Rescue: Cultural Representations of U.S. Evacuation from Vietnam," *Journal of American & Canadian Studies* 30 (2012): 55–84.

28 **"We have a saying in Vietnam"** Marjorie Margolies and Ruth Gruber, *They Came to Stay: How a Single Parent Adopted Lee Heh from Korea and Holly from Vietnam* (New York: Coward, McCann & Geoghegan, 1976), 213. Conversation also detailed in Varzally, *Children of Reunion*, chap. 2.

28 **Historically in Việt Nam** Varzally, *Children of Reunion*, chap. 2; also detailed in Allison Varzally, "Vietnamese Adoptions and the Politics of Atonement," *Adoption & Culture* 2, no. 1 (2009): 159–201, https://doi:10.1353/ado.2009.0008. See also Judy Tzu-Chun Wu, *Radicals on the Road: Internationalism, Orientalism, and Feminism during the Vietnam Era* (Ithaca, NY: Cornell University Press, 2013), 268–69.

29 **By 1972, the Nixon administration** Liên-Hang T. Nguyen, *Hanoi's War: An International History of the War for Peace in Vietnam* (Chapel Hill: University of North Carolina Press, 2012), 375.

29 **In the final months of war** Stanley Karnow, *Vietnam: A History* (New York: Viking, 1983), 666.

29 **The US military's deadly policies** Trin Yarborough, *Surviving Twice: Amerasian Children of the Vietnam War* (Washington, DC: Potomac Books, 2005).

29 **Hugh Hefner, who provided** For photos documenting Hefner's efforts, see Operation Babylift exhibit, Gerald R. Ford Presidential Library and Museum, April 1975, https://www.fordlibrarymuseum.gov/museum/exhibits/babylift/photography/. See also Edward Zigler, "The Vietnamese Children's Airlift: Too Little and Too Late" (paper, 83rd Annual Meeting of the American Psychological Association, Chicago, August 30–September 3, 1975), https://files.eric.ed.gov/fulltext/ED119827.pdf.

29 **"kind of wrongheaded thinking"** Varzally, *Children of Reunion*, 52.

29 **who she said welcomed** Gloria Emerson, "Collecting Souvenirs: Operation Babylift," *New Republic*, April 1975, 8–10.

30 **"growing up in a good American home"** Varzally, *Children of Reunion*, 53.

30 **"This Western sense of knowing"** Jonathan Patrick Thompson, "China Elephants and Orphans: Operation Babylift and the White Savior Complex" (master's thesis, Southern New Hampshire University, 2019), ProQuest, https://www.proquest.com/docview/2198662224.

30 **In the years leading up to the end** Kimberley L. Phillips Boehm, *War! What Is It Good For? Black Freedom Struggles and the U.S. Military from World War II to Iraq,*

John Hope Franklin Series in African American History and Culture (Chapel Hill: University of North Carolina Press). See also Simon Hall, "Black Power and the Anti-Vietnam War Movement," in *The Routledge History of World Peace since 1750*, ed. Christian Philip Peterson, William M. Knoblauch, and Michael Loadenthal (New York: Routledge, 2019), 132–41; and Vincent J. Intondi, *African Americans against the Bomb: Nuclear Weapons, Colonialism, and the Black Freedom Movement* (Stanford, CA: Stanford University Press, 2020).

30 **Inspired by the Black Panthers** Rychetta Watkins, *Black Power, Yellow Power, and the Making of Revolutionary Identities* (Jackson: University Press of Mississippi, 2012); and Diane C. Fujino, "Black Militants and Asian American Model Minorities: Contesting Oppositional Representations; or, On Afro-Asian Solidarities," *Kalfou: A Journal of Comparative and Relational Ethnic Studies* 2, no. 1 (2015), https://doi.org/10.15367/kf.v2i1.54.

30 **"We are a racist society"** James Baldwin, *The Cross of Redemption: Uncollected Writings*, ed. Randall Kenan (New York: Pantheon, 2010), 103–4.

30 **Just as Langston Hughes** Intondi, *African Americans against the Bomb*.

31 **In his 1967 "Beyond Vietnam" speech** Martin Luther King Jr., "Beyond Vietnam: A Time to Break Silence" (speech, April 4, 1967), YouTube, https://www.youtube.com/watch?v=AJhgXKGldUk.

31 **adoption advocates claimed** Sachs, *Life We Were Given*, chap. 4.

31 **"But what about the mixed-race children"** Margolies, *They Came to Stay*, 200–201. See also Nancy Hicks, "Black Agencies Charge Injustice in Placing of Vietnam Children," *New York Times*, April 19, 1975; and "Rescuing Vietnam Orphans: Mixed Motives," *Christian Century*, April, 16, 1975.

31 **Some family members in Việt Nam** Varzally, *Children of Reunion*, chap. 2.

32 **"Foreigners, who see only orphanages"** Varzally, chap. 2.

Chapter Five: Liên

This chapter is drawn from interviews primarily with Liên, both in person in Việt Nam and virtually, in 2017, 2019, and 2020, translated by Khuyên Tường Thị Tú.

34 **After its troops withdrew** Christopher Parsons and Pierre-Louis Vézina, "Migrant Networks and Trade: The Vietnamese Boat People as a Natural Experiment," *Economic Journal* 128, no. 612 (2018): F210–34, https://doi.org/10.1111/ecoj.12457.

34 **Other nations also denied assistance** Henry Kamm, "Exodus of Vietnam 'Boat People' Climbing Back to 1979 Levels, *New York Times*, June 26, 1981; and Nghia M. Vo, *The Vietnamese Boat People, 1954 and 1975–1992* (Jefferson, NC: McFarland, 2006).

37 **The Solimene family received** Letter provided by the Solimene family.

Chapter Six: Rô and Tuyết

This chapter is drawn from interviews primarily with Rô and Tuyết, both in person in Việt Nam and virtually, translated by their daughter, Hà.

42 **Tuyết's siblings also each had** For more on ID cards, see Research Directorate, Immigration and Refugee Board of Canada, Ottawa, "Vietnam: Whether an

Individual's Rights to Obtaining a Passport, Employment, Education and Other Civil Rights Are Affected if He or She Does Not Have Household Registration Documentation," February 27, 2009, UNHCR: The UN Refugee Agency, Refworld, https://www.refworld.org/docid/4b7cee8c38.html.

Chapter Seven: Cuckoo Birds

46 **In the nineteenth century** Francis Galton, "The History of Twins," *Journal of the Anthropological Institute of Great Britain and Ireland* 5, no. 3 (1876): 391–406.

48 **At a time when adopting** Barbara Melosh, *Strangers and Kin: The American Way of Adoption* (Cambridge, MA: Harvard University Press, 2006), Kindle.

48 **"For social workers"** Melosh, location 669, Kindle.

48 **The first pair of identical twins** Paul Popenoe, "Twins Reared Apart," *Journal of Heredity* 13, no. 3 (1922): 142–44.

48 **Popenoe was also a white supremacist** Kathy J. Cooke, "Duty or Dream? Edwin G. Conklin's Critique of Eugenics and Support for American Individualism," *Journal of the History of Biology* 35, no. 2 (June 2002): 365–84. See also Nidhi Subbaraman, "Caltech Confronted Its Racist Past. Here's What Happened," *Nature*, November 10, 2021, 194–98, https://doi.org/10.1038/d41586-021-03052-x; and Michael Hiltzik, "Caltech Faces Reckoning over Its Links to Eugenics and Sterilization Movement," *Los Angeles Times*, July 7, 2020.

49 **"Three generations of imbeciles"** Jason Morgan Ward, "Three Generations, No Imbeciles: Eugenics, the Supreme Court, and Buck v. Bell/Segregation's Science: Eugenics and Society in Virginia," *Virginia Magazine of History and Biography* 117, no. 3 (2009): 302–4.

49 **Under Hitler's regime** Robert Jay Lifton, "What Made This Man? Mengele: The Nazi Doctor's Potential for Evil Became Actual within the Environment of Auschwitz. Possessed by the Vision of a Perfect Race, Mengele Targeted His Research on Twins," *New York Times*, July 25, 1981. See also Lawrence Wright, *Twins: And What They Tell Us about Who We Are* (New York: John Wiley, 1997), 18–23.

50 **In the 1930s** Melosh, *Strangers and Kin*, chap. 1, Kindle. Read also Gabrielle Glaser, *American Baby: A Mother, a Child, and the Shadow History of Adoption* (New York: Viking, 2021), chap. 9; and "Confidentiality and Sealed Records," Adoption History Project, Department of History, accessed October 2021, University of Oregon, Eugene, https://darkwing.uoregon.edu/~adoption/topics/confidentiality.htm.

50 **Like twin studies** Barbara Stoddard Burks, "What Makes Jack a Bright Boy: Home or Heredity?" *North American Review* 228, no. 5 (November 1929): 599–608.

50 **Science is a reflection** Angela Saini, *Superior: The Return of Race Science* (Boston: Beacon Press, 2019), 58–59, 215.

50 **Another extreme theory** M. Rilling, "How the Challenge of Explaining Learning Influenced the Origins and Development of John B. Watson's Behaviorism," *American Journal of Psychology* 113, no. 2 (Summer 2000): 275–301. See also Susan M. Schneider and Edward K. Morris, "A History of the Term Radical Behaviorism: From Watson to Skinner," *Behavior Analyst* 10, no. 1 (1987): 27–39.

Chapter Eight: Isabella

This chapter is drawn from interviews primarily with Isabella. Olivia and Keely provided supplementary details.

52 **The Solimenes lived in Barrington** John McCarron, "Chicago Has Both Poorest, Richest Suburb," *Chicago Tribune*, June 5, 1989; and John Handley, "Barrington Country Upscale Area of Pastures and Paddocks," *Chicago Tribune*, July 9, 1988.

52 **The 2000 US Census** QuickFacts, Barrington Village: Illinois, US Census Bureau, accessed October 2021, https://www.census.gov/quickfacts/fact/table/barringtonvillageillinois/PST045219.

53 **Ferdinand the gender-nonconforming bull** Bruce Handy, "'The Story of Ferdinand' Became Fodder for the Culture Wars of Its Era," *New Yorker*, December 15, 2017. See also Michael Patrick Hearn, "Ferdinand the Bull's 50th Anniversary," *Washington Post*, November 9, 1986.

Chapter Nine: Cloth Monkeys

59 **By 1939, the British psychologist** Lenny van Rosmalen, René van der Veer, and Frank C. P. van der Horst, "The Nature of Love: Harlow, Bowlby and Bettelheim on Affectionless Mothers," *History of Psychiatry* 31, no. 2 (2020), https://doi.org/10.1177/0957154X19898997. See also Karen Robert, *Becoming Attached: First Relationships and How They Shape Our Capacity to Love* (New York: Oxford University Press, 1998); René A. Spitz, *The First Year of Life: A Psychoanalytic Study of Normal and Deviant Development of Object Relations* (New York: International Universities Press, 1965); Harry Bakwin, "Loneliness in Infants," *American Journal of Diseases in Children* 63, no. 1 (1942): 30–40; Harry Bakwin, "The Hospital Care of Infants and Children," *Journal of Pediatrics* 39, no. 3 (September 1951): 383–90; Melvin Konner, *The Evolution of Childhood: Relationships, Emotion, Mind* (Cambridge, MA: Belknap Press, 2010).

60 **In 1958, a professor of psychology** Stephen J Suomi, Frank C. P. van der Horst, and René van der Veer, "Rigorous Experiments on Monkey Love: An Account of Harry F. Harlow's Role in the History of Attachment Theory," *Integrative Psychological & Behavioral Science* 42, no. 4 (December 2008): 354–69, https://doi.org/10.1007/s12124-008-9072-9. See also Marga Vicedo, "The Evolution of Harry Harlow: From the Nature to the Nurture of Love," *History of Psychiatry* 21, no. 82(pt. 2) (2021): 190–205; and Frank C. P. van der Horst, and René van der Veer, "Loneliness in Infancy: Harry Harlow, John Bowlby and Issues of Separation," *Integrative Psychological & Behavioral Science* 42, no. 4 (September 2008): 225–35. Also read Deborah Blum, *Love at Goon Park : Harry Harlow and the Science of Affection* (New York: Perseus, 2002).

61 **A colleague of Harlow's** Stephen J. Suomi, "Risk, Resilience, and Gene-Environment Interplay in Primates," *Journal of the Canadian Academy of Child and Adolescent Psychiatry* 20, no. 4 (November 2011): 289–97. See also David Moreau, Brooke N. Macnamara, and David Z. Hambrick, "Overstating the Role of Environmental Factors in Success: A Cautionary Note," *Current Directions in Psychological Science: A Journal of the American Psychological Society* 28, no. 1 (November 2018): 28–33, https://doi.org/10.1038/d41586-018-01023-3.

61 **This shift helped overturn** Barbara Melosh, *Strangers and Kin: The American Way of Adoption* (Cambridge, MA: Harvard University Press, 2002), chap. 1, Kindle.

61 **"Give me a dozen healthy infants"** Frances Degen Horowitz, "John B. Watson's Legacy: Learning and Environment," *Developmental Psychology* 28, no. 3 (May 1992): 360–67.

61 **"Give me a child until he is seven"** "The Election of a Jesuit to St Peter's Throne Has Focused Attention on the Society of Jesus's Famous Motto, 'Give Me a Child at the Age of Seven, and I Shall Give You the Man,'" *Spectator* 321, no. 9630 (1828): 1–3.

62 **"Give me a child," as the viral adage goes** Bryn Farnsworth, "What Is Behavioral Psychology?" *iMotions Blog*, August 28, 2018, https://imotions.com/blog/behavioral-psychology/. See also B. F. Skinner Quotes, Brainy Quote, https://www.brainyquote.com/quotes/b_f_skinner_378139.

Chapter Ten: Olivia

This chapter is drawn from interviews primarily with Olivia. Isabella and Keely provided supplementary details.

Chapter Eleven: Wonderful Beginnings

70 **a white mother in Washington, DC** Susan J. Grossman, "A Child of a Different Color: Race as a Factor in Adoption and Custody Proceedings," *Buffalo Law Review* 17 (1968): 314–16. See also *In re* Adoption of a Minor, 228 F.2d 446 (DC Cir. 1955), Justia, https://law.justia.com/cases/federal/appellate-courts/F2/228/446/404375/.

70 **Throughout the nineteenth** Shari O'Brien, "Race in Adoption Proceedings: The Pernicious Factor," *Tulsa Law Journal* 21, no. 3 (0000): 1–4.

70 **though African American families** Evan B. Donaldson Adoption Institute, "Finding Families for African American Children: The Role of Race & Law in Adoption from Foster Care," May 2008, National Center on Adoption and Permanency, https://www.nationalcenteronadoptionandpermanency.net/post/finding-families-for-african-american-children-the-role-of-race-law-in-adoption-from-foster-care.

71 **In 1851, the Adoption of Children Act** Alice Bussiere, "The Development of Adoption Law," *Adoption Quarterly* 1, no. 3 (1998): 3–25, https://doi.org/10.1300/J145v01n03_02.

71 **Black children were frequently labeled** Bernice Q. Madison and Michael Schapiro, "Black Adoption: Issues and Policies: Review of the Literature," *Social Service Review* 47, no. 4 (1973): 1–3.

71 **Eventually, in the 1940s** Barbara Melosh, *Strangers and Kin: The American Way of Adoption* (Cambridge, MA: Harvard University Press, 2009), chap. 2, Kindle. For additional readings on racial "matching" history, see R. R. Banks, "The Color of Desire: Fulfilling Adoptive Parents' Racial Preferences through Discriminatory State Action," *Yale Law Journal* 107 (1998): 875–964, https://digitalcommons.law.yale.edu/ylj/vol107/iss4/1.

71 **"they were not deliberately advocating"** Valerie Phillips Hermann, "Transracial Adoption: 'Child-Saving' or 'Child-Snatching,'" *National Black Law Journal* 13, no. 1 (1993): 147–61.

71 **In a post–World War II society** Catherine Ceniza Choy, *Global Families: A History of Asian International Adoption in America* (New York: New York University Press, 2013),

introduction. See also Kim Park Nelson, *Invisible Asians, Korean American Adoptees, Asian American Experiences, and Racial Exceptionalism* (New Brunswick, NJ: Rutgers University Press, 2016), chap. 3; and Elizabeth Yoon Hwa Raleigh, *Selling Transracial Adoption: Families, Markets, and the Color Line* (Philadelphia: Temple University Press, 2018).

71 **"It is evidently common"** F. James Davis, *Who Is Black? One Nation's Definition* (University Park: Pennsylvania State University Press, 1991), 129.

72 **They eventually turned to orphanages** Choy, *Global Families*, chap. 1. See also Jodi Kim, "An 'Orphan' with Two Mothers: Transnational and Transracial Adoption, the Cold War, and Contemporary Asian American Cultural Politics," *American Quarterly* 61, no. 4 (December 2009): 855–80.

72 **In 1952, there were around five thousand** Hyoue Okamura, "The Language of 'Racial Mixture' in Japan: How Ainoko Became Haafu, and the Haafu-Gao Makeup Fad." *Asia Pacific Perspectives* 14, no. 2 (Spring 2017): 41–79.

72 **The US government did not openly acknowledge** Catherine Ceniza Choy, "Race at the Center: The History of American Cold War Asian Adoption," *Journal of American-East Asian Relations* 16, no. 3 (2009): 163–82.

72 **Yet the country's leaders understood** Kim, "An 'Orphan' with Two Mothers."

73 **In 1949, the white American writer** Emily Cheng, "Pearl S. Buck's 'American Children': U.S. Democracy, Adoption of the Amerasian Child, and the Occupation of Japan in *The Hidden Flower*," *Frontiers* 35, no. 1 (2014): 181–210.

73 **Meanwhile, another American, Harry Holt** SooJin Pate, *From Orphan to Adoptee: U.S. Empire and Genealogies of Korean Adoption*, Difference Incorporated (Minneapolis: University of Minnesota Press, 2014), introduction.

74 **The Holt Adoption Program appealed** Arissa H. Oh, "A New Kind of Missionary Work: Christians, Christian Americanists," *Women's Studies Quarterly* 33, nos. 3–4 (2005): 161–88.

74 **"Christian Americanism"** Arissa H. Oh, *To Save the Children of Korea: The Cold War Origins of International Adoption* (Stanford, CA: Stanford University Press, 2015), 8.

74 **Around thirty-five thousand children** Rachel Rains Winslow, *The Best Possible Immigrants: International Adoption and the American Family* (University Park: University of Pennsylvania Press, 2017), introduction.

74 **But the adoptive families and agencies** Eleana Jean Kim, *Adopted Territory: Transnational Korean Adoptees and the Politics of Belonging* (Durham, NC: Duke University Press, 2010), 263–64.

74 **It was not until 1965** Mae M. Ngai, "Hart-Celler at Fifty: Lessons for Immigration Reform in Our Time," *Labor* 12, no. 3 (September 2015): 1–4.

74 **LGBTQ immigrants were often deemed** Jessica Ordaz and Alejandra Portillos, "Immigration and Customs Enforcement's #Pride Tweet Conceals a Violent History," *Washington Post*, June 28, 2021.

74 **And until 1967, Asians** Deenesh Sohoni, "Unsuitable Suitors: Anti-Miscegenation Laws, Naturalization Laws, and the Construction of Asian Identities," *Law & Society Review* 41, no. 3 (2007): 587–618. See also Arica L. Coleman, "'Tell the Court I Love My

[Indian] Wife' Interrogating Race and Self-Identity in Loving v. Virginia," *Souls* 8, no. 1 (2006): 67–80.

75 **"wonderful beginnings and happy endings"** Choy, *Global Families*, 12–13.

75 **"not live or [would] have nothing"** Choy, 30.

75 **Critics of transracial adoption** Choy, 125–28. In the 1950s, the National Urban League and other organizations began recruiting more Black adoptive parents to adopt Black children. In one case, the Holt Adoption Program placed an African American and Korean adoptee with a white family in a white neighborhood. International Social Service-USA, wrote Choy, eventually learned that "the family was selling their home and moving away because the people of that section would not accept the little girl," 94–95.

75 **Between 1958 and 1967** Randall Kennedy, *Interracial Intimacies: Sex, Marriage, Identity, and Adoption* (New York: Vintage Books, 2003). See also Stephanie Woodard, "Native Americans Expose the Adoption Era and Repair Its Devastation: A Story about the Harmful Effects of the Indian Adoption Project," Indian Country Today, updated September 13, 2018, https://indiancountrytoday.com/archive/native-americans-expose-the-adoption-era-and-repair-its-devastation; and Terry L. Cross, "Child Welfare in Indian Country: A Story of Painful Removals," *Health Affairs* 33, no. 12 (2014): 2256–59, https://doi.org/10.1377/hlthaff.2014.1158; and "Indian Child Welfare Act," Association on American Indian Affairs, accessed October 2021, https://www.indian-affairs.org/indian-child-welfare-act.html

76 **government institutions forcibly removed** *Native Words, Native Warriors*, National Museum of the American Indian, accessed October 2021, https://americanindian.si.edu/nk360/code-talkers/boarding-schools/. See also Mary Annette Pember, "Death by Civilization: Thousands of Native American Children Were Forced to Attend Boarding Schools Created to Strip Them of Their Culture. My Mother Was One of Them," *Atlantic*, March 8, 2019, https://www.theatlantic.com/education/archive/2019/03/traumatic-legacy-indian-boarding-schools/584293/.

76 **The number of white babies** Steven Roberts, "Supply of Adoptable White Babies Shrinks: Officials of Agencies Warn on Growth of Private Channels Demand Could Lead to Private Deals and High Fees," *New York Times*, July 18, 1971.

76 **the National Children's Bureau estimated** Rita J. Simon, "Black Attitudes toward Transracial Adoption," *Phylon* 39, no. 2 (1978): 135–42, https://doi.org/10.2307/274508.

76 **"The supply of white children"** "National Association of Black Social Workers, 'Position Statement on Transracial Adoption,' September 1972," Adoption History Project, Department of History, University of Oregon, Eugene, https://pages.uoregon.edu/adoption/archive/NabswTRA.htm.

77 **Sociologists Rita Simon and Howard Altstein** Rita J. Simon, "Adoption and the Race Factor: How Important Is It?" *Sociological Inquiry* 68, no. 2 (1998): 274–79.

77 **But the researchers overwhelmingly focused** Park Nelson, *Invisible Asians*, 82–83.

77 **In 1978, the Indian Child Welfare Act** Kennedy, *Interracial Intimacies*, chap. 12.

77 **Against the backdrop of this dialogue** "Fostering and Foster Care," Adoption History Project, Department of History, University of Oregon, Eugene, accessed October 2021, https://pages.uoregon.edu/adoption/topics/fostering.htm.

77 **And while fewer babies** Choy, *Global Families*, 47–48.

78 **By the 1990s** Read Kathryn Joyce, *The Child Catchers: Rescue, Trafficking, and the New Gospel of Adoption* (New York: Public Affairs, 2013).

Chapter Twelve: Keely

This chapter is drawn from interviews primarily with Keely; her mother, Jacqueline; and her husband, Mick. Journal entries and Christmas card image shared by Keely. Photo of Loan provided by the Solimenes.

Chapter Thirteen: Baby Brokers and Viral Adoptions

88 **In the United States, a "viral"** Kathryn Joyce, *The Child Catchers: Rescue, Trafficking, and the New Gospel of Adoption*, New York: Public Affairs, 2013). See also Arissa H. Oh, *To Save the Children of Korea: The Cold War Origins of International Adoption* (Stanford, CA: Stanford University Press, 2015).

88 **An illicit international adoption underworld** Dan Eaton, "Dozens of Couples in Limbo as Cambodia Halts Foreign Adoptions," Agence France-Presse, June 22, 2000; Bill Bainbridge and Lon Nara, "Adoptions 'Like Selling Goods,'" *Phnom Penh Post*, December 7, 2001; Sara Corbett, "Where Do Babies Come From?" *New York Times*, June 16, 2002; and Ethan B. Kapstein, "The Baby Trade," *Foreign Affairs*, November 1, 2003.

88 **In 1999, nine people** Freddie Balfour, "Nine Convicted for Smuggling 199 Vietnamese Babies Abroad for Adoption," Agence France-Presse, January 21, 2000; and "Vietnam Court to Try Ring Accused of Selling Babies," Reuters, November 22, 2001.

89 **"By heading to a poor"** E. J. Graff, "The Problem with Saving the World's 'Orphans,'" *Boston Globe*, December 11, 2008. For Graff's investigative series on adoption, see the Schuster Institute for Investigative Journalism, Brandeis University, Waltham, MA, https://www.brandeis.edu/investigate/adoption/index.html.

89 **In 1999, the *Wall Street Journal*** Sam Marshall, "Vietnam's Youngest Export," *Wall Street Journal*, May 21, 1999.

90 **By this point, an estimated** "Seven People in Vietnam Charged with Involvement in Baby Trafficking Ring," Associated Press, November 23, 2001.

90 **By 2003, Việt Nam's adoption program** Schuster Institute for Investigative Journalism, "Adoption in Vietnam," accessed February 2021, https://www.brandeis.edu/investigate/adoption/vietnam.html; and "Vietnam to Halt U.S. Adoptions after Report," Associated Press, April 28, 2008.

90 **But by 2008, those agreements** "Adoption in Vietnam," Schuster Institute for Investigative Journalism, Brandeis University, Waltham, MA, accessed October 2021, https://www.brandeis.edu/investigate/adoption/vietnam.html; and Associated Press, "Vietnam to halt U.S. adoptions after report," April 28, 2008.

90 **Moratoriums on intercountry adoptions** E. J. Graff, "The Lie We Love," *Foreign Policy*, November–December 2008, 58–66, https://www.brandeis.edu/investigate/adoption/docs/FPFinalTheLieWeLove.pdf.

Chapter Fourteen: "Is the Baby Okay?"

This chapter is drawn from interviews with Sue Fallon and Keely. Photo of the baby dressed in a white romper, the child listing in May 1999, and emails from the Santa Barbara attorney provided by Sue.

92 **had worked with the same facilitator** One woman, Carrie West of Roswell, Georgia, who met Mai-Ly LaTrace through an Ohio adoption agency that used her as its facilitator in Việt Nam, traveled to the country in 2000 expecting to meet a three-year-old girl they had seen in photos, according to an investigative report in the *Tampa Bay Times*. West ended up meeting Latrace's mother, Marie LaTrace, in Việt Nam, who told her the child she thought she was going to adopt had tuberculosis and was not available after all. West traveled back to Việt Nam a year later to try again, this time meeting Mai-Ly LaTrace, who asked her for donations for the child she never adopted, claiming she was still suffering from tuberculosis. LaTrace then helped West adopt a different two-year-old girl. When West returned home, she shared her story online, which attracted the attention of another adoptive mother living in Saipan, a US commonwealth in the western Pacific. It turned out that this mother seemed to have actually adopted the child West had first planned to adopt. It was the same file. Same photo. Yet the child did not have tuberculosis. See Julie Hauserman, "Vietnam Adoption Nightmares," *Tampa Bay Times*, September 17, 2002; R. Kit Roane, "Pitfalls for Parents: International Adoption Has Become Big Business, but Regulation Still Lags," *US·News & World Report*, May 29, 2005; and E. J. Graff, "Anatomy of an Adoption Crisis," *Foreign Policy*, September 12, 2010, https://foreignpolicy.com/2010/09/12/anatomy-of-an-adoption-crisis/.

92 **The Vietnamese Embassy issued** Then, in 2003, the US Department of State provided Carrie West with a letter from the birth mother of the child she had instead adopted. In it, the mother stated that someone had offered to pay her $500 if she gave away her baby. In news reports, LaTrace denied ever paying or coercing the birth mother. In 1997, LaTrace worked with a California adoption agency to set up a Việt Nam program and asked for $35,000 to open the facility. But the orphanage was never built, and the agency claimed it did not know where the money went. A year later, LaTrace was hired by an adoption agency in Jacksonville, Florida, to work as a facilitator. But at least five clients complained to the agency, saying "LaTrace was referring children to them who weren't available." One family traveled to Việt Nam in June 2002, meeting LaTrace to adopt a girl. They were expecting a three-month-old. But they were given a newborn. LaTrace insisted it was the child they had come for, but the couple was suspicious, noting there were five different birth dates on her documents. They complained to the Florida Department of Children and Families and to the state's attorney general's office. They thought the baby might have been stolen. The Florida agency was cited for licensing and record-keeping violations. It shuttered in 2003. Hauserman, "Vietnam Adoption Nightmares"; and Julie Hauserman, "Alleging Fraud, State Moves to Close Adoption Agency," *Tampa Bay Times*, November 20, 2002.

93 **In some cases, it made more sense** In 2011, Việt Nam signed the Hague Convention on Protection of Children, an international treaty designed to safeguard international adoptions and prevent trafficking. Special Commission of 2022, "Adoption Section,"

Hague Conference on Private International Law, accessed October 2021, https://www.hcch.net/en/instruments/conventions/specialised-sections/intercountry-adoption; and "Viet Nam Joins Hague Intercountry Adoption Convention," Hague Conference on Private International Law, World Organization for Cross-border Co-operation in Civil and Commercial Matters, November 14, 2011, https://www.hcch.net/en/news-archive/details/?varevent=238.

Chapter Fifteen: A Twin Who Walks Alone

102 **At fourteen weeks of gestation** Umberto Castiello, Cristina Becchio, Stefania Zoia, Cristian Nelini, Luisa Sartori, Laura Blason, et al., "Wired to Be Social: The Ontogeny of Human Interaction," *PLoS ONE* 5, no. 10 (2010): e13199, https://doi.org/10.1371/journal.pone.0013199.

103 **Segal founded the Twin Studies Center** Erika Hayasaki, "Identical Twins Hint at How Environments Change Gene Expression," *Atlantic*, May 15, 2018, https://www.theatlantic.com/science/archive/2018/05/twin-epigenetics/560189/. See also Nancy L. Segal, *Born Together—Reared Apart: The Landmark Minnesota Twin Study* (Cambridge, MA: Harvard University Press, 2012); Nancy L. Segal, *Indivisible by Two: Lives of Extraordinary Twins* (Cambridge, MA: Harvard University Press, 2005); and Nancy L. Segal, *Entwined Lives: Twins and What They Tell Us about Human Behavior* (New York: Dutton, 1999).

104 **My uncle, whose twin died** Erika Hayasaki, *Dead or Alive*, Kindle Single, January 24, 2017.

105 **In 2007, identical twin** Neela Banerjee, "A Singular Pain: When Death Cuts the Bond of Twins," *New York Times*, March 1, 2007.

105 **The Jicarilla Apache tribe** Emily C. McIlroy, "One Half Living for Two: Cross-Cultural Paradigms of Twinship," *Omega: Journal of Death and Dying* 64, no. 1 (February 2012): 1–13, https://dx.doi.org/10.2190/om.64.1.a.

105 **oríkì praise poem** McIlroy, 4.

Chapter Sixteen: Blindly Searching

This chapter is drawn from interviews with Keely, Sue Fallon, and Tuyết Hồ. Emails sent from the orphanage director's daughter, Joy Degenhardt, and Tuyết Hồ, provided by Keely.

Chapter Seventeen: Fairy Tales

110 **Once upon a time** Indigo Willing, "The Adopted Vietnamese Community: From Fairy Tales to the Diaspora," in "Vietnam beyond the Frame," special issue, *Michigan Quarterly Review* 43, no. 4 (Fall 2004): 648–64, https://ssrn.com/abstract=2032832.

110 **I am descended from dragons** Alessandra Chiricosta, "Following the Trail of the Fairy-Bird: The Search for a Uniquely Vietnamese Women's Movement," in *Women's Movements in Asia*, ed. Mina Roces and Louise Edwards (New York: Routledge), 124–25.

110 **It's such a beautiful story** Direct quotes from Zoom interview with Indigo Willing, November 2020.

111 **Thinking they were abandoned** Willing, "Adopted Vietnamese Community: From Fairytales to the Diaspora," 649.

112 **In Red Thread narratives** Frayda Cohen, "Tracing the Red Thread: Chinese-U.S. Transnational Adoption and the Legacies of 'Home,'" *Anthropologica* 57, no. 1 (2015): 41–52. See also Leslie K. Wang, *Outsourced Children: Orphanage Care and Adoption in Globalizing China* (Stanford, CA: Stanford University Press), chap. 7.

112 **"Fairy tales transform"** M. Garcia Gonzalez and E. Wesseling, "The Stories We Adopt By: Tracing 'The Red Thread' in Contemporary Adoption Narratives," *The Lion and the Unicorn* 37, no. 3 (2013): 257–76, https://doi.org/10.1353.uni.2013.0021.

112 **Color blindness fueled** Elizabeth Yoon Hwa Raleigh, *Selling Transracial Adoption: Families, Markets, and the Color Line* (Philadelphia: Temple University Press, 2018).

112 **Adopted Vietnamese International** For information about the organization, see the website at www.adoptedvietnamese.org/. See also Indigo Willing, Anh Đào Kolbe, Dominic Golding, Tim Holtan, Cara Wolfgang, Kev Minh Allen, et al., *Vietnamese. Adopted: A Collection of Voices* (CQT Media & Publishing, 2015).

Chapter Eighteen: The Letters

This chapter is drawn from interviews with Keely, Isabella, and Olivia. Emails from Joy and letters from Liên and Nguyễn Thị Mùa provided by the Solimenes.

Chapter Nineteen: Storms

This chapter is drawn from interviews with Hà, Tuyết, and Rô.

122 **Monsoons feed off imbalances** See "Learning with the Times: What Causes the Monsoon?" *Times of India*, July 12, 2010; and NASA Viz Team, "The Science of Monsoons," July 8, 2016, NASA's Goddard Space Flight Center, https://svs.gsfc.nasa.gov/12303.

122 **Typhoons are not born** National Oceanic and Atmospheric Administration, "What Is the Difference between a Hurricane and a Typhoon?" National Ocean Service, accessed October 2021, https://oceanservice.noaa.gov/facts/cyclone.html.

123 **The typhoon had brought with it** "Natural Disasters in Vietnam: Typhoons, Storms, Tornadoes, and an Earthquake," Facts and Details, accessed October 2021, https://factsanddetails.com/southeast-asia/Vietnam/sub5_9h/entry-3489.html; and "Typhoon Lekima Slams Vietnam," Associated Press, October 3, 20017, https://www.cbsnews.com/news/typhoon-lekima-slams-vietnam/.

Chapter Twenty: The Fog

129 **The thought of a child** Based on interviews with Isabella.

129 **This process, known in the adoptee community** Haley Radke, host, "Coming Out of the Fog with Lesli A. Johnson, MFT," episode 49, Healing series, *Adoptees On* podcast, November 24, 2017, https://www.adopteeson.com/listen/outofthefog. See also Mark Hagland, "Coming Out of the Adoptee Fog," Intercountry Adoptee Voices, November 1, 2019, https://intercountryadopteevoices.com/2019/11/01/coming-out-of-the-adoptee-fog/.

130 **"a very convoluted, complex journey"** Direct quotes from Zoom interview with Lynelle Long, November 2020. See also ICAV's video series produced by Long, which includes interviews with intercountry adoptees, https://intercountryadopteevoices. com/video-resource-for-professionals/.

130 **"Children are not offered up"** Direct quotes from phone interview with Victoria DiMartile, November 2020. Hear more from DiMartile on Francie Ryan Frisbie, host, "Exploring Black History Month and Transracial Adoption with Victoria DiMartile," *Adoption Advocacy Podcast*, February 15, 2021, https://podcasts.apple.com/us/podcast/ february-2021-exploring-black-history-month-and/id1447905024?i=1000509048414; and Angela Tucker, host, "Torie DiMartile: Amy Coney Barrett and the White Savior Narrative," *The Adoptee Next Door* podcast, October 20, 2020, https:// podcasts.apple.com/us/podcast/torie-dimartile-amy-coney-barrett-and-the-white/ id1525068563?i=1000495518387.

131 **There are high rates** Margaret A. Keyes, Stephen M. Malone, Anu Sharma, William G. Iacono, and Matt McGue, "Risk of Suicide Attempt in Adopted and Nonadopted Offspring," *Pediatrics* 132, no. 4 (October 2013): 639–46, https://doi.org/10.1542/ peds.2012-3251.

132 **"You've got to be able to tolerate"** Direct quotes from phone interview with Amanda L. Baden, November 2019. See also Baden's research, including Amanda L. Baden, Judith L. Gibbons, Samantha L. Wilson, and Hollee McGinnis, "International Adoption: Counseling and the Adoption Triad," *Adoption Quarterly* 16, nos. 3–4 (2013): 218–37, https://doi.org/10.1080/10926755.2013.79440; Amanda L. Baden, "'Do You Know Your Real Parents?' and Other Adoption Microaggressions," *Adoption Quarterly* 19, no. 1 (2016): 1–25, https://doi.org/10.1080/10926755.2015.1026012; and Amanda L. Baden, Doug Shadel, Ron Morgan, Ebony E. White, Elliotte S. Harrington, Nicole Christian, et al., "Delaying Adoption Disclosure: A Survey of Late Discovery Adoptees," *Journal of Family Issues* 40, no. 9 (2019): 1154–80, https:// doi.org/10.1177/0192513X19829503.

Chapter Twenty-One: "I Got Her"

This chapter is drawn from interviews with Tuyết Hồ over video calls; interviews with Liên, translated by Khuyên Tưởng Thị Tú; and interviews with Keely. Tuyết Hồ's emails provided by Keely.

Chapter Twenty-Two: Strangers in the Village

This chapter is drawn from my interviews with Tuyết Hồ, Hà, and Keely. Photographs of the visit provided by Keely.

Chapter Twenty-Three: "They Love Her"

This chapter is drawn from my interviews with Tuyết Hồ and Keely.

146 **A *PBS NewsHour*** film crew, "Girl Up Campaign Helps Teens Empower Peers around the Globe," *PBS News Hour*, August 8, 2011.

Chapter Twenty-Four: They Are Coming

This chapter is drawn from my interviews with Rô, Tuyết, Hà, Tuyết Hồ, and Dung Hồ, over video calls, and Dick McKenzie, in person in Việt Nam.

149 **Dick wrote emails** Postcards and updates from McKenzie posted on the website of the "Leapers of 52," the Class of 1952 of New Castle High School, New Castle, PA, http://frogpond52.homestead.com/Vietnam_Postcards_3.html.

151 **Dick emailed Keely** Emails provided by Keely.

Chapter Twenty-Five: Motion Sickness

This chapter is drawn from my interviews with Rô, Tuyết, Hà, Tuyết Hồ, and Dung Hồ, over video calls, and Dick McKenzie, in person in Việt Nam.

153 **Under a sunroof** Descriptions of their villa confirmed via photos posted on the website of the "Leapers of 52," the Class of 1952 of New Castle High School, New Castle, PA. See Dick McKenzie, "At Home in Vietnam," FrogPond52, January 24, 2006, frogpond52.homestead.com/McKenzie-Christening.html; and letters and postcards from Dick.

Chapter Twenty-Six: The Cold

This chapter is drawn primarily from my interviews with Isabella, Keely, and Hà. Scenes of the reunion also confirmed in interviews with Kevin German, the photographer who was present in Los Angeles, and through photos he took in the van, the airport, and the hotel and around Nha Trang. He also photographed the list of questions that Isabella could ask.

Chapter Twenty-Seven: The Night

This chapter is drawn primarily from my interviews with Olivia and Keely; Arianna and Alexandra; and photographer Kevin German, with scenes confirmed from his photos, including video footage he showed me of the iPad reunion. The letter written to Olivia's grandmother was provided by Keely.

Chapter Twenty-Eight: "Harder than This"

This chapter is drawn primarily from my interviews with Isabella, Keely, and Hà. Scenes supplemented by photo images from Keely.

176 **Adoptive parents, though well meaning** Phone interview with Amanda L. Baden, September 2019 and November 2020.

176 **The choice to look for birth families** Interview with Lynelle Long, November 2020.

176 **"You can't connect the dots"** " 'You've Got to Find What You Love,' Jobs Says," Stanford News, June 14, 2005, https://news.stanford.edu/2005/06/14/jobs-061505/.

177 **Hà explained to Keely how controlling** Note from Dick and Dung: They remembered they made the choice to end the relationship with Hà and her family on their own instead and did not feel they were controlling. They felt like Hà did not want to work hard, and they did not care for Tuyết and Rô and thought the Solimenes should provide financial support for Liên instead, which is why they severed ties.

178 **slammed the door in her face** Note from Dick: He did not recall the flowers or slamming the door in Hà's face, but he added: "It sounds like me. I can be a bit of an ass."

Chapter Twenty-Nine: Always Loan

This chapter is drawn primarily from my interviews with Hà. Isabella, Keely, Hà, Tuyết, Rô, Dick, and Dung provided supplementary details. Emails from Dick provided by Keely.

Chapter Thirty: "Where I Am From"

This chapter is drawn primarily from my interviews with Isabella.

179 **in Việt Nam in history classes** "Teaching the Vietnam War," PBS LearningMedia, accessed December 2021, https://ca.pbslearningmedia.org/collection/teaching-the-vietnam-war/.

183 **"I am from a world"** Poem provided by Isabella.

Chapter Thirty-One: "Be with Us"

This chapter is drawn primarily from my interviews with Olivia. Keely provided supplementary details.

Chapter Thirty-Two: Goodbye

This chapter is drawn from my interviews with Hà, Tuyết, and Rô.

Chapter Thirty-Three: "I Will Come Back"

This chapter is drawn from my interviews with Hà, Tuyết, and Rô. Letter from a lawyer from Baker & McKenzie provided by the Solimenes.

Chapter Thirty-Four: America

This chapter is drawn primarily from my interviews with Hà, Keely, Isabella, Victoria, and Olivia. Details supplemented with photographs taken that day by the Solimene family.

Chapter Thirty-Five: "We're Still Here"

This chapter's scenes and narrative sections are drawn from my interviews with Hà, Keely, Isabella, and Olivia.

214 **her family started to hear reports** Camila Domonoske, "As Adoptee in U.S. Awaited Deportation, His Korean Birth Mother Studied English," *The Two-Way* (NPR blog), November 17, 2016, https://www.npr.org/sections/thetwo-way/2016/11/17/502413247/as-adoptee-in-u-s-awaits-deportation-his-korean-birth-mother-is-studying-english. See also Maggie Jones, "Adam Crapser's Bizarre Deportation Odyssey," *New York Times Magazine*, April 1, 2015, https://www.nytimes.com/2015/04/01/magazine/adam-crapsers-bizarre-deportation-odyssey.html.

214 **The Child Citizenship Act** E. Tammy Kim, "Adoptees Have the Same Right to Citizenship as Biological Children," op-ed, *New York Times*, September 23, 2021.

214 **The federal government** Marisa Kwiatkowski, "'You Love This Country, and It's Taken from You': Adoption Doesn't Guarantee US Citizenship," *USA Today*, December 16, 2020. See also Charles "Chuck" Johnson, Russell Moore, and Nancy Kay Blackwell, "Statement on Immigrants as Essential Workers During Covid-19 and the Adoptee Citizenship Act of 2019, Submitted to the House Committee on the Judiciary on Immigration and Citizenship," September 22, 2020, https://docs.house.gov/meetings/JU/JU01/20200923/111028/HHRG-116-JU01-20200923-SD005.pdf.

215 **The Adoptee Rights Campaign** See "US Adoptees without Citizenship National and State-by-State Estimates," Adoptee Rights Campaign, June 2019 interim update, https://adopteerightscampaign.org/research/.

215 **Taneka Jennings, a Chicago-based** Direct quotes from Zoom interview with Taneka Jennings, October 2021.

216 **By 2015–16, the mainstream media** Choe Sang-Hun, "Deportation a 'Death Sentence' to Adoptees after a Lifetime in the U.S," *New York Times*, July 2, 2017; and Chris Fuchs, "Deported Adoptee's Death Heightens Calls for Citizenship Bill," NBC News, June 2, 2017.

217 **Adam and Phillip galvanized** Emma [Jade] Wexler, "Invisible Immigrants: The Politics of Transnational/racial Asian American Adoptees" (honors thesis, Brown University, 2020), https://brown.digication.com/emma-wexler-ethnic-studies-2020/thesis.

217 **The Adoptee Citizenship Act of 2021** Direct quotes from Zoom interview with Jennings. For deeper research, read Eleana Kim and Kim Park Nelson, "'Natural Born Aliens': Transnational Adoptees and US Citizenship," *Adoption & Culture* 7, no. 2 (2019): 257–79.

218 **a powerful educational video series** Zoom interview with Lynelle Long, November 2020. See also ICAV's video series produced by Long, which includes interviews with intercountry adoptees, https://intercountryadopteevoices.com/video-resource-for-professionals/.

218 **In the mid-2000s, the field of critical adoption studies** Margaret Homans, Peggy Phelan, Janet Mason Ellerby, Eric Walker, Karen Balcom, Kit Myers, et al., "Critical Adoption Studies: Conversation in Progress," *Adoption & Culture* 6, no. 1 (2018): 1–49.

219 **A growing group of scholars** Wexler, "Invisible Immigrants." See also Hannah Hyun White, "Between Two Worlds: A Phenomenological Study of the Lived Experiences of Asian American Transracial/Transnational Adoptees Engaging in Activism and Advocacy Work" (master's thesis, University of Arizona, 2019), https://repository.arizona.edu/handle/10150/633190?show=full.

219 **Rebecca Kinney, a professor** Direct quotes from Zoom interview with Rebecca Kinney, October 2021.

220 **In 1790, the Supreme Court passed** The brief history of US immigration policy detailed in this and the two paragraphs that follow are documented in Deenesh Sohoni, "Unsuitable Suitors: Anti-Miscegenation Laws, Naturalization Laws, and the Construction of Asian Identities," *Law & Society Review*, 41, no. 3 (2007): 587–618; Jane H. Hong, *Opening the Gates to Asia: A Transpacific History of How America Repealed Asian Exclusion* (Chapel Hill: University of North Carolina Press, 2019), introduction;

and Erika Lee, "The 'Yellow Peril' and Asian Exclusion in the Americas," *Pacific Historical Review* 76, no. 4 (2007): 537–62.

220 **the case of Takao Ozawa** Steven C. Tccl, "Lessons on Judicial Interpretation: How Immigrants Takao Ozawa and Yick Wo Searched the Courts for a Place in America," *OAH Magazine of History* 13, no. 1 (1988): 41–49. Listen also to Rebecca Kinney interview, "What Is the Work and How Do You Know if You're Doing It? On Asian American History, Activism, and Solidarity with Rebecca Kinney," *Adopted Feels* podcast, October 11, 2021, https://podcasts.apple.com/au/podcast/what-is-the-work-and-how-do-you-know-if-youre-doing-it/id1463322441?i=1000538197115.

221 **There are more than two hundred thousand** Eleana Kim, *Adopted Territory: Transnational Korean Adoptees and the Politics of Belonging* (Durham, NC: Duke University Press, 2010), 22 and 270.

221 **Some adoptees have also become involved** Adoptee advocacy groups and campaigns, discussed in this paragraph and the one that follows, are documented in Wexler, "Invisible Immigrants."

221 **After Donald Trump's 2016 election** Kathryn Joyce, "The Threat of International Adoption for Migrant Children Separated from Their Families," *Intercept*, July 1, 2018.

224 **"I hereby declare, on oath"** "Naturalization Oath of Allegiance to the United States of America," US Citizenship and Immigration Services, US Department of Homeland Security, accessed December 2021, https://www.uscis.gov/citizenship/learn-about-citizenship/the-naturalization-interview-and-test/naturalization-oath-of-allegiance-to-the-united-states-of-america.

Chapter Thirty-Six: Switched

This chapter is drawn primarily from my interviews with Hà, Isabella, and Olivia.

227 **Isabella had been assigned** Scenes rendered from photos provided by Isabella from Nepal.

Chapter Thirty-Seven: Powerful Marks

232 **In the 1960s** Gabrielle Glaser, *American Baby: A Mother, a Child, and the Shadow History of Adoption* (New York: Viking, 2021); and Nancy L. Segal, *Deliberately Divided: Inside the Controversial Study of Twins and Triplets Adopted Apart* (Lanham, MD: Rowman & Littlefield, 2021).

232 **"You have to talk about"** "Lessons From a Controversial Study that 'Deliberately Divided' Twins," Cal State Fullerton, October 18, 2021.

233 **Identical twins (also known as monozygotic twins)** Erika Hayasaki, "Identical Twins Hint at How Environments Change Gene Expression," *Atlantic*, May 15, 2018, https://www.theatlantic.com/science/archive/2018/05/twin-epigenetics/560189/.

233 **Since 1922, there have been 1,894 cases** Hayasaki.

234 **But for today's twin researchers** Direct quotes and sections about Segal from various in-person, Zoom, and phone interviews with her between 2017 and 2020.

234 **Non-shared experiences can also exist** Lavinia Gordon, Jihoon E. Joo, Joseph E. Powell, Miina Ollikainen, Boris Novakovic, Xin Li, et al., "Neonatal DNA Methylation Profile in Human Twins Is Specified by a Complex Interplay between Intrauterine Environmental and Genetic Factors, Subject to Tissue-Specific Influence," *Genome Research* 22, no. 8 (August 2012): 1395–1406, https://doi.org/10.1101/gr.136598.111.

235 **A lifetime of experiences and habits** Mario F. Fraga, Esteban Ballestar, Maria F. Paz, Santiago Ropero, Fernando Setien, Maria L. Ballestar, et al., "Epigenetic Differences Arise during the Lifetime of Monozygotic Twins," *Proceedings of the National Academy of Sciences* 102, no. 30 (July 2005): 10604–10609, https://doi.org/10.1073/pnas.0500398112; Romain Barrès, Jie Yan, Brendan Egan, Jonas Thue Treebak, Morten Rasmussen, Tomas Fritz, et al., "Acute Exercise Remodels Promoter Methylation in Human Skeletal Muscle," *Cell Metabolism* 15, no. 3 (March 2012): 405–11, https://doi.org/10.1016/j.cmet.2012.01.001; Marie E. Gaine, Snehajyoti Chatterjee, and Ted Abel, "Sleep Deprivation and the Epigenome," *Front Neural Circuits* 12, no. 14 (February 2018), https://doi.org/10.3389/fncir.2018.00014; B. P. F. Rutten, E. Vermetten, C. H. Vinkers, G. Ursini, N. P. Daskalakis, E. Pishva, et al., "Longitudinal Analyses of the DNA Methylome in Deployed Military Servicemen Identify Susceptibility Loci for Post-traumatic Stress Disorder," *Molecular Psychiatry* 23, no. 5 (May 2018): 1145–56, https://doi.org/10.1038/mp.2017.120; Andrew E. Teschendorff, James West, and Stephan Beck, "Age-Associated Epigenetic Drift: Implications, and a Case of Epigenetic Thrift?" *Human Molecular Genetics* 22, no. R1 (October 2013): R7–15, https://doi.org/10.1093/hmg/ddt375; Moshe Szyf, "The Early Life Environment and the Epigenome," *Biochimica et Biophysica Acta* 1790, no. 9 (September 2009): 878–85, https://doi.org/10.1016/j.bbagen.2009.01.009; Sheng Li, Francine E. Garrett-Bakelman, Stephen S. Chung, Mathijs A. Sanders, Todd Hricik, Franck Rapaport, et al., "Distinct Evolution and Dynamics of Epigenetic and Genetic Heterogeneity in Acute Myeloid Leukemia," *Nature Medicine* 22, no. 7 (July 2016): 792–99, https://doi.org/10.1038/nm.4125; and Lionel A. Poirier, "The Effects of Diet, Genetics and Chemicals on Toxicity and Aberrant DNA Methylation: An Introduction," *Journal of Nutrition* 132, no. 8 (Suppl.) (August 2002): 2336S–39S, https://doi.org/10.1093/jn/132.8.2336S.

235 **For twins raised together** Nicole Pelletiere, "Infant Twins Share Heartbreaking Cancer Diagnosis," ABC News, September 10, 2015; Jaye Watson, "Identical Twins Battling Dramatically Different Versions of ALS," 11Alive, updated November 28, 2017, https://www.11alive.com/article/news/health/identical-twins-battling-dramatically-different-versions-of-als/85-495238319; and Mark Lieber, "Liver Transplant Saves One Teen, but Identical Twin Dies," CNN, March 23, 2018.

236 **In 2020, Cynthia and Michelle Racanati** Stefan Sykes, Yasmine Salam, and Mohammed Syed, "Twin Sisters on Front Lines Contract Covid; Only One Survives," NBC News, December 18, 2020.

236 **Rare pairs have "discordant" diagnoses** Rasmus Ribel-Madsen, Mario F. Fraga, Stine Jacobsen, Jette Bork-Jensen, Ester Lara, Vincenzo Calvanese, et al., "Genome-Wide Analysis of DNA Methylation Differences in Muscle and Fat from Monozygotic Twins Discordant for Type 2 Diabetes," *PLoS ONE* 7, no. 12 (2012): e51302, https://doi.org/10.1371/journal.pone.0051302; C. C. Y. Wong, E. L. Meaburn, A. Ronald, T. S. Price, A. R. Jeffries, L. C. Schalkwyk, et al., "Methylomic Analysis of Monozygotic

Twins Discordant for Autism Spectrum Disorder and Related Behavioural Traits," *Molecular Psychiatry* 19, no. 4 (2014): 495–503, https://doi.org/10.1038/mp.201341; Christina A. Castellani, Benjamin I. Laufer, Melkaye G. Melka, Eric J. Diehl, Richard O'Reilly, and Shiva M. Singh, "DNA Methylation Differences in Monozygotic Twin Pairs Discordant for Schizophrenia Identifies Psychosis Related Genes and Networks," *BMC Medical Genomics* 8, no. 17 (May 2015), https://doi.org/10.1186/s12920-015-0093-1; Namitha Mohandas, Sebastian Bass-Stringer, Jovana Maksimovic, Kylie Crompton, Yuk J. Loke, Janet Walstab, et al., "Epigenome-Wide Analysis in Newborn Blood Spots from Monozygotic Twins Discordant for Cerebral Palsy Reveals Consistent Regional Differences in DNA Methylation," *Clinical Epigenetics* 10, no. 25 (2018), https://doi.org/10.1186/s13148-018-0457-4; and Paul E. Young, Stephen Kum Jew, Michael E. Buckland, Roger Pamphlett, and Catherine M. Suter, "Epigenetic Differences between Monozygotic Twins Discordant for Amyotrophic Lateral Sclerosis (ALS) Provide Clues to Disease Pathogenesis," *PLoS ONE* 12, no. 8 (2017): e0182638, https://doi.org/10.1371/journal.pone.0182638.

Chapter Thirty-Eight: Similar Scars

237 **"What if one day you woke up"** "Twin Sisters Separated at Birth Reunite on 'GMA,'" YouTube, January 11, 2017, https://www.youtube.com/watch?v=QHeNKMxsqYE.

239 **"What we find with twins raised apart"** "Twins Separated at Birth," CBS News, February 5, 2017, https://www.cbsnews.com/video/twins-separated-at-birth/#x.

Similarities and differences quotes from in-person interviews with Isabella and Hà in Arlington Heights, Illinois.

Chapter Thirty-Nine: Unspoken

243 **Professor Nancy Segal would eventually** Nancy L. Segal, Francisca J. Niculae, Erika N. Becker, and Emmy Y. Shih, "Reared-Apart/Reared-Together Chinese Twins and Virtual Twins: Evolving Research Program and General Intelligence Findings," *Journal of Experimental Child Psychology* 207 (July 2021): 105106, https://doi.org/10.1016/j.jecp.2021.105106.

243 **The IQ scores of virtual twins** Direct quotes and context of study from Zoom interview with Segal, 2021.

243 **IQ tests, however, are imperfect** Angela Saini, *Superior: The Return of Race Science* (Boston: Beacon Press, 2019), 193–94.

244 **New research shows that identical twins** Hakon Jonsson, Erna Magnusdottir, Hannes P. Eggertsson, Olafur A. Stefansson, Gudny A. Arnadottir, Ogmundur Eiriksson, Ogmundur, et al., "Differences between Germline Genomes of Monozygotic Twins," *Nature Genetics* 53, no. 1 (2021): 27–34, https://doi.org/10.1038/s41588-020-00755-1.

244 **Environmental variables are influenced** Lucas J. Matthews and Eric Turkheimer, "Across the Great Divide: Pluralism and the Hunt for Missing Heritability," *Synthese* 198, no. 3 (2019): 2297–311, https: doi.org/10.1007/s11229-019-02205-w; and Eric Turkheimer, "Weak Genetic Explanation 20 Years Later: Reply to Plomin et al. (2016)," *Perspectives on Psychological Science* 11, no. 1 (2016), https://doi.org/10.1177/1745691615617442.

245 **"We think we know who we are"** Lawrence Wright, *Twins: And What They Tell Us about Who We Are* (New York: John Wiley, 1997), 37–38.

Chapter Forty: Grandma

249 **In 2017, Isabella returned** Drawn from interviews with Isabella and Hà, as well as photos of their trip.

250 **Isabella and Hà again returned** Scenes are from my notes, photos, and recorded videos.

Chapter Forty-One: Where It Feels Safe

254 **Before we left Việt Nam** I was present during this trip with Olivia to visit her birth family. Scenes are rendered from notes, interviews and videos. Direct quotes are from interviews with Olivia.

Chapter Forty-Two: Climb Out

This chapter is reconstructed based on interviews primarily with Hà and Isabella. Keely provided supplemental details.

Epilogue

This chapter is drawn primarily from interviews with Olivia, Hà, Isabella, and Keely.

265 **"Why are these costs ethical?"** Jennifer Morton, *Moving Up without Losing Your Way : The Ethical Costs of Upward Mobility* (Princeton, NJ: Princeton University Press, 2019), 7–8.

SELECTED BIBLIOGRAPHY
& SUGGESTED RESOURCES

Adopted Feels podcast. https://adopted-feels.simplecast.com.

Adoptees for Justice. https://adopteesforjustice.org/about-us/.

Adoptee Rights Campaign. https://adopteerightscampaign.org/.

"Adoption in Vietnam." Schuster Institute for Investigative Journalism. https://www.brandeis.edu/investigate/adoption/vietnam.html.

Babe, Ann. "Korean Adoptees Felt Isolated and Alone for Decades. Then Facebook Brought Them Together." *Rest of World*, May 13, 2021. https://restofworld.org/2021/stranger-than-family/.

Baden, Amanda L. "'Do You Know Your Real Parents?' and Other Adoption Microaggressions." *Adoption Quarterly* 19, no. 1 (2016): 1–25.

Baden, Amanda L., Judith L. Gibbons, Samantha L. Wilson, Samantha, and Hollee McGinnis. "International Adoption: Counseling and the Adoption Triad." *Adoption Quarterly* 16, nos. 3–4 (2013): 218–37.

Baden, Amanda L., Doug Shadel, Ron Morgan, Ebony E. White, Elliotte S. Harrington, Nicole Christian, et al. "Delaying Adoption Disclosure: A Survey of Late Discovery Adoptees." *Journal of Family Issues* 40, no. 9 (2019): 1154–80.

Baldwin, James. *The Cross of Redemption: Uncollected Writings*. Edited by Randall Kenan. New York: Pantheon Books, 2010.

———. *The Fire Next Time*. New York: Vintage, 1993. Originally published 1963.

Blum, Deborah. *Love at Goon Park : Harry Harlow and the Science of Affection*. New York: Basic Books, 2011.

Cheng, Emily. "Pearl S. Buck's 'American Children': U.S. Democracy, Adoption of the Amerasian Child, and the Occupation of Japan in *The Hidden Flower*." *Frontiers* (Boulder), vol. 35, no. 1 (2014): 181–210.

Choy, Catherine Ceniza. *Global Families: A History of Asian International Adoption in America*. New York: New York University Press, 2013.

Chung, Nicole. "My White Adoptive Parents Struggled to See Me as Korean. Would They Have Understood My Anger at the Rise in Anti-Asian Violence?" *Time*, March 22, 2021. https://time.com/5948949/anti-asian-racism-white-adoptive-family/.

———. "Stories of Transracial Adoptees Must Be Heard—Even Uncomfortable Ones." *Guardian*, April 4, 2019. https://www.theguardian.com/commentisfree/2019/apr/04/transracial-adoption-listen-understand.

Cohen, Frayda. "Tracing the Red Thread: Chinese-U.S. Transnational Adoption and the Legacies of 'Home.'" *Anthropologica* 57, no. 1 (2015): 41–52.

Davis, F. James. *Who Is Black?: One Nation's Definition*. University Park: Pennsylvania State University Press, 1991.

Dominus, Susan. "The Mixed-Up Brothers of Bogotá." *New York Times Magazine*, July 12, 2105. https://www.nytimes.com/2015/07/12/magazine/the-mixed-up-brothers-of-bogota.html.

Evan B. Donaldson Adoption Institute. "Finding Families for African American Children: The Role of Race & Law in Adoption from Foster Care," May 2008, National Center on Adoption and Permanency. https://www.nationalcenteronadoptionandpermanency.net/post/

finding-families-for-african-american-children-the-role-of-race-law-in-adoption-from-foster-care.

Futerman, Samantha, and Ryan Miyamoto, directors. *Twinsters.* Ignite Channel, 2015.

Garcia Gonzalez, M., and E. Wesseling. "The Stories We Adopt By: Tracing 'The Red Thread' in Contemporary Adoption Narratives." *The Lion and the Unicorn* 37, no. 3 (2013): 257–76.

Glaser, Gabrielle. *American Baby: A Mother, a Child, and the Shadow History of Adoption.* New York: Viking, 2021.

Goetz, Kaomi. *Adapted* podcast. http://adaptedpodcast.com/.

Graff, E. J. "Anatomy of an Adoption Crisis." *Foreign Policy*, September 10, 2010. https://foreignpolicy.com/2010/09/12/anatomy-of-an-adoption-crisis/.

———. "The Lie We Love." *Foreign Policy*, November–December 2008, 58–66. https://www.brandeis.edu/investigate/adoption/docs/FPFinalTheLieWeLove.pdf.

Guida-Richards, Melissa. *What White Parents Should Know About Transracial Adoption: An Adoptee's Perspective on its History, Nuances, and Practices.* Berkeley, California: North Atlantic Books, 2021.

Harness, Susan Devan. *Bitterroot: A Salish Memoir of Transracial Adoption.* American Indian Lives. Lincoln: University of Nebraska Press.

Hauserman, Julie. "Vietnam Adoption Nightmares." *Tampa Bay Times*, September 17, 2002. https://www.tampabay.com/archive/2002/09/17/vietnam-adoption-nightmares/.

Hayasaki, Erika. "Identical Twins Hint at How Environments Change Gene Expression." *Atlantic*, May 15, 2018. https://www.theatlantic.com/science/archive/2018/05/twin-epigenetics/560189/.

Hermann, Valerie Phillips. "Transracial Adoption: 'Child-Saving' or 'Child-Snatching.'" *National Black Law Journal* 13, no. 1 (1993): 147–61.

Homans, Margaret, Peggy Phelan, Janet Mason Ellerby, Eric Walker, Karen Balcom, Kit Myers, et al. "Critical Adoption Studies: Conversation in Progress." *Adoption & Culture* 6, no. 1 (2018): 1–49.

Hong, Jane H. "Introduction." In *Opening the Gates to Asia: A Transpacific History of How America Repealed Asian Exclusion*, 1–20. Chapel Hill: University of North Carolina Press, 2019.

Hopgood, Mei-Ling. *Lucky Girl: A Memoir.* Chapel Hill, NC: Algonquin Books, 2009.

Intercountry Adoptee Voices (ICAV). https://intercountryadopteevoices. com/. ICAV's video series, interviews with intercountry adoptees. https://intercountryadopteevoices.com/video-resource-for-professionals/.

Jones, Maggie. "Adam Crapser's Bizarre Deportation Odyssey." *New York Times Magazine*, April 1, 2015. https://www.nytimes.com/2015/04/01/magazine/adam-crapsers-bizarre-deportation-odyssey.html.

Joseph, Jay. *The Trouble with Twin Studies: A Reassessment of Twin Research in the Social and Behavioral Sciences.* New York: Routledge, 2016.

Joyce, Kathryn. *The Child Catchers: Rescue, Trafficking, and the New Gospel of Adoption.* New York: Public Affairs, 2013.

———. "The Threat of International Adoption for Migrant Children Separated from Their Families." *Intercept*, April 27, 2018.

Karen, Robert. *Becoming Attached: First Relationships and How They Shape Our Capacity to Love.* New York: Oxford University Press, 1998.

Kennedy, Randall. *Interracial Intimacies: Sex, Marriage, Identity, and Adoption.* New York: Vintage Books, 2003.

Keyes, Margaret A., Stephen M. Malone, Anu Sharma, William G. Iacono, and Matt McGee, Matt. "Risk of Suicide Attempt in Adopted and Nonadopted Offspring." *Pediatrics* 132, no. 4 (October 2013): 639–46. https://doi.org/10.1542/peds.2012-3251.

King, Martin Luther, Jr. "Beyond Vietnam: A Time to Break Silence." Speech, April 4, 1967. https://www.youtube.com/watch?v=AJl1gXKGldUk.

Kim, Claire Jean. "The Racial Triangulation of Asian Americans." *Politics & Society* 27, no. 1 (March 2999): 105–38.

Kim, Eleana. *Adopted Territory: Transnational Korean Adoptees and the Politics of Belonging.* Durham, NC: Duke University Press, 2010.

Kim, Eleana, and Kim Park Nelson. "'Natural Born Aliens': Transnational Adoptees and US Citizenship." *Adoption & Culture* 7, no. 2 (2019): 257–79.

Kim, Jodi. "An 'Orphan' with Two Mothers: Transnational and Transracial Adoption, the Cold War, and Contemporary Asian American Cultural Politics." *American Quarterly* 61, no. 4 (December 2009): 855–80.

Konner, Melvin. *The Evolution of Childhood: Relationships, Emotion, Mind.* Cambridge, MA: Belknap Press, 2010.

Lee, Erika. "The 'Yellow Peril' and Asian Exclusion in the Americas." *Pacific Historical Review* 76, no. 4 (2007): 537–62.

Marshall, Sam. "Vietnam's Youngest Export." *Wall Street Journal*, May 21, 1999.

Melosh, Barbara. *Strangers and Kin: The American Way of Adoption.* Cambridge, MA: Harvard University Press. Kindle.

Morton, Jennifer. *Moving Up without Losing Your Way: The Ethical Costs of Upward Mobility.* Princeton, NJ: Princeton University Press, 2019.

Nagle, Rebecca, host. *This Land* podcast. Season 2. https://crooked.com/podcast-series/this-land/#all-episodes.

National Association of Black Social Workers. "National Association of Black Social Workers Position Statement on Trans-Racial Adoptions,' September 1972." Adoption History Project,

Department of History, University of Oregon, Eugene. https:// pages.uoregon.edu/adoption/archive/NabswTRA.htm.

Oh, Arissa H. "A New Kind of Missionary Work: Christians, Christian Americanists." *Women's Studies Quarterly* 33, nos. 3–4 (2005): 161–88.

———. *To Save the Children of Korea: The Cold War Origins of International Adoption*. Stanford, CA: Stanford University Press, 2015.

Park Nelson, Kim. *Invisible Asians, Korean American Adoptees, Asian American Experiences, and Racial Exceptionalism*. New Brunswick, NJ: Rutgers University Press, 2016.

Pate, SooJin. *From Orphan to Adoptee, U.S. Empire and Genealogies of Korean Adoption*. Difference Incorporated. Minneapolis: University of Minnesota Press, 2014.

Phillips Boehm, Kimberley L. *War! What Is It Good For? Black Freedom Struggles and the U.S. Military from World War II to Iraq*. John Hope Franklin Series in African American History and Culture. Chapel Hill: University of North Carolina Press.

Radke, Haley, host. *Adoptees On* podcast. https://www.adopteeson.com/.

Raleigh Yoon Hwa, Elizabeth. *Selling Transracial Adoption: Families, Markets, and the Color Line*. Philadelphia: Temple University Press, 2018.

Sachs, Dana. *Life We Were Given: Operation Babylift, International Adoption, and the Children of War in Vietnam*. Boston: Beacon Press.

Saini, Angela. *Superior: The Return of Race Science*. Boston: Beacon Press, 2019.

Segal, Nancy L. *Born Together—Reared Apart: The Landmark Minnesota Twin Study*. Cambridge, MA: Harvard University Press, 2012.

———. *Deliberately Divided: Inside the Controversial Study of Twins and Triplets Adopted Apart.* Lanham, MD: Rowman & Littlefield, 2021.

———. *Entwined Lives: Twins and What They Tell Us about Human Behavior.* New York: Dutton, 1999.

———. *Indivisible by Two: Lives of Extraordinary Twins.* Cambridge, MA: Harvard University Press, 2005.

———, and Montoya, Yesika S. *Accidental Brothers: The Story of Twins Exchanged at Birth and the Power of Nature and Nurture.* New York: St. Martin's Press, 2018.

Skinner, B. F. *Science and Human Behavior.* New York: Simon & Schuster, 1965.

Sohoni, Deenesh. "Unsuitable Suitors: Anti-Miscegenation Laws, Naturalization Laws, and the Construction of Asian Identities." *Law & Society Review* 41, no. 3 (2007): 587–618.

Sorosky, Arthur D., Annette Baran, and Reuben Pannor. *The Adoption Triangle: The Effects of the Sealed Record on Adoptees, Birth Parents, and Adoptive Parents.* Garden City, NY: Anchor Press, 1978.

Teel, Steven C. "Lessons on Judicial Interpretation: How Immigrants Takao Ozawa and Yick Wo Searched the Courts for a Place in America." *OAH Magazine of History* 13, no. 1 (1988): 41–49.

Tucker, Angela, host. *The Adoptee Next Door* podcast. https://www.angelatucker.com/podcast.

Varzally, Allison. *Children of Reunion: Vietnamese Adoptions and the Politics of Family Migrations.* Chapel Hill: University of North Carolina Press.

Wardle, Tim, director. *Three Identical Strangers.* Universal Pictures Home Entertainment, 2018.

Watkins, Rychetta. *Black Power, Yellow Power, and the Making of Revolutionary Identities.* Jackson: University Press of Mississippi, 2012.

Wexler, Emma [Jade]. "Invisible Immigrants: The Politics of Transnational/racial Asian American Adoptees." Honors thesis, Brown University, April 2020. https://brown.digication.com/emma-wexler-ethnic-studies-2020/thesis.

White, Hannah Hyun. "Between Two Worlds: A Phenomenological Study of the Lived Experiences of Asian American Transracial/Transnational Adoptees Engaging in Activism and Advocacy Work." Master's thesis, University of Arizona, 2019. https://repository.arizona.edu/handle/10150/633190?show=full.

Willing, Indigo. "The Adopted Vietnamese Community: From Fairy Tales to the Diaspora." In "Vietnam beyond the Frame." Special issue, *Michigan Quarterly Review* 43, no. 4 (Fall 2004): 648–64. https://ssrn.com/abstract=2032832.

———, Anh Đào Kolbe, Dominic Golding, Tim Holtan, Cara Wolfgang, Kev Minh Allen, et al. *Vietnamese.Adopted: A Collection of Voices.* CQT Media & Publishing, 2015.

Winslow, Rachel Rains. "Introduction." In *The Best Possible Immigrants: International Adoption and the American Family*, 7–13. University Park: University of Pennsylvania Press, 2017.

Wright, Lawrence. *Twins: And What They Tell Us about Who We Are.* New York: John Wiley, 1997

Wu, Judy Tzu-Chun. *Radicals on the Road: Internationalism, Orientalism, and Feminism during the Vietnam Era.* Ithaca, NY: Cornell University Press, 2013.

Yarborough, Trin. *Surviving Twice: Amerasian Children of the Vietnam War.* Washington, DC: Potomac Books, 2005.

ACKNOWLEDGMENTS

THIS PROJECT WOULD not have been possible without the generous participation of the mothers, sisters, and daughters whose lives I have tried to portray in these pages. My deepest gratitude goes to Hà, Isabella, Olivia, Keely, Liên, Rô, and Tuyết. It takes courage to open one's life to a journalist. Thank you for trusting me to tell this story through multifaceted perspectives and for understanding my commitment to hold to truth, which can sometimes look or feel different depending on where you are standing. Thank you to all the other individuals interviewed in this book who were willing to pass on knowledge, memories, context, history, and commentary. And to Nancy Segal for introducing me to the Solimenes and for providing deep background and encyclopedic knowledge about twin research over the years.

I am especially grateful for the support and insight of the following people who offered invaluable suggestions, fact-checks, and criticisms and helped the manuscript mature: Jade Wexler, Mei-Ling Hopgood, Ann Babe, Addie Tsai, Thúy Võ Đặng, Joie Norby Lê, Catherine Bliss, and a special thanks to Khuyên Tưởng Thị Tú, who also provided fact-checking, translation, and diacritics (along with Hà's assistance), as well as guidance in Việt Nam and beyond. Thank you to the adoptee leaders and experts, including Indigo Willing, Lynelle Long, Taneka Jennings, Victoria DiMartile, Rebecca Kinney, and others, who spent time with me sharing their knowledge and insights.

This project would not have survived without the editorial guidance, friendship, and emotional strength of my "writing support system": Leslie Schwartz, a brilliant writer and editor who helped me through my hardest days; Lubov Demchuk, who read multiple drafts and offered thoughtful feedback; Steve Padilla, for his close reading, guidance, mastery of craft, and love for stories; and to my longform tribe—Rebecca Tuhus-Dubrow, Mona Gable, Melissa Chadburn, Eileen Guo, Haley Cohen Gilliland, Jaeah Lee, Katherine Reynolds Lewis, Frances Kai-Hwa Wang, Valeria Fernandez, Sylvia A. Harvey, Kerra Bolton, Chandra Whitfield, Ruxandra Guidi, and Grace Hwang Lynch.

Thank you especially to Barry Siegel for helping provide a pathway into book writing for me, for believing in me, and for reminding me that "all narrative is an argument, in how we select and order a story." And to Richard E. Meyer for being an ongoing inspiration, champion, and insightful narrative teacher who taught me that a writer's job is to "part the curtain on humanity." Thank you also to Miriam Pawel for over two decades of journalism mentorship and guidance and for giving me my shot.

I am deeply grateful to my agent, David Halpern, for believing in this project from its inception, encouraging me, and always having my back. And to my sharp, flexible and incredibly caring Algonquin editors, Betsy Gleick and Madeline Jones, for reading multiple drafts with patience and expert guidance and for their thoughts on improvement at every stage (of which there were many).

In addition, I appreciate the support provided by Margaret Engel at the Alicia Patterson Foundation, which backed my research on epigenetics and twin studies, and the Knight-Wallace Reporting Fellowship under the guidance of Lynette Clemetson and Robert Yoon, who have offered an abundance of faith, encouragement, and expertise. These fellowships allowed me to finish my various reporting projects over the last five years and helped cover travel, research, and especially childcare, without which I could not have completed this work. I am also grateful to the Literary Journalism Program and the English Department of the University of California, Irvine, for supporting my research, along with Judy Tzu-Chun Wu and Amanda Swain at the

Humanities Center there, and the School of Humanities Dean, Tyrus Miller, for awarding me a manuscript workshop grant. And especially to my students and mentees who shine so brightly in my life—they are the audience I envision I am writing for.

I am indebted to the people who have stepped in to help with childcare when we needed it most, always with compassion and love: Elizabeth Anaya Jr. and Elizabeth Anaya Sr., Monica Tanwar and her wonderful staff, Gianna Jacquette, Leilah and Reinah Villegas; and of course the grandmas, Bev Harris, Meletia Coombs, and Lisa Hayasaki; and the aunties, including Mia Hayasaki, Tamalyn Dallal, and Hillie Coombs.

To my closest and dearest friends, who make me laugh, humble and inspire me, and always lift me up: Sandra Murillo, Marjorie Hernandez, Jia-Rui Chong-Cook, Melissa Murillo, Tanya Miller, Kenyatta Willis, David and Tessa Pierson, Garrett Therolf, Thúy Ngô, Shermaine Alya Riehl, Rachana Rathi, Poukhan Philavanh, Nisa Williams, and Kenisha Revish. In addition, I treasure and appreciate Portia Marcelo, who took my photos, and Roxan Tucker-Browne, who helped me stay mentally and physically healthy.

My family has always encouraged my work with an abundance of love. I am endlessly thankful to my mother for her emotional and intellectual support; to my father, Yoshi Hayasaki, always my most inspiring coach; and to Casey and Emily Hayasaki, Megan and Gavin McNeely, and the entire Coombs clan.

To my kids, Takara, Akyn, and Kai, thank you for giving me cuddles and helping me see and experience the world in new and surprising ways. And to G. Hayward Coombs, my love and life partner, who champions my ambitions and helps make all this possible.

Erika Hayasaki, a journalist based in Southern California, is the author of *The Death Class* and a professor in the literary journalism program at the University of California, Irvine. A former *Los Angeles Times* national correspondent, her writing has appeared in the *New York Times Magazine*, the *Atlantic*, *Wired*, and other publications. She has been a Knight-Wallace Reporting Fellow and an Alicia Patterson Fellow, and she has received awards and recognition from the Association of Sunday and Feature Editors, the Society for Features Journalism, the American Society of Newspaper Editors, and *The Best American Science and Nature Writing 2019*. She is the mother of a daughter and twin boys.